Friendships
in Normal
and Handicapped
Children

Friendships in Normal and Handicapped Children

Edited by

Tiffany Field
University of Miami

Jaipaul L. Roopnarine
Syracuse University

Marilyn Segal
Nova University

ABLEX PUBLISHING CORPORATION
Norwood, New Jersey 07648

Library of Congress Cataloging in Publication Data
Main entry under title:

Friendships in normal and handicapped children.

  Bibliography: p.
  Includes index.
    1. Handicapped children—Attitudes—Addresses, essays,
lectures. 2. Childhood friendship—Addresses, essays,
lectures. 3. Interpersonal relations—Addresses, essays,
lectures. 4. Socialization—Addresses, essays, lectures.
I. Field, Tiffany. II. Roopnarine, Jaipaul. III. Segal,
Marilyn M.
HV888.F74 1984   362.4′088054   84-11173
ISBN 0-89391-221-2

Printed in the United States of America.

ABLEX Publishing Crporation
355 Chestnut Street
Norwood, New Jersey 07648

Contents

I

METHODOLOGIES FOR STUDYING FRIENDSHIPS IN CHILDREN

1

Issues in the Assessment of Social Skills of Normal and Handicapped Children

2

Sociometric, Social–Cognitive, and Behavioral Measures for the Study of Friendship and Popularity

III

RESEARCH STUDIES ON FRIENDSHIPS
IN NORMAL AND HANDICAPPED CHILDREN

Contributors

Numbers in parentheses indicate the pages on which the authors' contributions begin.

Nicholas J. Anastasiow (209), Hunter College, 695 Park Avenue, New York, New York 10021

Steven R. Asher (53), Bureau of Educational Research, University of Illinois at Urbana-Champaign, Champaign, Illinois 61820

Thomas J. Berndt (31), Department of Psychology, University of Oklahoma, Norman, Oklahoma 73019

Tiffany Field (89, 153), Mailman Center for Child Development, University of Miami, Miami, Florida 33101

Wyndol Furman (3), Department of Psychology, University of Denver, Denver, Colorado 80207

Carollee Howes (163), Graduate School of Education, University of California, Los Angeles, Los Angeles, California 90024

Michael J. Guralnick (139), The Nisonger Center, Ohio State University, Columbus, Ohio 43209

Jaipaul L. Roopnarine (81, 89), Department of Child, Family, and Community Studies, Syracuse University, Syracuse, New York 13210

Judith Rubenstein (99, 125), Tufts Medical School, Newton, Massachusetts 02158

Carol Rubin (99), New England Medical Center Hospital, Boston, Massachusetts 02111

Phillip S. Strain (187), Children and Youth Programs, 3411 Belmont Road, Nashville, Tennessee 37215

Angela R. Taylor (53), College of Education, Institute for Child Study, University of Maryland, College Park, Maryland 20742

Preface

In 1982 the Society for Research in Child Development funded a study group entitled, *Friendships in normal and handicapped children*. This volume is an outgrowth of that study group. Developmental and clinical psychologists who had been studying friendships in normal children, handicapped children or both met for a two-day symposium at the Mailman Center for Child Development, University of Miami. The purpose of the meeting was to share current data, to discuss implications of current research, and to formulate ideas for future studies on friendship formation among young children. Many of these issues are summarized in a commentary by Judith Rubenstein in Chapter 7, and by Nicholas Anastasiow in Chapter 12.

The volume is divided into three parts: Methodologies for Studying Friendships in Children; Research Studies on Friendships in Normal Children; and Research Studies on Friendships in Normal and Handicapped Children. In the first chapter, Wyndol Furman presents issues on the assessment of social skills in normal and handicapped children, or how to determine why it is that some children have friends whereas others do not. Advantages and disadvantages of measures of social competence, social skills, and performance—including interaction rates, teacher ratings, and sociometric ratings—are discussed, and a model of skill components underlying social behavior is presented.

Thomas Berndt then offers a critical review and theoretical chapter on methods for studying children's friendships versus methods for investigating their popularity or sociometric status. He illustrates the parallels between the measurement of children's friendships and popularity and also suggests ways to integrate these two research areas. He concludes that an integration of sociometry, social cognition, and behavioral observations of popular, neglected, and rejected children may provide more adequate answers to the questions surrounding popularity and friendships.

In the final chapter in the methodology section Angela Taylor and Steven Asher discuss the importance that goals play in children's social competence, and how maladaptive motivational and goal-orientation patterns of retarded children may contribute to their difficulties relating to nonretarded peers. They review research in which a game-playing situation has been used to investigate children's goals and social interactions and as an intervention context for promoting the social competence and peer acceptance of retarded and low-status non-retarded children.

In Chapter 4, the first chapter of Part II, Jaipual Roopnarine presents a study on the acquaintanceship process in nursery classrooms. Changes in the play behaviors and playmate preferences of preschool children were noted to occur during their first two weeks of acquaintanceship, suggesting a fairly rapid formation of friendships even at this young age.

In the following chapter, Jaipaul Roopnarine and Tiffany Field present data on preschool children who have or do not have close friends. Preschool children who were close friends appeared to be similar in physical characteristics, including age, sex, and height. Those children who had close friends were more extraverted and verbal, engaged in more fantasy play, and appeared to take turns being dominant and submissive. Children who did not have close friends appeared to spend their time watching those who had close friends.

In Chapter 6, older children's fantasies of interaction with same and opposite sex peers are illustrated in data and drawings presented by Judith Rubenstein and Carol Rubin. Analyses of children's drawings indicated sex differences in children's perceptions of the nature of peer relationships and in the impact of male and female peers on boys and girls.

Judith Rubenstein summarizes these two sections of the volume in Chapter 7. She discusses the definition and functions of friendship and how they are affected by sex differences, developmental changes, different situations, and motivational factors. She concludes that relatively little is known about peer attachment, even though "there is little more consistently important across the life span than the capacity for friendship."

In Part III, Michael Guralnick reviews data on peer interaction deficits in specialized and mainstreamed settings and proposes possible explanations for minimal effects of mainstreaming. He concludes that ". . . there is probably no substitute for the richness, diversity, and responsivity found in mainstreamed programs [but that] systematic programming must occur."

Tiffany Field then presents data suggesting that handicapped children do form friendships even with normal children in mainstreamed preschool settings. Those handicapped children who had more friends than their handicapped peers were more extraverted and more assertive in initiating, leading, and terminating play interactions. They were also more verbal and affectively responsive. Similar distributions of children who had and did not have close friends and similar distributions of behavior were noted for the samples of normal and handicapped children.

In Chapter 10 Carollee Howes presents data on social interactions and friendships in normal, emotionally disturbed, and abused children. Although the abused children showed higher levels of physical aggression and the emotionally disturbed children formed relationships less frequently, once friendships were established they were remarkably similar across different groups of children.

A study comparing the social interactions of handicapped preschoolers in integrated and segregated settings is then presented by Phillip Strain. His data demonstrate that greater social participation occurs in integrated than segregated preschool settings. But the level of handicapped children's social behavior only approached that of normal children when the normal children were asked to interact with the handicapped children, thus highlighting the value of peer-mediated intervention.

In the final chapter, Nicholas Anastasiow discusses the concerns of the special educator and the problems of designing optimal intervention programs. If the normal child typically relates to the handicapped child as an adult does to a child, how can friendships between these two groups of children be facilitated.

As in any volume of research, the questions posed loom larger than the answers found. We hope, however, that we have provided some suggestions and perspectives for future research and interventions for facilitating friendships of normal and handicapped children.

I

METHODOLOGIES FOR STUDYING FRIENDSHIPS IN CHILDREN

Issues in the Assessment of Social Skills of Normal and Handicapped Children*

Wyndol Furman

Why do some children have friends whereas others do not? A common answer to this question is that some children are more socially skilled than others. Those who are socially skilled are more able to gain peer acceptance and develop friendships than those who are not skilled. Similarly, many handicapped children encounter difficulties in peer relations because they lack the necessary social skills. The social skills model of adjustment has proven to be valuable. Considerable progress has been made in identifying the skills associated with socially competent performance and in developing intervention programs for fostering such skills (see Asher & Renshaw, 1981; Furman, 1979, in press; Gresham, 1981; Hops, 1982; Hops & Greenwood, 1981). While this progress is encouraging, we believe that several major conceptual and methodological issues in the assessment of social skills have not been adequately addressed. In the present chapter, we will discuss some of these important yet neglected issues.

THE CONCEPT OF SOCIAL COMPETENCE

Social skills are usually thought of as discrete elements of a broader construct of social competency. Although efforts to specify the general construct of social competency have met with limited success (Ander-

* Appreciation is expressed to Tom Berndt and my fellow members of the University of Denver group on relationships for stimulating my interest on this topic.

son & Messick, 1974), investigators in the field of peer relations have relied on two primary indices—global patterns of social behavior, and judgments by other individuals.

The most common behavioral index of social competence has been overall rate of peer social interaction. That is, children who interact infrequently with their peers are thought to be experiencing problems in social adjustment (Hops, 1982; Strain, Kerr, & Ragland, 1981). This index seems intuitively plausible in that withdrawn children may be deprived of the important learning experiences obtained in peer interactions (Hartup, 1976). On the other hand, the empirical data are not very compelling (Asher, Markell, & Hymel, 1981). Although some types of nonsocial behavior may not be adaptive (Furman & Garcia, 1983; Rubin, 1982), most nonsocial behavior consists of appropriate, healthy activities, such as constructive solitary play (Moore, Evertson, & Brophy, 1974). Similarly, a few studies have found social withdrawal to be associated with subsequent problems in school adjustment (Kohn & Rosman, 1972; Victor & Halverson, 1976), but others have not found rate of interaction to be related to current or subsequent adjustment (see Asher et al., 1981; Furman, in press). Most importantly, only a limited number of studies have directly addressed this question. Thus, it seems premature to conclude that simple social withdrawal is (or is not) indicative of poor social competence.

Rates of positive interactions have been found to associate with sociometric status and other indices of adjustment (see Hartup, in press). Since the vast majority of peer interactions take this form, one could use these results to argue that low rates of interaction are indicative of problems (Hops, 1983). That is, socially withdrawn children are missing the important experiences that occur in positive peer interactions. Alternatively, it seems more compelling to argue that children's social competency should be determined by assessing the specific types of social or nonsocial behavior associated with adjustment, rather than assessing overall rates of interaction. As yet, few investigators have done so.

The other primary index of social competence has been the judgments of other individuals. In some cases, teachers have been asked to evaluate the peer relations of children (Greenwood, Walker, Todd, & Hops, 1979), but, more commonly, the peers themselves have been asked who their friends are or how much they like various classmates (Asher & Hymel, 1981). Two groups of children are thought to be experiencing difficulties: (a) socially rejected children—those who are actively disliked by their peers, and (b) socially isolated children—those who have few friends or are not particularly liked, but are not actively disliked either. Cross-sectional and longitudinal studies provide clear

evidence that sociometric status is associated with concurrent and subsequent adjustment (see Hartup, in press). Children who are unaccepted by their peers, particularly those who are actively disliked, do
seem to be socially incompetent. At the same time, several issues concerning the determination of social competence on the basis of sociometric status have not been adequately addressed. Three basic concerns can be raised: (a) the fact that specific skills are only distally
related to sociometric status, (b) the implicit adherence to a contrast
group approach for validating specific skills, and (c) the absence of
information about why sociometric status is important.

First, it is important to remember that any specific social skill or
behavior is not going to be linked closely with sociometric status; in
fact, even general patterns of behavior are not highly predictive of
sociometric status. Sociometric status is affected by factors such as
physical attractiveness, intelligence, and expertise, as well as by social
behavior (Asher, Oden, & Gottman, 1977). The distal nature of ties
between social behaviors or skills and sociometric status has several
important implications. When evaluating validational evidence concerning a specific skill or behavior, one should expect its relationship
with sociometric status to be moderately strong at best. Low sociometric status also does not necessarily indicate a problem in social
skilos or behavior; the reason for being unaccepted could lie elsewhere.
Consequently, it is important to include more direct measures of social
skill or behavior. By the same logic, it seems unwise to use sociometric
measures as the sole index for assessing treatment effects. If changes in
sociometric status occur, one does have impressive evidence that the
treatment is effective. If changes are not observed, it could mean that
the program is ineffective, but it could also mean that the sociometric
measure is not sufficiently sensitive to the changes that occurred. Perhaps we would be more successful in identifying treatment effects by
asking specifically how much they like the target's children's social
behavior, rather than asking how much they generally like them.

The use of sociometric measures also has implications for the procedure used to demonstrate that specific social skills or behaviors are
important elements of social competence. Two distinct approaches exist. One can either contrast the behavior of groups of socially competent
and incompetent individuals, or one can determine whether the consequences of specific social behaviors tend to be desirable or undesirable
ones. When sociometric measures are used as the index of social competence, we are implicitly advocating the use of the contrast group
approach. That is, behaviors that are more typical of popular children
would be considered desirable, while those that are more typical of
unpopular children would be considered undesirable. Although this

approach will result in the identification of many important behaviors, mistakes can occur. Some of the differences between popular and un-popular children may not be particularly important ones, and some may be a consequence of being popular rather than a cause. Moreover, one should not assume that, if unpopular children were to act in the same manner as popular children do, their acceptance by peers would be enhanced. For example, unpopular children may first need to learn how to get peers to like them, rather than how to act toward peers who already like them. It may even be inappropriate for unpopular children to act as if their peers already liked them.

Rather than studying groups where status is already established, some investigators have begun to examine the process of acquaintan-ceship or friendship formation (Furman & Willems, 1982; Gottman & Parkhurst, 1980). By comparing the means that popular and unpopular children use to make friends, one may be able to specify the behaviors that foster peer acceptance. This approach is promising because it re-duces the problem of inadvertently identifying behaviors that are a consequence of peer acceptance rather than a cause. However, it too has a subtle, but important, limitation. Even if unpopular children were to engage in the same behaviors that popular children do, they may not be successful. Special compensatory skills may be required to over-come the stigma of being unaccepted or disliked. This point is particu-larly important when one is concerned with fostering the social compe-tence of exceptional children. Handicapped children may need additional skills to make up for the limitations imposed by their phys-ical or emotional disability. As yet, the potential moderating effect of status (e.g., handicapped versus nonhandicapped, popular versus un-popular) on the effectiveness of various skills or behaviors has received little attention.

Although the contrast group approach is an appropriate means for identifying important social behaviors, we believe that the alternative approach of assessing outcomes of different behaviors has not received sufficient attention in the study of peer relations. In that approach, behaviors that lead to positive outcomes would be considered desirable ones, while those that lead to negative outcomes would be undesirable. Perhaps the best known example is the work of Patterson and his col-leagues on the consequences of aggressive and coercive behaviors (Pat-terson & Cobb, 1973; Patterson, Littman, & Bricker, 1967). Many of the limitations of the contrast group approach are avoided in this ap-proach, although often only the immediate outcomes have been exam-ined. In some instances, the short-term and long-term consequences of a behavior may differ. For example, aggressive acts are usually suc-cessful in the short-run (Patterson et al., 1967), but eventually the aggressive child may pay the cost of being disliked. Conversely, resisting inappropriate peer pressure may have immediate negative consequences, but it could ultimately foster appropriate social development.

Although it may not be possible to determine the long-term consequences of behaviors through direct observations, such outcomes can be indirectly determined by subjective judgments of likely outcomes. This process is incorporated in Goldfried and D'Zurilla's (1969) model for assessing competency. Four steps are involved: (a) situational analysis, (b) response enumeration, (c) response evaluation, and (d) instrument development. First, a large, representative sample of concrete problematic situations are obtained through interviews, surveys, or observational procedures. Next, a sample of likely responses to each problematic situation are collected. Then, a set of judges evaluate the adequacy of each of these responses, taking into account the likely outcomes both (short-term and long-term). Finally, an instrument is developed in which the different problem situations are presented, and a number of responses ranging from competent to incompetent are provided. An excellent illustration of this approach is the research of McFall and his colleagues on skills deficits in adolescent delinquents (Freedman, Rosenthal, Donahoe, Schlundt, & McFall, 1978; Gaffney & McFall, 1981).

Finally, we believe that it is time to take a closer look at what it is about sociometric status that is important. Although peer rejection is predictive of subsequent problems in adjustment, it may be that the causal determinants of such difficulties are the factors that lead to peer rejection, rather than peer rejection per se. For example, aggressive children tend to be rejected by their peers (see Hartup, in press). Is it the peer rejection or the aggressive behavior that puts them at risk? If sociometric status has no causal impact, it would be more appropriate to conceptualize and assess competence in terms of the relevant causal variables rather than in terms of the indirect correlate.

On the other hand, we do believe that sociometric status is likely to be one of the causal determinants of adjustment or maladjustment. For example, children who are unaccepted by their peers may be deprived of important learning experiences that occur in peer interactions. Similarly, the repeated experience of rejection may lead to poor self esteem. Finally, some children who are unaccepted by their peers may be at risk because they have few or no close friends. The experience of having a close friend may be critical for appropriate social development (Furman, 1982; Sullivan, 1953). Even if some of these arguments are correct, the need to understand the causal processes manifested in ratings of sociometric status still exists. One would target different children and design different treatment programs depending upon whether the problem is seen as one of aggressiveness, a deprivation of important learning experiences, the experience of being rebuffed frequently, or an absence of friendship. For that matter, each of these potential causal factors also needs to be scrutinized carefully. For example, what is it about friendships that is important? It could be the companionship, the affection, the enhancement of worth, or some other social provision commonly received in these relationships, but as yet that has not been determined (Furman & Buhrmester, 1982).

We do not mean to imply that sociometric status is an inappropriate index of social competence. That approach has served the field well, but we believe that it is time to obtain a more complete picture of the nature of social competence. When assessing social competence, one should incorporate other variables, such as measures of the qualitative features of interactions or relationships. Additionally, few investigators in the field of peer relations have thought of social adjustment in terms of traditional clinical criteria such as behavioral symptomatology (except for aggressiveness) or prevalent emotional feelings, such as feeling loved (versus lonely) or happy (versus depressed). Examination of the ties between peer relations and these variables may help foster the integration of the fields of developmental and child clinical psychology (Furman, 1979).

SOCIAL SKILLS AND SOCIAL PERFORMANCE

We have discussed some of the issues concerning the conceptualization of social competence, and we will now turn to social skills, that is, the discrete elements incorporated in the broad construct of competence. One basic issue is whether social skills should refer to actual social behaviors or to the abilities to behave in socially appropriate manners, be they fully manifested in behavior or not. Previous definitions have varied in this respect. For example, Rinn and Markle (1979) define social skills as "a repertoire of verbal and nonverbal behaviors by which children affect the responses of other individuals. . . . The extent to which they are successful in obtaining desirable outcomes and avoiding or escaping undesirable ones without inflicting pain on others is the extent to which they are considered socially skilled" (p. 108). In contrast, Combs and Slaby (1977) propose that social skills refer to the "ability to interact with others in a given social context in specific ways that are socially acceptable or valued and at the same time personally beneficial, mutually beneficial, or beneficial primarily to others" (p. 162).

We believe that it is important to distinguish among social performance, maximal social performance, and social skills. Here, *social per-formance* refers to a person's typical pattern of behavior, while *max-imal social performance* refers to a person's pattern of behavior when the conditions are optimal. Finally, *social skills* are defined as the underlying competencies or abilities that affect a person's social perfor-mance. A person's typical social performance may not provide a ver-idical representation of the person's maximal social performance (and skills). Certainly, one's level of social skills imposes an upper ceiling on the person's level of performance, but other variables, such as moti-vation or environmental feedback, may cause a person to act at less than optimal levels. In contrast, maximal social performance does pro-vide a veridical representation of the person's skill level. That is, when the conditions are optimal (e.g., when the necessary motivation and feedback are present), the observed performance should reflect the per-son's underlying level of social skills. Our distinction between social skills and maximal performance is one between underlying abilities and the product of such abilities when they are fully expressed. Such a differentiation is made because social skills affect social performance even when the conditions are not optimal.

What implications do these distinctions have for assessing social competency? Almost all measures of social skills are either direct or indirect assessments of a person's typical social performance. As noted earlier, assessments of typical performance do not necessarily reflect skill levels. An investigator may infer a skill deficit is present when some other factors may be inhibiting performance. For example, Schwartz and Gottman (1976) found that unassertive adults knew how to respond assertively and were able to do so in hypothetical situations; but they were not likely to respond assertively in actual situations. It is also possible that assessments of typical social performance could mask differences in maximal performance or skills. That is, the dif-ference between socially competent and socially incompetent children may be greater when the conditions are optimal than when typical.

These distinctions are important theoretically as well. For exam-ple, Bandura (1969) hypothesized that acquisition of new behaviors or skills is largely dependent upon stimulus contiguity, while the level of actual performance is primarily determined by reinforcement contin-gencies.

Finally, the distinctions have important implications for designing interventions. Coaching or behavioral rehearsal programs seem based on the assumption that the person lacks the requisite skills. Conse-quently, these programs have included components that teach the per-son such skills. If the individual does not have a skill deficit, however, the instructional components in the coaching programs may not be as important as performance enhancement components, such as positive feedback. Moreover, one may want to design different programs for individuals with skill and performance deficits.

THE MANIFESTATION OF SKILLFULNESS

Typically, the skillfulness of one's social interactions has been considered to be a function of the frequency of various molecular response components (Bellack, 1979; Michelson & Wood, 1981). For example, skillfulness in heterosexual interactions has been assessed in terms of the frequency of eye contact, verbalizations, appropriate gestures, and so on. While this approach has often proved to be valuable, it may not fully capture the concept of skillful performance.

Differences in social competency may be reflected in sequences of behavior as well as frequencies of single acts. For example, a disagreement or negative behavior by an unpopular child is more likely to escalate into a series of negative exchanges than a similar behavior by a popular child (Asarnow, 1982; Putallaz & Gottman, 1981). Similarly, skillful performance may be a function of when certain behaviors occur rather than how often they occur. In one of the few empirical investigations of this possibility, Fischetti, Curran, and Wessberg (1977) had socially unskilled and skilled males engage in a structured interaction with a female. Unskilled males were found to respond to the female's comments as frequently as the skilled males did, but the timing of their responses was judged to be less appropriate.

Moreover, studies of discrete behaviors or even sequences of discrete behaviors may not always prove to be the best means of identifying differences in the degree of skillfulness in social interactions. For example, numerous investigators have tried to identify specific behaviors that distinguish high and low daters (e.g., Arkowitz, Lichtenstein, McGovern, & Hines, 1975; Glasgow & Arkowitz, 1975). Although a few components, such as the number of silences, have been identified, the yield of this approach has been relatively meager. In contrast, partners or observers consistently judge high daters to be more skillful and attractive than low daters. Thus, judges appear to be evaluating skillfulness on some basis other than the frequencies of specific behaviors. Perhaps skillful or unskillful performance is a function of organized global clusters of behavior. For example, high daters may be more likely to discuss interesting topics, talk fluently about a topic, or present themselves as having a "good" personality or smooth style (Conger, Wallander, Mariotto, & Ward, 1980). Similarly, interaction strategies of positive self-presentation or focusing on one's partner may foster interpersonal attraction (Scott & Edelstein, 1981). Certainly, judgments about global interpersonal strategies are based on observations of discrete behaviors, but any specific behavior may not be highly related to such judgments. Instead, the organization or inferred consistencies of behavior may be better indices of such judgments. To the best of our knowledge, empirical studies of global strategies in peer relationships have not been conducted, although several developmental investigators have suggested that the relative merits of global versus molecular analyses should be reconsidered (Bakeman & Brown, 1980; Furman, 1983; Waters, 1978).

OVERT BEHAVIORS
AND UNDERLYING VARIABLES

Regardless of whether the focus is on molecular behaviors or global strategies, research should not be limited to the examination of overt acts. An unskillful behavior or pattern of behaviors may reflect deficits in any of a number of underlying components. For example, a socially withdrawn child's failure to initiate a conversation with another may reflect a lack of motivation to interact with the other, a misperception that the situation is not conducive to conversation, or a lack of skills for identifying effective means of conversing.

In the following section, a model of the clusters of *individual difference* variables that underlie social performance will be described. This model is based on Argyle and Kendon's (1967) work, but it incorporates recent advances in developmental and social psychology. The principal components are depicted in Figure 1; components that are hypothesized to be closely related are connected with lines. The use of lines instead of causal arrows is intentional. Our purpose here is simply to delineate some of the major individual differences variables that lead to variation in general patterns of social behavior; this model is not sufficiently complex to serve as a model of the processes underlying any specific social act. Certainly, the different components delineated here may have causal roles, but many more links and intermediary variables would be required to describe the actual processes involved. A causal model (versus an individual differences model) seems beyond the reach of our current state of knowledge.

The first component in the model is *motivation*. It refers to children's general intentions or goals for social interchanges. Clearly, goals or intentions will markedly influence patterns of behavior. For example, the motive to approach success vs. avoid failure has been found to affect achievement (Heckhausen, 1968). With the exception of some

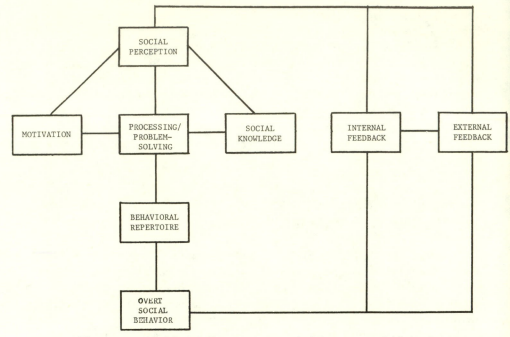

Figure 1. *A model of skill components underlying overt social behavior.*

research on cooperative and competitive motives (Bryant, 1975), however, this component has received remarkably little attention in studies
of children's social behavior. As Taylor and Asher (this volume), we
believe that the concept of goals or motivation is essential for understanding social behavior (Furman & Buhrmester, 1982).

Social perception refers to the identification and interpretation of
social inputs or social situations. For example, it includes the ability to
discriminate and label the other's emotional or internal state. This component also incorporates interpretations of behavior, such as the causal
attributions that children use to explain others' actions. For example,
some children may attribute social failures to their lack of ability, while
others may attribute them to situational influences. Social perceptions
and interpretations may be influenced by such variables as the ability
to take the perspective of the other. A significant amount of research
has been done on recognition of emotions, attributional styles, and
perspective-taking ability (see Shantz, 1975), but little work has been
done on their interrelations or their relations with other skill components.

Any social input is perceived and processed in the context of previously existing *social knowledge.* This knowledge may be about the specific person(s) with whom one is interacting, or about social behavior in general. It includes information about the meaning of an act, social mores, social routines, and socially acceptable behavior. While limited in number, the existing studies provide evidence that social knowledge is linked to social competence. For example, popular children have greater knowledge about how to go about making a new friend, or about the common ways to help a peer (Gottman, Gonso, & Rasmussen, 1977; Ladd & Oden, 1979). Children's conceptions of friendship have also been studied extensively, although the primary focus has been on developmental changes rather than individual differences (see Bigelow & LaGaipa, 1980; Selman, 1980).

Perhaps the most complex component is *processing or problem solving.* It refers to the abilities involved in translating one's social perceptions and motives into a course of social action. Spivack, Platt, and Shure (1976) delineated a series of such social cognitive competencies. These include

(a) Problem recognition—accurately identifying the social problem or situation (incorporated in this model's perception component)
(b) Alternative thinking—being able to generate multiple solutions to a problem
(c) Causal thinking—the ability to relate one event to a later one with regard to the "why" that might have precipitated that act
(d) consequential thinking—identifying the likely consequences of a social act
(e) means–end thinking—identifying the sequence of steps required to reach an outcome.

In the last decade, numerous studies have examined the ties between these problem solving skills and social competence (Spivack et al., 1976; Spivack & Shure, 1982).

The *behavioral repertoire* is the array of available verbal and motor behaviors. This component should be differentiated from *overt social behaviors.* The former refers to the behaviors that the child could potentially display, whereas the latter refers to the behaviors that actually do occur. Although the overt behavior must be in the repertoire, it is affected by *all* of the components in the model. Thus, overt behavior is best understood as the observed product of the components—not a component per se. The behavioral repertoire has not been studied very often, but overt responses have. Investigators have found that popular and unpopular children's social performance differs in numerous respects (see Asher, Oden, & Gottman, 1977; Hartup, in press). Perhaps these findings do reflect differences in popular and unpopular children's behavioral repertoires, but they could result from differences in any of the other components.

The final two components are *external* and *internal feedback*. These refer to the response of the environment and the evaluation of the person in question. They both include feedback about the manner of performance and about the response to that performance. Numerous studies have documented the major effects of peer reinforcement and punishment on children's behavior (Hartup, 1977). Research also suggests that popular and unpopular children often receive very different feedback, even when they display the same behavior (Bierman & Furman, in press). Similarly, recent theorists have recognized that self-evaluations and self-reinforcement influence children's behavior and their perceptions of their social competence (see Harter, in press). Moreover, positive or negative feedback is likely to affect one's motivation and expectancies or perceptions of the situation.

A simple example can illustrate the importance of these various components in determining social behavior. Consider a situation in which a child is standing near a small group of peers playing a game together. Some children may generally be *motivated* to join such a group, while others may typically prefer to play alone. Among those motivated to join, the children may differ in the accuracy of their *perceptions* of whether it is possible to join the group. Of course, such perceptions will be related to their prior *knowledge* of the nature of the play and the participants involved. If they decide it is appropriate to join the play, the children may differ in their ability to generate effective means for joining or in their ability to anticipate the consequences of different means (i.e., the *social processing/problem-solving* component). Some children may have a greater *repertoire* of "joining behaviors" than others do. Peers may tend to respond differently to various requests or even the same request, depending upon who says it (i.e., *external feedback*). Finally, the children may differ in their evaluations of their own behavior or ability (i.e., *self-feedback*). Those who tend to be critical of their own efforts may give up quickly, or not even try to join. This example illustrates how differences in social performance may reflect differences in any of a number of components. Conversely, the same social performance may occur even when children differ on some of these variables; that is, strengths in one component may compensate for deficits in another.

Finally, it should be noted that all of the components except external feedback and perhaps motivation involve abilities or skills. Such skills, however, may not always be fully exercised. For example, children who regularly receive negative feedback may not process social inputs as effectively as they could if they tended to receive positive feedback. We believe that the motivational, social perceptions, and feedback components contain some of the primary variables that lead to a difference between typical and maximal social performance. The study of such variables may lead to a better understanding of the links between performance and competence.

Implications

This model is principally designed to serve as a heuristic device to guide subsequent research or theory. It is unlikely that the present model or other potential models will actually "carve nature at its joints." The components described here can and should be further differentiated. Moreover, the focus has principally been on individual differences variables. We do not mean to denigrate the role of the other person's behavior or situational factors; a discussion of these variables is contained in a subsequent section. While aware of the limitations of proposing such a model, we do believe that, it can help organize and integrate the research on social competence.

In proposing the different components, we hope to identify some of the important factors that affect social behavior. Some of the components, such as motivation or social knowledge, have not been studied as extensively as they should be. Similarly, the specification of various components may help organize seemingly unrelated work. For example, the identification of emotions, perspective-taking, and attributional processes all involve social perception, but the similarities among them have not been fully appreciated.

More generally, one of our major goals of this model is to encourage investigators to examine the range of components that underlie social performance. Few such studies currently exist. As noted previously, many investigations have focused on overt social performance alone. Other investigations have examined underlying components, but, usually, these studies only examine the relationship between one component variable and some criterion variable (e.g., sociometric status). Not surprisingly, the relationships that have been found tend to be modest in size. Too many variables lie between any one component and a broad criterion variable. By looking at the ties among the components, we may be able to observe stronger relationships, and ultimately identify the set of variables required to predict our criteria.

Additionally, different components have been examined by different disciplines. Most of the work on external feedback has been done by behavioral clinical psychologists, while the work on social perception and processing has been conducted by developmental psychologists. Clearly, there is a need to integrate the work of developmental and clinical psychologists (Furman, 1979).

Finally, the present model has important clinical implications. Extensive assessments of these components would provide a rich picture of the specific deficits a child may have. Such assessments could guide treatment or preventive programs by pinpointing the specific components that need to be targeted. Programs that target the specific underlying deficit may have more generalized and maintained effects than either those that provide the same kind of component skill training for all children or those that solely focus on the overt behaviors that result from such deficits (Furman, in press).

SOCIAL SKILLS AND SOCIAL RELATIONSHIPS

The preceding section provided a description of the role that underlying variables, particularly social skills, play in determining social behavior. Clearly, other variables, such as the characteristics of the other person or situational factors, also affect the nature of social interactions. In the following section, I will present a general model of the major classes of variables that affect social interactions in relationships. For the sake of simplicity, the focus will be on dyadic relationships, although the same general considerations would apply to relationships in which more than two people are involved. After the model has been described, the implications for the assessment of social competency will be discussed.

Table 1 presents a list of the major classes of variables that generally affect patterns of interaction. The first one is the *characteristics of the target individual*. It would incorporate all of the variables in the previous model except for the one of external feedback. In addition to these social competency variables, it would include other trait or person variables, such as personality or cognitive characteristics. I intend this term to refer to the person's characteristics—not the person's actual behavior. The person's behavior is not only affected by his or her own characteristics, but by the other variables in the model; conversely, the target person's characteristics affects the partner's behavior as well as his or her own. Additionally, my term "characteristic" is not intended to be identical to the classic concept of traits. Some individuals may want to think of individual characteristics in terms of broad traits (e.g., assertiveness), while others may want to think in terms of more situationally specific or time-limited characteristics (e.g., current tendency to refuse inappropriate requests in work settings). In either case, however, the person is attributing some characteristic to the individual—

Table 1
Major Classes of Variables Affecting Patterns of Interaction

1. *Characteristics of the Individual*—skill components, personality, and cognitive characteristics of the person.
2. *Characteristics of the Partner*—skill components, personality, and cognitive characteristics of the other.
3. *Interaction of the Characteristics of the Two Individuals*—product of the first two terms.
4. *Relationship-Specific Characteristics*—history of the relationship, specific attitudes and feelings toward each other, expectancies for the future of the relationship.
5. *Situational Characteristics*—environmental variables that affect social interactions.
6. *Interactions among Preceding Classes*—characteristics of individual by relationship-specific characteristics, characteristics of individual by situational variables, characteristic of partner by relationship-specific characteristics, characteristic of partner by situational variables, relationship-specific characteristics by situational variables, interactions of the characteristics of the two by relationship specific characteristics, interactions of the two by situational variables, characteristics of the individual by relationship-specific characteristics by situational variables, characteristics of the partner by relationship-specific characteristics by situational variables, interactions of the two by relationship-specific characteristics by situational characteristics.

the concept I am trying to capture here. Thus, I believe that the present model is applicable regardless of one's views about the size, stability, or causal status of traits or dispositional variables.

The second class of variables is identical to the first, except that it refers to the *partner's characteristics*. Of course, when one is interested in a target person's interactions in a number of relationships, these characteristics will vary from relationship to relationship.

The third class is the *interaction of the characteristics of the two individuals*. It is the simple multiplicative product of the first two terms. In some conceptualizations, this interaction term incorporates relationship-specific characteristics (e.g., the amount of affection felt toward a specific person), but I prefer to distinguish between those variables and the interaction of the general characteristics of the two individuals.

The *relationship-specific variables* are incorporated in my fourth category. This group is the most difficult one to specify, yet it is one of the most critical ones. At a minimum it would seem to incorporate the effects of previous interactions (i.e., the history of the relationship), the participants' specific attitudes and feelings toward each other, and their expectations for the future of the relationship.

The fifth category incorporates *situational or environmental variables* that affect the nature of social interactions. Finally, the sixth category refers to the *interactions* among the preceding categories. The most commonly discussed one is the target person by situation interaction, although other interactions (e.g., partner by situation) also play important roles.

Each of these six categories generally affect the *pattern of interaction* in a relationship. By pattern of interaction, I mean the general characteristics of interaction, such as the amount of interaction, degree of intimacy in the interaction, and so on. The characteristics of interest here are general tendencies or patterns, however, rather than any specific social act.

A simple example can be used to illustrate this model. Consider the amount of self-disclosure that occurs in a relationship between two people. First, it may be affected by each of the two people's general tendencies to be self-disclosing. It may also be affected by the interaction of their general tendencies. For example, if either person tends to disclose frequently, the level of disclosure may be greater than expected from simply averaging the two individuals' tendencies to disclosure (Jourard & Resnick, 1970). Additionally, the degree of intimacy may be affected by the previous history of self-disclosure in the relationship, their feelings of affection toward each, and their expectations about how the relationship may go in the future. Similarly, interactions that occur in formal situations, such as work settings, may be characterized by less disclosure than those that occur in informal settings. Finally, interactions among the different categories may have an impact. For example, some individuals may tend to be very disclosing in intimate situations, but very impersonal at work; such differences may not be as marked for others.

Although it may appear that I am proposing a process model of social interaction, such is not intended. Like the first model, this one is concerned with the ties between general characteristics of individuals (or relationships) and general patterns of interaction. A model of the processes determining specific social acts would need all of these variables, but it would also need to contain other variables, such as the pattern of interaction that immediately preceded the present act. Studies of social processes may also be successful by examining the role of specific beliefs and values rather than general individual differences (Fishbein & Ajzen, 1975). That is, general individual characteristics do affect social interactions, but their effect may occur through their impact on variables such as expectancies and perceived valence.

Implications for Assessing Social Competence

The present model points out a fundamental problem in the assessment of social skills or social competence. These assessments typically rely on the observation of social interactions. Social interactions, however, are affected by all of the categories in the model, and not just an individual's social competence. In other words, social competencies are usually conceptualized as characteristics of the individual, and yet what is usually observed—patterns of social interaction—are characteristics of the dyad or relationship. This difference in the level of conceptualization seriously complicates the assessment of social competency.

In the present section, I will review the common strategies of assessing social competency and determine whether they do provide veridical indices of the individual's social characteristics or competence. For the sake of simplicity, it will initially be assumed that relationship-specific characteristics do not affect patterns of interaction. The complications brought on by the inclusion of that class of variables will be discussed in the next section.

The basic question is whether the assessment techniques eliminate or control for the contributions of the partner's social characteristics, the interchange between partner and target person, the situational variables, and the interactions among the different classes of variables. First, consider the use of observational techniques in either a naturalistic or experimental setting. The situational variables are usually controlled for by standardizing the situation in which children are observed. For example, we could observe children during free-play or during dyadic conversations. The standardization of situations seems essential, although situational factors may not be totally eliminated. That is, any global setting, such as a playground, may contain a number of smaller settings within it. Some children may tend to play in the sandbox, while others may play on the merry-go-round. The different play material may tend to elicit different kinds of behavior. Moreover, regardless of how homogenous or restricted the situation is, the situation by individual characteristic interaction would still remain in the equation. That is, some children may perceive a sandbox as a place for social interaction, while others perceive it as a place for individual play. One could, however, consider the situation by individual characteristic interaction variables to be an aspect of the individual's social competence. This is, in fact, implicit in behavioral psychologists' argument that individual characteristics should be construed as situation specific.

Even if the situation were fully standardized, the partner, and the interaction between partner and target, would still remain as determinants of the pattern of interaction. One solution has been to observe a child in interactions with a number of other children. While the approach often seems necessary, it is based on the questionable assumption that, over the course of time, different children play equally with different partners. If, however, popular children tend to play with other popular children, and unpopular children with unpopular (Parkhurst & Gottman, 1981), then random sampling will not result in an even distribution of partners. The contribution of partner, and the interaction between partner and subject, would be reduced but not fully eliminated.

One means of eliminating the contribution of the partner would be to observe target children in interactions with a fixed set of partners. For example, we could observe children's interactions with Johnny, Peter, and Susan. This approach does eliminate the main effect of partner type, but the subject by partner interaction component would still remain. For example, partners may interact differently toward popular and unpopular children, not only because of the differences in the target children's characteristics, but because of how those characteristics mesh with their own. One could argue that such interaction effects are an aspect of the person's social competence, but the implications of this decision have not been carefully considered.

A second means of evaluating social competence is to ask for ratings or judgments from others (e.g., teachers or peers), or from the individuals themselves. This approach encounters many of the same difficulties that observational procedures do, because such judgments will be based on observations of patterns of social interaction. Perhaps in their evaluation of a person's characteristics or competency, judges could try to correct for the influence of other factors, such as situational variables, although research on attributional biases suggests that, if anything, judges will overattribute behaviors to the characteristics of the person (Jones & Nisbett, 1972).

A third approach is to try to use role-playing or analogue measures in which the partner's behavior is standardized. For example, we have asked children to converse with another person who has a fixed script and a series of rules to guide responses (Kelly, Furman, Phillips, Hathorn, & Wilson, 1979). This approach does eliminate the contribution of the partner's characteristics, but, unfortunately, it may have other limitations. The major concern has been whether individuals act in the same manner when role-playing as they do in more naturalistic interactions. For example, role playing a behavior has minimal consequences, unlike engaging in behavior in naturalistic settings. Several studies have examined the patterns of correlations between behavior when role-playing heterosexual interactions and behavior when interacting with a confederate in a waiting room (Bellack, Hersen, & Lamparski, 1979; Kern, 1982; Wessberg, Mariotto, Conger, Farrell, & Conger, 1979). Sometimes, high correlations have been found, but in other instances only low ones have been observed. In most of these studies, however, the criterion situation itself has been an analogue; it is not clear if behavior in a waiting room really reflects a person's behavior in heterosexual situations, which makes it difficult to draw conclusions from either high or low correlations.

An interesting question is whether conceptually we should expect behavior in a role-playing situation to be highly correlated with behavior in naturalistic settings. First, it is not clear if role-playing measures are designed to assess maximal social performance or typical social performance. Moreover, unlike role-playing measures, naturalistic interactions will be affected by variation in the characteristics of the partners different individuals select. Thus, even if the role-playing or analogue measure is valid, one may expect to find moderate correlations. One may need to assess the ecological validity of these measures by determining if socially competent and incompetent individuals differ in role-playing situations. Although it is difficult to make direct comparisons, studies that have used such a contrast group approach have tended to yield more positive results than those that tried to examine patterns of correlation between settings (see McNamara & Blumer, 1982).

One important, yet relatively unexamined, question is whether the standardization of the partner's response in analogue or role-playing measures distorts the process of social interaction. Socially incompetent behaviors may lead to different responses than social competent ones, and such responses may lead to different subsequent behaviors on the part of the subject (see Snyder, Tanke, & Berscheid, 1977, for a relevant illustration). The standardization of the partner's responses may either seem artificial or may underestimate the differences between socially competent and incompetent individuals. Unfortunately, the reverse possibility of exaggerated differences also exists. Imagine talking to a socially shy person. One may compensate for this person's shyness by talking more or making greater efforts to engage him or her in a conversation. Thus, the difference observed in a standardized interaction with this person would not be evident in a naturalistic interaction, if compensatory influences occur. This point gives rise to the interesting conceptual question of whether one should control for the differential responses elicited by individuals. In effect, the issue here is

whether the interaction between the individual's and partner's characteristics should be thought of as an aspect of the individual's social
competency. If not, the analogue approach may provide an appropriate
assessment procedure. If so, the naturalistic procedures may be more
appropriate.

A final means of assessing social competency is to use a questionnaire or structured test that does not involve interacting with another
person. For example, Shure and Spivack (1974) assess problem-solving
ability by interviewing children about what they would do in a series of
social situations. Since no partner is involved, these procedures are not
faced with the issues analogue or role-playing measures encounter by
standardizing the partner's response, but a similar criterion problem
exists. That is, how well should these measures predict a person's
behavior in naturalistic settings where variables such as the partner's
characteristics have an impact? If significant relations are observed,
one has good validational evidence, but if they are not observed, it does
not necessarily indicate that the measures are invalid. Again, it may be
more appropriate to expect competent and incompetent individuals to
respond differently on these measures.

Social Skills in Relationships

The issues become even more complex when we consider the effect
that the relationship-specific variables may have on patterns of social
interactions. Consider the assessment strategies described previously.
If one observes children in a naturalistic or experimental setting, the
observed interactions would not only be a function of the characteristics of the target children, partners, the interaction of the two, and
the setting, but they would also be a function of the relationships between the target children and the partners. Children interact differently
with a friend than with an acquaintance or enemy because of the impact of the personal relationship. The contribution of the characteristics of the partners could be eliminated by observing all children
interacting with a fixed set of partners, but the relationship-specific
variables would remain. That is, it is unlikely that all children would
have the same kind of relationships with some set of partners, unless
all were strangers.

One could eliminate or at least reduce the relationship-specific
variables by observing all children interacting with their friends, for
example. Unfortunately, this solution reintroduces the partner's characteristics. That is, it seems unlikely that the friends of popular and
unpopular children will have the same kinds of characteristics. Thus,
matching on the relationship-specific variables seems to lead to mis-

matching on the partner characteristic variables, and vice-versa. Finally, with either of these solutions, the interactions between target child and partner characteristics and between target child characteristics and the relationship-specific variables would still remain in the equation. As noted earlier, however, one may want to conceptualize these interaction terms as aspects of the target children's social competence. These issues would also arise concerning the impact of relationship-specific variables on observation assessments if one used ratings or evaluations by judges.

Structured analogue or role-playing situations also encounter serious difficulties. The standardization of the partner's responses does seem to eliminate both the partner characteristics and the relationship specific variables, but the issues concerning ecological validity remain. In fact, it seems very questionable whether a person's behavior in a role-playing situation is representative of behavior in the context of an ongoing relationship. Is it reasonable to expect that a role-played conversation with a stranger is typical of the naturalistic conversations they have with a friend? Similarly, the standardization of the partner's responses seems particularly likely to distort the process of social interaction that occurs between individuals who have an ongoing relationship.

The relationship-specific factor may also indirectly affect the results yielded from questionnaires or structured tasks that do not involve social interactions. Although children do not directly interact with someone in this case, the nature of the relationship described in the problem situations may alter their responses. Different solutions may be provided, depending upon whether the problem is in an interaction with a friend or a parent. Moreover, some children may find problems in certain relationships more difficult to solve than those in other relationships (i.e., a person by relationship-specific interaction). It seems important to consider systematically varying the context of the relationship presented in the social problems.

Several alternative strategies for assessing social competency in relationships also warrant consideration. For example, one should consider asking the participants in a relationship about their own social skills or their partners' social skills. As members of an ongoing relationship, they may be in a unique position to know the history of the relationship and evaluate the competencies of those involved. Certainly, their perceptions may be biased, but an insider's perspective can reveal information about a relationship that no outsider can obtain (Furman, 1983; Olson, 1977).

Finally, in some instances it may be valuable to reconceptualize social competencies as characteristics of dyads rather than as characteristics of individuals. That is, one may think in terms of the social competency of a parent–child relationship rather than in terms of the social competency of the parent and child separately. This solution avoids many of the problems described above, because the characteristics of the partner, interaction between partner and subject, and relationship-specific components are all meaningful aspects of the dyad's characteristics. This reconceptualization seems very appropriate when the members of the relationship are "fixed," such as in parent–child or sibling relationships. When the relationships are not as fixed or stable, as in the case of friendships, the reconceptualization is not as compelling. It is reasonable to evaluate the social competencies of friendship dyads, and develop intervention programs for enhancing the characteristics of those dyads that are deficient in some respect (Furman, in press). For example, we could assess the amount of intimate disclosure in a friendship and, when appropriate, try to foster such disclosure. On the other hand, we are not only concerned with teaching children the social skills that foster the development or maintenance of their current friendships, but we also want to teach the individual children the skills necessary for developing and maintaining subsequent friendships. That is, we are interested in enhancing social competencies at the level of the individual as well as at the level of the dyad. Perhaps, however, intervening with existing friendship dyads may prove to be a valuable means of fostering the skills children need in their subsequent friendships.

In summary, these considerations point out some of the conceptual issues involved in assessing the competencies of individuals when our procedures must rely on social interactions that occur in the context of relationships. No completely satisfactory solution is evident to us, but several of the approaches should prove valuable. Further progress can be made by studying the role of the characteristics of individuals and the relationship specific variables on patterns of interaction. Current research on handicapped and normal children's friendships indicates that the relationship-specific variables do have a major effect on patterns of interactions (Asher & Gottman, 1981; Furman, 1982; Hartup, in press). Once we have a better picture of how the relationship-specific variables and the other "confounding" factors affect social interactions, we should be in a better position to assess the social competencies of individuals.

The Changing Nature of Skills in Relationships

The most neglected characteristic of relationships is that they are dynamic processes (Furman & Childs, 1981). All relationships are in a constant process of change or development. Even a relationship between the best of friends continues to grow over the course of time; in fact, if a relationship does not seem to be "going anywhere," it may decline as a result.

One of the principal reasons for including a relationship specific category is to account for temporal changes in relationships. This category contains the elements of the history of the relationship, the current perceptions of the relationship, and the expectations for the future. Clearly, all of these elements change as relationships develop.

Although the relationship-specific variables may be the major means of accounting for temporal changes in interactions, the other classes of variables may also contribute. The characteristics of the individual or the partner that affect patterns of interaction may vary depending upon the stage of the relationship. For example, assertiveness may be important in initiating a relationship, but it may be less important in full-blown relationships. Conversely, the experience of the relationship may lead to changes in the participants' individual characteristics. For example, Sullivan (1953) hypothesized that the development of chumships fosters feelings of self-worth and altruism. Finally, as relationships develop, the situations in which interactions occur may change. For example, in the early stages of a friendship, two children may spend a good deal of their time engaged in shared play activities with other peers present, while later, when the relationship becomes more fully developed, they may spend more time alone in intimate dyadic conversations.

What implications does the dynamic nature of friendships have for the assessment of social competency? First, it underscores the importance of examining the role of the relationship-specific variables in determining patterns of interactions. Additionally, it suggests that different social competencies may be important at different relationship stages. Most research on social skills, however, has focused on assertiveness skills and, in particular, relationship initiation skills. We expect that these skills are primarily important in interactions with strangers or new acquaintances. In fact, in a recent longitudinal study of the transition of college, initiation skills were found to strongly relate to measures of adjustment during the transitional fall period (i.e., when new relationships were being established); they were not very related, however, during the stable periods of the summer before college or later in the school year (Shaver, Furman, & Buhrmester, in press).

In subsequent research (Buhrmester & Furman, 1983), we were able to identify five distinct skill domains: (a) relationship initiation, (b) negative assertiveness, (c) self-disclosure, (d) support and guidance, and (e) conflict resolution skills. Although relationship initiation skills may decline in importance once a relationship is established, some of these other skills, such as self-disclosure and support and guidance, may be important factors in the later stages of a relationship.

CONCLUSION

Clearly, the assessment of social skills or social competence is a complicated matter. In the present paper we have emphasized a series of five important issues to consider: (a) the limitations of our current indices of social competence in peer relations, (b) the differences among typical social performance, maximal performance, and social skills, (c) the idea that skills are not only manifested in terms of frequencies of molecular acts, but may be reflected in the sequence or timing of acts or in global strategies that incorporate a range of discrete acts, (d) the large number of skill components or other variables that underlie overt performance, and (e) the fact that we have to infer social competence from direct or indirect observations of social interactions, but that variables other than the individual's social competence affect patterns of interactions. Although it is easier to point out the problems than the solution, it is hoped that the present chapter will stimulate further work on these topics. Clearly, both handicapped and nonhandicapped children will benefit as we develop a better understanding of the role of social competencies in friendships.

REFERENCES

Anderson, S., & Messick, S. (1974). Social competency in young children. *Developmental Psychology, 10,* 282–293.

Argyle, M., & Kendon, A. (1967). The experimental analysis of social performance. In L. Berkowitz (Ed.), *Advances in Experimental Social Psychology* (Vol. 3). New York: Academic Press.

Arkowitz, H., Lichtenstein, E., McGovern, K., & Hines, P. (1975). The behavioral assessment of social competence in males. *Behavior Therapy 6,* 3–13.

Asarnow, J. R. (1982). *Children with peer problems: Sequential and nonsequential analysis of behavior.* Paper presented at American Psychological Association, Washington, DC.

Asher, S. R., & Gottman, J. M. (Eds.). (1981). *The development of children's friendship.* Cambridge, England: Cambridge University Press.

Asher, S. R., & Hymel, S. (1981). Children's social competence in peer relations: Sociometric and behavioral assessment. In J. D. Wine & M. D. Smye (Eds.), *Social competence.* New York: Guilford Press.

Asher, S. R. Markell, R. A., & Hymel, S. (1981). Identifying children at risk in peer relations: A critique ofthe rate of interaction approach to assessment. *Child Development 52,* 1239–1245.

Asher, S. R., Oden, S. L., & Gottman, J. M. (1977). Children's friendships in school settings. In L. G. Katz (Ed.), *Current topics in early-childhood education* (Vol. 1). Norwood, NJ: Ablex.

Asher, S. R., & Renshaw, P. D. (1981). Children without friends: Social knowledge and social skill training. In S. R. Asher & J. M. Gottman (Eds.), *The development of children's friendship*. Cambridge, England: Cambridge University Press.

Bakeman, R., & Brown, J. V. (1980). Early interaction: Consequences for social and mental development at three years. *Child Development 51*, 437–447.

Bandura, A. (1969). *Principles of behavior modification*. New York: Holt, Rinehart & Winston.

Bellack, A. S. (1979). A critical appraisal of strategies for assessing social skill. *Behavioral Assessment, 1*, 157–176.

Bellack, A. S., Hersen, M., & Lamparski, D. (1979). Role play tests for assessing social skills. Are they valid? Are they useful? *Journal of Consulting and Clinical Psychology 47*, 335–342.

Bierman, K. L., & Furman, W. (in press). The effects of social skills training and peer involvement on the social adjustment of preadolescents. *Child Development*.

Bigelow, B. J., & La Gaipu, J. J. (1980). The development of friendship values and choice. In H. C. Foot, A. J. Chapman, & J. R. Smith (Eds.), *Friendship and social relations in children*. New York: John Wiley.

Bryant, J. H. (1975). Children's co-operation and helping behaviors. In E. M. Hetherington (Ed.), *Review of Child Development Research* (Vol. 5). Chicago: Univ. of Chicago.

Buhrmester, D., & Furman, W. (1983). *Perceived social skillfulness and socio-emotional adaptation during college*. Manuscript in preparation.

Combs, M. L., & Slaby, D. A. (1977). Social-skills training with children. In B. B. Lahey & A. E. Kazdin (Eds.), *Advances in Clinical Child Psychology* (Vol. 1). New York: Plenum.

Conger, A. J., Wallander, J. L., Mariotto, M. J., & Ward, D. (1980). Peer judgments of heterosexial-social anxiety and skill:What do they pay attention to anyhow? *Behavioral Assessment 2*, 243–259.

Fischetti, M., Curran, J. P., & Wessberg, H. W. (1979). Sense of timing: A skill deficit in heterosexual socially anxious males. *Behavior Modification 1*, 179–194.

Fishbein, M., & Ajzen, I. (1975). *Belief, attitude, intention and behavior: An introduction to theory and research*. Reading, MA: Addison-Wesley.

Freedman, B. J., Rosenthal, L., Donahoe, C. P., Jr., Schlundt, D. G., & McFall, R. M. (1978). A social-behavioral analysis of skill deficits in delinquent and nondelinquent adolescent boys. *Journal of Consulting and Clinical Psychology, 46*, 1448–1462.

Furman, W. (1979). Promoting social development: Development implications for treatment. In B. B. Lahey & A. E. Kazdin (Eds.), *Advances in Clinical Child Psychology* (Vol. 3). New York: Plenum.

Furman, W. (1982). Children's friendships. In T. Field, G. Finley, A. Huston, H. Quay, & L. Troll (Eds.), *Review of Human Development*. New York: John Wiley.

Furman, W. (1983). Some observations on the study of personal relationships. In J. C. Masters & K. L. Yarkin-Levin (Eds.), *Boundary areas in psychology: Developmental and social*. New York: Academic Press.

Furman, W. (in press). Enhancing peer relations and friendships. In S. Duck (Ed.), *Personal relationships V: Repairing personal relationships*. London: Academic Press.

Furman, W., & Burhmester, D. (1982). *A motivational approach to the study of personal relationships and social networks*. Paper presented at the Second Annual Conference on Naturalistic Studies of Social Interaction, Nags Head, NC.

Furman, W., & Childs, M. K. (1981). *A temporal perspective on children's friendship*.

Paper presented at Meeting of Society for Research in Child Development, Boston, MA.

Furman, W., & Garcia, D. (1984). *The stability and predictability of social isolation.* Paper in preparation, University of Denver.

Furman, W., & Willems, T. (1982). *The acquaintanceship process in middle childhood.* Paper presented at the International Conference on Personal Relationships, Madison, WI.

Gaffney, L. R., & McFall, R. M. (1981). A comparison of social skills in delinquent and nondelinquent adolescent girls. *Journal of Consulting and Clinical Psychology, 49,* 959–967.

Glasgow, R. E., & Arkowitz, H. (1975). The behavioral assessment of male and female social competence in dyadic heterosexual interactions. *Behavior Therapy 6,* 488–498.

Goldfried, M. R., & D'Zurilla, T. J. (1969). A behavioral-analytic model for assessing competence. In C. D. Spielberger (Ed.), *Current topics in clinical & community psychology* (Vol. 1). New York: Academic Press.

Gottman, J., Gonso, J., & Rasmussen, B. (1975). Social interaction, social competence, and friendship in children. *Child Development 45,* 709–718.

Gottman, J. M., & Parkhurst, J. T. (1980). A developmental theory of friendship and acquaintenceship processes. In W. A. Collins (Ed.), *Minnesota Symposium on Child Psychology* (Vol. 13). Hillsdale, NJ: Erlbaum.

Greenwood, C. R., Walker, H. M., Todd, N. M., & Hops, H. (1979). Selecting a cost-effective screening device for the assessment of preschool social withdrawal. *Journal of Applied Behavioral Analysis 12,* 639–652.

Gresham, F. M. (1981). Social skills training with handicapped children. *Review of Educational Research 51,* 139–176.

Harter, S. (in press). Developmental perspectives on the self-system. In P. H. Mussen (Editor-in-chief) and E. M. Heatherington (Ed.), *Carmichael's manual of child psychology* (4th edition, Vol. 4). New York: John Wiley.

Hartup, W. W. (1976). Peer interaction and the behavioral development of the individual child. In E. Schopler & R. J. Reichler (Eds.), *Psychopathology and child development.* New York: Plenum.

Hartup, W. W. (1977). Peer interaction and the processes of socialization. In M. J. Guralnick (Ed.), *Early intervention and the integration of handicapped and non-handicapped children.* Baltimore: University Park Press.

Hartup, W. W. (in press). The peer system. In P. H. Mussen (Editor-in-chief) & E. M. Heatherington (Ed.), *Carmichael's manual of child psychology* (4th edition, Vol. 4). New York: John Wiley.

Heckhausen, H. (1968). Achievement motive research: Current problems and some contributors toward a general theory of motivation. In W. Arnold (Ed.), *Nebraska Symposium on Motivation.* Lincoln, NE: Univ. of Nebraska Press.

Hops, H. (1983). Children's social competence and skill: Current research practices and future directions. *Behavior Therapy 14,* 13–18.

Hops, H. (1982). Social skills training for socially withdrawn/isolated children. In P. Karoly & J. Steffen (Eds.), *Advances in child behavior analysis and therapy (Vol. 2): Intellectual and social deficiencies.* New York: Gardner Press.

Hops, H., & Greenwood, C. R. (1981). Social skills deficits. In E. J. Mash & L. G. Terdal (Eds.), *Behavioral assessment of childhood disorders.* New York: Guilford Press.

Jones, E. E., & Nisbett, R. E. (1972). The actor and the observer: Divergent perceptions of the causes of behavior. In E. E. Jones, D. E. Kanouse, S. Valins, & B. Weiner (Eds.),

Attribution: Perceiving the causes of behavior. Morristown, NJ: General Learning Press.

Jourard, S. M. & Resnick, J. L. (1970). Some effects of self-disclosure among college women. *Journal of Humanistic Psychology 10*, 84–93.

Kelly, J. A., Furman, W., Phillips, J., Hathorn, S., & Wilson, T. (1979). Teaching conversational skills to retarded adolescents. *Child Behavior Therapy 1*, 36–43.

Kern, J. M. (1982). The comparative external and concurrent validity of three role-plays for assessing heterosocial performance. *Behavior Therapy 13*, 666–680.

Kohn, M., & Rosman, B. L. (1972). Relationship of preschool socio-emotional functioning to later intellectual achievement. *Developmental Psychology 6*, 445–452.

Ladd, G. W., & Oden, S. L. (1979). The relationship between peer acceptance and children's ideas about helpfulness. *Child Development 50*, 402–408.

McNamara, J. R., & Blumer, C. A. (1982). Role playing to assess social competence. Ecological validity considerations. *Behavior Modification 6*, 519–549.

Michelson, L., & Wood, R. (1980). Behavioral assessment and training of children's social skills. In M. Hersen, P. Miller & R. Eisler (Eds.), *Progress in behavior modification* (Vol. 9). New York: Academic Press.

Moore, N. V., Evertson, C. M., & Brophy, J. E. (1974). Solitary play: Some function reconsiderations. *Developmental Psychology 10*, 830–834.

Olson, P. H. (1977). Insiders' and outsiders' views of relationships: Research studies. In G. Levinger & H. L. Rausch (Eds.), *Close relationships: Perspectives on the meaning of intimacy.* Amherst, MA: Univ. of Massachusetts Press.

Patterson, G. R., & Cobb, J. A. (1973). Stimulus control for classes of noxious behavior. In J. F. Knutson (Ed.), *The control of aggression: Implications from basic research.* Chicago: Aldine.

Patterson, G. R., Littman, R. A., & Bricker, W. (1967). Assertive behavior in children: A step toward a theory of aggression. *Monographs of the Society for Research in Child Development 32*, Whole No. 113.

Putallaz, M., & Gottman, J. M. (1981). An interactional model of children's entry into peer groups. *Child Development, 52*, 986–994.

Putallaz, M., & Gottman, J. M. (1981). Social skills and group acceptance. In S. R. Asher & J. M. Gottman (Eds.), *The development of children's friendships.* Cambridge, England: Cambridge University Press.

Rinn, R. C., & Markel, A. (1979). Modification of social skills deficits in children. A. S. Bellack & M. Hersen (Eds.), *Research & practice in social skills training.* New York: Plenum.

Rubin, K. H. (1982). Social and social cognition developmental characteristics of young isolate, normal, and sociable children. In K. H. Rubin & H. S. Ross (Eds.), *Peer relationships and social skills in childhood.* New York: Springer-Verlag.

Selman, R. L. (1980). *The growth of interpersonal understanding: Developmental and clinical analyses.* New York: Academic Press.

Schwartz, R. M., & Gottman, J. M. (1976). Toward a task analysis of assertive behavior. *Journal of Consulting and Clinical Psychology 44*, 910–920.

Scott, W. O. N., & Edelstein, B. A. (1981). The social competence of two interaction strategies: An analog evaluation. *Behavior Therapy 12*, 482–492.

Shantz, C. W. (1975). The development of social cognition. In E. M. Hetherington (Ed.), *Review of child development research* (Vol. 5). Chicago: University of Chicago.

Shaver, P., Furman, W., & Buhrmester, D. (in press). Aspects of a life transition: Network changes, social skills, and loneliness. In S. Duck & Perlman, D. (Eds.). *The Sage series in personal relationships*, Vol. 1. London: Sage.

Shure, M. B., & Spivack, G. (1974). *Preschool Interpersonal Problem-solving (PIPS) Test:*

Manual. Philadelphia, Dept. of Mental Health Sciences, Hahnemann Community Mental Health/Mental Retardation Center.

Snyder, M., Tanke, E. D., & Berscheid, E. (1977). Social perception and interpersonal behavior: On the self-fulfilling nature of social stereotypes. *Journal of Personality and Social Psychology 35*, 656–666.

Spivak, G., Platt, J. J., & Shure, M. B. (1976). *The problem-solving approach to adjustment.* San Francisco: Jossey-Bass.

Spivack, G., & Shure, M. B. (1982). The cognition of social adjustment: Interpersonal cognitive problem-solving thinking. In B. B. Lahey & A. E. Kazdin (Eds.), *Advances in clinical child psychology* (Vol. 5). New York: Plenum.

Strain, P. S., Kerr, M. M., & Raglund, E. U. (1981). The use of peer social initiations in the treatment of social withdrawal. In P. S. Strain (Ed.), *The utilization of classroom peers as behavior change agents.* New York: Plenum.

Sullivan, H. S. (1953). *The interpersonal theory of psychiatry.* New York: W. W. Norton.

Victor, J. B., & Halverson, C. F., Jr. (1976). Behavior problems in elementary school children: A follow-up study. *Journal of Abnormal Child Psychology 4*, 17–29.

Waters, E. (1978). The reliability and stability of individual differences in infant-mother attachment. *Child Development 49*, 483–494.

Wessberg, H. W., Mariotto, M. J., Conger, A. J., Farrell, A. D., & Conger, J. C. (1979). Ecological validity of role plays for assessing heterosexual anxiety and skill of male college students. *Journal of Consulting and Clinical Psychology 47*, 525–535.

2

Sociometric, Social–Cognitive, and Behavioral Measures for the Study of Friendship and Popularity*

Thomas J. Berndt

During the past decade, research on children's friendships and peer relationships has increased dramatically (see Asher & Gottman, 1981; Duck & Gilmour, 1981; Foot, Chapman, & Smith, 1980; K. H. Rubin & Ross, 1982; Z. Rubin, 1980). At the same time, the variety and the sophistication of methods for assessing these relationships has increased. This chapter presents an overview of the most common techniques for assessing friendships and other peer relationships during childhood and adolescence.

Relatively equal emphasis is given to methods for studying children's friendships and methods for studying their popularity or sociometric status. Although friendship refers to a relationship and popularity refers to a child's position in a social group, there are important connections between the two concepts. For instance, a child who has no friends is unpopular, and a child who has many friends is popular. In addition, the same measurement techniques can be used to assess children's friendships (e.g., who are their friends) and their popularity (e.g., how many friends they have). Finally, the consideration of both topics in the same chapter may not only illustrate the parallels between them, but also expose opportunities for integration of the two research areas.

* Preparation of this chapter was supported in part by grant number 1R01-MH38093 from the National Institute of Mental Health, and by a grant from the W. T. Grant Foundation. Their support is gratefully acknowledged.

The chapter is divided into three major sections. The methods and procedures described in the first section are traditionally included in the domain of sociometry. These techniques are used primarily for identifying children's friends or determining their popularity with classmates. Evidence on the reliability and validity of these techniques is discussed. The second section describes methods for exploring the facet of children's social cognition that involves their ideas about peer relationships. Methods for examining children's conceptions of friendship and their impressions of popular and unpopular classmates are reviewed. The third section describes techniques for observing children's behavior with friends and other classmates, either in settings controlled by an experimenter or in natural settings. The value of studying children's social interactions in both types of settings is illustrated with specific examples.

CURRENT SOCIOMETRIC METHODS

For nearly 50 years, psychologists have asked children and adolescents to name their best friends, the children they like, or the children they would choose as playmates (see Renshaw, 1981). These questions about social relationships and social preferences constitute the basic elements of sociometric methodology. Children's responses to the questions are essential data for research on friendship and on popularity.

Identifying Best Friends

In studies of friendship, sociometric methods are used to determine who are a child's close friends. The earliest studies employed a simple definition of friendship: A best friend is someone whom a child names as a best friend. In many studies (e.g., Horrocks & Buker, 1951), children were told to name a fixed number of best friends, and often three names were requested. Although the assessment of friendships by means of best-friend nominations clearly has face validity, there are both conceptual and methodological problems with this method.

First, children may name as best friends other children who are not actually their best friends. In standard usage, friendship refers to a relationship of strong and mutual liking or esteem. That is, friendship is a reciprocal relationship that must be affirmed by both parties. Nominations by a single child are, therefore, not a good basis for identifying close friends. Children often name more popular classmates as best friends, but they seldom are named in return (Ball, 1981; Leinhardt,

1972). Such "choosing up" assures that unilateral best-friend nominations do not always correspond to actual friendships.

Second, biases and errors can be introduced when children are told to name a fixed number of friends. For example, if all children are told to name three best friends, children who have only one close friend must include the names of children who are not really their friends, and children who have more than three best friends must exclude some of them. Even if a number is not specified, biases can be introduced by children's tendency to name other children who are sitting near them, or their tendency to overlook children who are absent on the day that the questions are asked (Hallinan, 1981).

Finally, nominations provide a fairly insensitive measure of friendship because they constitute a dichotomous response scale. A child either names another child as a friend or does not. Along with the other problems, this insensitivity of measurement places a limit on the reliability of measures derived from best-friend nominations.

Despite these problems, using nominations to identify friendships can be the method of choice under certain circumstances. Nominations can be obtained more easily and efficiently than the alternative methods that will be discussed next. In studies with large samples, the gain in efficiency may offset the losses in reliability. Valuable data have been obtained in several recent studies where the primary measures of friendship were best-friend nominations. For example, Kandel (1978) used data on adolescents' best-friend nominations to demonstrate the influence of friendship on adolescents' educational aspirations, drug use, and other behaviors. Epstein (1983) surveyed several thousand students from the fifth to the twelfth grade on two occasions a year apart. She found that the changes in students' grades over the year were related to the initial grades of their friends. Students who had nominated children with higher grades as friends showed an increase in their own grades.

In research with smaller samples, or in cases where greater reliability of measurement is necessary, best-friend nominations may provide less adequate measures of friendship than alternative methods. Hallinan (1981) identified best friends by giving children lists of their classmates and asking them to name the ones who were their best friends, their friends, and not their friends. Because the categories of best friends, friends, and nonfriends can be viewed as roughly ordered by degree of liking, this method can be regarded as a partial ranking technique. The technique leads to reliable data, if reliability is judged by the stability of children's rankings. In one study with fourth through sixth graders (Hallinan & Tuma, 1978), more than 70% of the children listed as best friends at one time were listed again six weeks later. Using the same technique, Eder and Hallinan (1978) discovered intriguing differences in the formation of friendships by boys and girls. For example, girls were less likely than boys to expand an existing dyadic friendship to include a third child, suggesting that the girls had more exclusive friendships.

One disadvantage of Hallinan's procedure is that the scale of measurement still is relatively crude. Even best friendships differ in their intensity or closeness, but these differences cannot be captured when the underlying response scale is dichotomous (i.e., best friend versus not a best friend). To circumvent this problem, my co-workers and I have identified best friends by a combination of best-friend nominations and ratings of liking on a 5-point scale (Berndt, 1981a, 1981b, 1982b). The lowest point on the scale is labeled "don't like"; the highest point is labeled "like very much, as much as a best friend." Children are considered close friends if either one or both of them nominated the other as a best friend, and their ratings of liking average 4.0 or better on the 5-point scale. With these criteria, friends may not have reciprocal nominations, but reciprocity of liking is required. Moreover, in all studies a majority of the pairs of friends actually did name each other as best friends.

The most elaborate set of criteria for identifying close friends was used by Mannarino (1976, 1979). His research was designed as a test of Sullivan's (1953) hypotheses about the effects of intimate and sensitive friendships in the preadolescent or early adolescent years. Sullivan referred to such a close friend as a "chum," and Mannarino attempted to identify relationships that fit Sullivan's description. To be credited with having a chum, children had to select the same classmate as a best friend on two occasions two weeks apart (and, in the 1979 study, be selected in return); say that they preferred to spend their free time with the chum alone, rather than with a group of friends; and respond positively to a series of specific items concerning various features of their relationship, such as their sharing and helping with the chum and the intimacy of their conversations with him or her.

Mannarino's criteria represent the most detailed and precise measures for identifying close friends, but these characteristics may be a disadvantage. He noted that less than one-third of the fifth and sixth graders in his samples had such a chumship. It appears, therefore, that he did not have a representative sample of friendships. Instead, he had identified a specific type of friendship that is theoretically important but atypical. For most purposes, it probably is preferable to separate two assessments that Mannarino confounded. Friendships first could be identified by one of the methods described earlier. Then the features of these friendships, such as their intimacy, could be evaluated with

Mannarino's other measures or the measures discussed later in this chapter.

Finally, it is important to note that preschool children do not always give consistent answers to sociometric questions (Hymel, 1983). During the preschool period, friendships might be identified more reliably by behavioral observations than by sociometric measures (see Howes, and Roopnarine & Field, this volume). Defining children as friends because they play together frequently, however, is a departure from the usual definition of friendship as a relationship indicated by children's own reports of strong and mutual liking.

Measuring Popularity

From this point of view of the children participating in a study, several of the methods for assessing children's popularity are the same as those used to identify pairs of friends. The methods differ only in the way that the responses are scored. For example, when children are asked to name their best friends, or to rate how much they like each of their classmates, the number of times a child is nominated or the mean rating of liking by classmates can serve as a measure of the child's popularity. As in the case of friendship, measures of popularity generally are more reliable when they are based on ratings rather than nominations (Hymel, 1983). The difference in reliability is most obvious in research with preschool children (Asher, Singleton, Tinsley, & Hymel, 1979).

Still greater reliability can be achieved by use of the paired-comparison technique. In this technique, children are shown pictures of all possible pairs of their classmates. When shown each pair, they are asked which child they like better. The major problem with this technique is the amount of testing time that is required when the peer group is at all large. In one study (Vaughn & Waters, 1981), preschool children took two or three 15-minute sessions to judge all possible pairs of their 22 classmates. For this reason, most investigators have avoided the paired-comparison technique, and have adopted either nominations, ratings, or some combination of the two.

Gresham (1981) suggested that nominations and ratings produce measures of sociometric status that are largely independent. If this conclusion were correct, comparisons between the findings of research using the two different methods would be difficult. The conclusion was based primarily on the results of a factor analysis of measures derived from peer ratings and peer nominations that were summed across three times of measurement. Although the two types of measures did load on different factors in this analysis, they loaded on the same factors at

Times 1 and 2. Moreover, when summed across all three times of measurement, the correlations between nominations and ratings ranged from .38 to .76 (all p < .01). These correlations are in the same range as the stability coefficients for the measures, and they establish the convergent validity of the measures.

In recent research, greatest attention has focused not on the methods for collecting sociometric data, but on the coding of the data and subsequent classification of children. Some researchers use a single dimension of social acceptance or social preference (e.g., Rubin & Daniels-Beirness, 1983). When ratings are used, a child's score on the dimension is the mean rating that the child received from peers. When nominations are used, the child's score is the sum of positive nominations minus negative nominations, divided by the number of children who made nominations.

Other researchers have revived distinctions made in the early sociometric literature between, for example, sociometric stars (i.e., popular children), isolates, and rejected children (see Renshaw, 1981). Peery (1979) defined children as popular if they had many positive nominations and few negative ones. He defined children as rejected if they had many negative nominations and few positive ones, as isolated if they had few nominations but mostly negative ones, and as amiable if they had few nominations but mostly positive ones.

Coie and Dodge (1983; Coie, Dodge, & Coppotelli, 1982; Dodge, Schlundt, Schocken, & Delugach, 1983) also distinguished between popular and rejected children, but they argued that children who had few nominations of either type should be described as neglected rather than isolated. They pointed out that children with few nominations were labeled as neglected in some early research (e.g., Northway, 1944). Moreover, recent research has established that these children are not always socially isolated or uninvolved in social interactions (cf. Asher, Markell, & Hymel, 1981). Coie and Dodge described another group of children as average in their sociometric status. They defined a final group of children as controversial because they received many positive nominations and many negative nominations.

Newcomb and Bukowski (1983) argued that the classification systems of Peery and of Coie and Dodge are problematic for several reasons. First, the criteria for classifying children do not produce mutually exclusive and exhaustive groups. Second, the classifications often are based on scores standardized within groups of children. These scores are not sensitive to differences between groups, and they do not provide a consistent frame of reference for comparing children in different groups.

In place of these systems, Newcomb and Bukowski recommended a system based on the probability of different patterns of scores. For example, children are judged as "stars" if they receive more positive nominations than would be expected by chance, given the size of their classroom group and the number of nominations made by each child. Children are judged as rejected if they receive more negative nominations than would be expected by chance. Similar criteria are used to define average, isolated (or neglected), and controversial children. Evidence on the stability of these classifications and on the reputations of children in the different groups suggests that this system results in more reliable and valid distinctions among children than the previous two systems.

The last word on classification schemes for use with sociometric data has probably not been written. Nevertheless, the recent studies attest to the vigor and the growing precision of sociometric research. Comparable gains have been made in research on the correlates of sociometric status (see Berndt, 1983). For example, differences in sociometric status have been related to the frequency of children's positive and negative interactions with peers (e.g., Masters & Furman, 1981); their social participation on the school playground (Ladd, 1983); their reputation as classmates who are cooperative or, conversely, cause fights (Coie & Dodge, 1983); teachers' ratings of their behavior problems (Rubin & Daniels-Beirness, 1983); their academic achievement (Green, Forehand, Beck, & Vosk, 1980); their physical attractiveness; and a host of other measures of personality and social behavior (Hartup, 1983). These correlations demonstrate the validity of sociometric measures and their utility as indicators of a child's social adjustment and peer relationships. The measures clearly will be an important tool in research for the foreseeable future.

SOCIAL COGNITION AND FRIENDSHIP

A common element in several apparently dissimilar research methods is the use of children as informants on their own relationships. For example, investigators have asked children to describe their conceptions of friendship, or to state their opinions of their own classmates. Because the data in this research reflect children's ideas about social relationships, the research methods can be classified within the general domain of social cognition.

Conceptions of Ideal Friendships

The current emphasis on children's friendships was partly sparked by social–cognitive research. Many researchers have asked children to describe what they expect from a friend, how they can tell that someone is a friend, or how friends act toward each other (Berndt, 1981c,

1982a; Bigelow & La Gaipa, 1980; Douvan & Adelson, 1966; Selman, 1981; Youniss, 1980). Most often, the questions focus not on the children's own friendships but on their conceptions of friendships. That is, the questions refer to a prototypical or ideal friendship.

Regardless of the specific form of the questions, there is considerable consistency in children's answers (Berndt, 1981c, 1982a). Most children and adolescents say that friends play together or do other activities together. Most children and adolescents assume that friends help each other and share with each other. Only in adolescence are there frequent references to intimacy and loyalty in friendships. References to intimacy and to the faithfulness of friends (i.e., "she won't leave me for someone else") are more common among girls than boys.

There is less argreement among researchers about the best way to code and interpret children's responses. Many investigators code the responses into mutually exclusive and exhaustive categories, using procedures comparable to standard content analysis (Berndt, 1981c; Bigelow & La Gaipa, 1980). Other investigators score the responses for the level of social perspective-taking that they seem to represent (Selman, 1981). For example, adolescents who comment about the disclosure of intimate information between friends obviously recognize that people can understand each other's thoughts and feelings. An appreciation of mutual or reciprocal understanding is assumed to reflect a high level of perspective taking. Still other investigators code responses into categories suggested by previous theories of friendship. From the theories of Piaget (1932/1965) and Sullivan (1965), Youniss (1980) derived the hypothesis that the nature and the importance of equality and reciprocity in friendship change between childhood and adolescence. He suggested that age changes in children's conceptions of friendship lend support to the hypothesis.

The contrasting interpretations of children's responses are valuable in highlighting distinct features of friendship. Nevertheless, the significance of these data is somewhat unclear. Although the age changes in children's comments about friendship cannot be attributed entirely to changes in their verbal fluency (see Furman & Bierman, in press), there is probably not an exact correspondence between children's conceptions of an ideal friendship and the features of their own friendships. Consequently, to determine what actual friendships are like, it is necessary to ask children about them directly.

Impressions of Actual Friendships

In one study (Berndt, 1982), fourth and eighth graders completed a sociometric questionnaire during the fall of the school year and then were paired with a close friend. The pairings were based on the combination of best-friend nominations and ratings of liking that was discussed earlier. Shortly after the pairs were formed, each child was interviewed individually. The interview began with a series of open-ended questions about the friend's personality (e.g., "Tell me all that you can about [friend's name], what kind of person he/she is and what kinds of things he/she likes to do"). Children were then asked a comparable series of questions about the friendship itself. They were asked about both positive and negative features of the friendship—what they liked best about being friends with their partner, and when it was hard to be friends with him or her.

Following the open-ended questions were closed-ended questions about several features of the friend's personality and the friendship itself. For example, children were asked how smart the friend was and how often he or she took their side in a fight or argument. The features of the friendship that were examined with specific questions were intimacy, loyalty, conflicts (or aggressive behavior between the friends), prosocial behavior, and similarity. A final set of five questions concerned the frequency of interaction between the friends (e.g., how often they went to each other's houses).

The interviews and observations were repeated in the spring of the same school year. The children were paired with the same partner as in the fall, regardless of whether or not they had remained close friends. The analysis of the sociometric data indicated that a sizable minority of the fall friendships did weaken or end during the school year. In the spring, only 69% of the pairs that were formed in the fall still met the original criteria for a close friendship. This percentage did not vary significantly with grade or sex.

As expected, comparable results were found for children's responses to the interviews (see Table 1). Children's responses to the open-ended questions about the friend's personality and the friendship were coded into mutually exclusive and exhaustive categories. There were separate sets of categories for positive comments and for negative comments. Ratings of the friendship and the friend's personality were scaled so that high scores indicated a more positive view of the friendship and the friend's personality. A high score on the measure for frequency of interaction indicated that the two children in a pair saw or talked to each other a great deal.

The weakening of children's friendships during the school year affected scores on all of the interview measures. Positive comments and ratings decreased over time; negative comments increased over time. The changes were statistically significant ($p < .05$) for all measures except that for positive comments about the friend's personality ($p < .06$).

Table 1
Mean Scores for Reports on the Friendship and the
‘Friend's Personality at Each Time

	Time	
Measures	Fall	Spring
Positive friendship categories	1.20	1.10
Negative friendship categories	.48	.60
Positive personality categories	.67	.57
Negative personality categories	.39	.50
Friendship ratings	2.85	2.69
Personality ratings	2.87	2.73
Frequency of interaction	11.17	9.33

These findings establish the validity of the interview measures as indicators of the children's friendships.

In a second analysis, correlations were computed between the interview measures and a friendship score for each pair of children based on whether or not each child had nominated the other as a best friend and how much each child had said he or she liked the other. Because all children were close friends with their partners in the fall, the correlations for the spring data are most meaningful.

Children who were better friends in the spring, as judged by their friendship scores, made more positive comments about their friendships, rated their friendships more positively on the closed-ended questions, and reported more frequent interactions with each other (Table 2). Although the magnitude of these correlations varied slightly for fourth and eighth graders, none of the differences was significant. The correlations with comments and ratings of the friend's personality

Table 2
Correlations of Spring Interview Responses with Friendship Scores

Interview Measure	Friendship Scores		
Positive friendship categories	.57**	.29	.43**
Negative friendship categories	−.07	−.19	−.16
Friendship ratings	.36	.43*	.41**
Frequency of interaction	.77***	.51*	.66***

*p < .05.
**p < .01.
***p < .001.

are not shown, because these correlations were not significant. In other words, the strength of children's friendships was more strongly related to their comments about the friendship itself than to their comments about each other's personality. These data provide further evidence for the validity of the friendship measures derived from the interviews.

The nonsignificant correlation of friendship scores with negative comments about the friendship was clarified by a more detailed examination of the results for specific categories. Apparently, only certain types of negative comments indicate problems in a relationship. Children who were better friends were less likely to talk about a lack of intimacy and loyalty in their relationship, but they were more likely to comment on the ways that they and their friend were dissimilar. Because better friends also made more comments about the ways they were similar to each other, the data as a whole suggest that close friends recognize their differences as well as their similarities (see Diaz & Berndt, 1982).

Taken together, the results indicate that children's interview responses were a valid reflection of their closeness to their partner. In addition, the results set the foundation for further refinements of the assessment technique. Additional research of this type could lead to the formulation of a semistructured, standardized measure of friendships during childhood and adolescence.

Sharabany, Gershoni, and Hofman (1981) used multiple items on several features of friendship to assess changes in same- and opposite-sex friendships between fifth and eleventh grade. Their measure would probably be difficult to use with younger children, however, because of the vocabulary in some of the items. Because the items are presented in a questionnaire given to groups of children, detecting misinterpretations of specific items would also be difficult. Finally, the use of closed-ended questions with a structured response format facilitates coding of the data, but rules out an exploration of the reasons for a child's responses.

For many purposes, an interview that includes both open- and closed-ended questions would be preferable to a written questionnaire. In addition, a more explicit theoretical focus for social–cognitive measures of friendship would be desirable. One alternative would be to select items that are relevant to hypotheses about the positive influence of friendships on children's development. In recent years, many researchers have explored the impact of social relationships on adults who are trying to cope with various life stresses (see Gottlieb, 1981). A systematic investigation of children's ideas about the support that they derive from their friendships would be valuable for both theory-oriented and applied research.

Impressions of Popular and Unpopular Children

When exploring children's ideas about their social world, researchers need not restrict their inquiry to a single friendship or even a few friendships. With suitable procedures, children can be asked about their impressions of all their classmates. Actually, such measures have been available for a long time, but they have usually been treated as peer-assessment techniques rather than social–cognitive measures. For example, Bower (1969) asked children to name classmates for positive roles (e.g., leader) and negative roles (e.g., someone who starts fights) in a hypothetical class play. The class play and similar measures are clearly parallel to interviews and questionnaires used to examine children's friendships; they differ mainly in the number of social relationships under investigation, that is, one friendship versus all possible relationships within an existing group.

Several researchers have since used instruments like the class play to examine children's impressions of peers who differ in their sociometric status. Coie and Dodge (1983) found that popular children are viewed by their classmates as cooperative and as leaders; rejected children are viewed as disruptive and as often starting fights. Neglected children are viewed as shy, and the "controversial" children who receive many positive nominations and many negative nominations are viewed both as leaders and as often starting fights (see also Newcomb & Bukowski, 1983).

The attributions that children make about popular and unpopular peers are an invaluable source of evidence on the reasons for individual differences in sociometric status (Berndt, 1983). Up to now, however, these measures have not been used in systematic tests of hypotheses about the origins of sociometric status. In addition, specific items for these measures have usually been selected on intuitive grounds, because they seem relevant to social adjustment. In the future, the selection of items because of their relevance to particular questions or hypotheses could be worthwhile.

An alternative technique for examining the social–cognitive correlates of popularity and unpopularity is focused less on children's judgments of their peers than on their judgments concerning social situations. Hypothetical situations that involve conflicts or other types of social problems are described to children, and then the children are asked how they would respond. The children's ability to generate appropriate responses to the situations is taken as a measure of their social problem-solving or social–cognitive skills. Training in social skills is regarded currently as one of the most promising techniques for experimental interventions with isolated or rejected children (see Asher & Renshaw, 1981; Conger & Keane, 1981; Ladd & Mize, 1983; Urbain &

Kendall, 1980). By changing children's ideas about problem situations and assuring that the children's behavior also changes, researchers expect to improve children's reputations and their relationships with peers.

The theoretical and practical significance of research on social problem-solving has been convincingly demonstrated (e.g., see Ladd & Mize, 1983). Nevertheless, the full value of this type of research may not yet have been realized, for two reasons. First, although children are asked about specific situations, the situational information is often lost when the data are coded. For example, popular children may be contrasted with unpopular children in terms of how often they choose friendly rather than hostile goals and strategies across all types of situations (Renshaw & Asher, 1983). In intervention research, greater attention to situational details could be beneficial. Children could be taught not simply what type of behavior is generally appropriate, but what behavior is most appropriate in the specific situations that are common and problematic for them. A focus on specific situations could also add precision and depth to current conceptions of the social world of children and adolescents.

Second, when children are asked about social conflicts, they are not usually told which specific children are involved. When such specific information is provided, the results can be extremely illuminating. For example, Dodge (1980; Dodge & Frame, 1982) showed that aggressive boys are especially likely to perceive an ambiguous act as intentionally aggressive if they are told that the act was directed toward them. Conversely, other boys are especially likely to perceive an ambiguous act as intentionally aggressive if it was performed by a boy who has a reputation as aggressive. These biased perceptions could increase the stability of aggressive behavior by functioning as self-fulfilling prophecies. Similar processes probably contribute to the stability of individual differences in sociometric status (cf. Coie & Dodge, 1983). Further research on children's ideas about their social world, for specific situations with specific actors, has great promise for explaining the crucial differences between children who have many satisfying social relationships with classmates and children who have few or none. Studies of this type would be most valuable if they were done in conjunction with observations of children's behavior in the specific situations under consideration.

FRIENDSHIPS, POPULARITY, AND BEHAVIORAL OBSERVATIONS

The methods employed for the observation of interactions between friends or the social behavior of popular and unpopular children are not intrinsically different from those typical in developmental research (see Cairns, 1979; Lamb, Suomi, & Stephenson, 1979; Sackett, 1978). The choice of a setting for behavioral observations is an issue in the research on friendship, however, because most of the recent research was done not in natural settings but in settings structured by an experimenter. For example, researchers have recorded the amount of sharing and helping between friends as they worked on various activities, such as coloring geometric designs (Berndt, 1981a, 1981b, 1982b; Staub & Noerenberg, 1981) or exploring an unusual object (Newcomb & Brady, 1982).

Structured Tasks and Everyday Life

The standard criticism of research that employs unusual, structured tasks in a setting under an experimenter's control is that the results may not validly reflect the behavior of children in natural settings. The validity of laboratory-experimental research has been vigorously debated for several years (e.g., Berkowitz & Donnerstein, 1982; Weisz, 1978), but no consensus on the question has emerged. One way to resolve the debate may be to consider more carefully the types of evidence that establish the validity of a measure. An example from the recent research on friendship can be used to illustrate the major issues.

In the short-term longitudinal study that was described earlier (Berndt, 1982b), pairs of friends were asked to work on a task that involved coloring geometric designs while sharing a special tracer (i.e., an artist's template). The children were told that they needed to share the tracer, but that the amount they shared was up to them.

After each trial, the children received nickels that indicated how well they were doing on the task. Children were not allowed to keep the nickels, but they were told that the number they received would determine what prize they got later. On each trial, children received two nickels if they colored more than their partner and one nickel if they colored less. In previous research (Berndt, 1981b), this research structure seemed to encourage kindergarten to fourth-grade boys to compete with their friends rather than to share equally with them.

In the fall, when the children in each pair were close friends, eighth graders shared more equally than fourth graders. This finding is consistent with several previous studies indicating that prosocial behavior and preferences for equality between peers increase with age (see Eisenberg, 1982; Damon, 1977).

In the spring, the amount of sharing by each pair of children varied with grade and with their current relationship to each other (Table 3). Children were judged to be still friends with each other if their responses on the spring sociometric questionnaire indicated that they still met the criteria for a close friendship. Fourth graders shared less with their partners if they were still close friends than if they were no longer close friends. These data match those from an earlier study with the same reward structure (Berndt, 1981b), although in this study both boys and girls shared less with close friends. Apparently, the fourth graders assumed that they would get fewer rewards than their partner and, in effect, lose the game to the partner if they shared the tracer for a long time. Rather than losing and seeming inferior to their partner, they chose to compete with him or her. In other words, the data demonstrate the intensity of competition between friends during middle childhood.

Eighth graders shared more when they were still friends than when they were no longer close friends. Moreover, the eighth graders paired with friends came closest to equal sharing of the tracer, which would have resulted in a score of 360 seconds. This finding suggests that competition is replaced by a preference for equality during the transition from childhood to adolescence.

The results that seem most inconsistent with common sense notions of friendship are those for fourth graders. Would fourth graders also compete rather than share with close friends in natural settings, or is the evidence on friends' interactions when working on a structured task completely unrepresentative of friends' behavior in everyday life? Additional data from the study clarify the answer.

Fourth graders who shared less with their partners when doing the structured task made more positive comments about their friendship during the interviews described earlier ($r = -.53$, $p < .05$). Eighth graders shared more when they made more positive comments about their friendship ($r = .35$, $p < .11$). Moreover, fourth graders who, during the interviews, made more specific comments about their helping and sharing with each other shared less than other fourth graders when working on the structured tasks ($r = -.61$, $p < .01$). The reverse was true at eighth grade ($r = .28$, ns). Although the positive correlations at eighth grade were nonsignificant, there was a significant difference between the correlations for the two grades in both these cases.

Table 3
Mean Number of Seconds for Sharing in the Spring

	Still Friends	No Longer Friends
Fourth Grade	261	317
Eighth Grade	334	300

The negative correlation at fourth grade between comments about sharing and actual sharing is particularly intriguing, because it simultaneously confirms two apparently contradictory propositions. First, friends' behavior on laboratory-type tasks reflects the closeness of their friendship as assessed by other methods less subject to experimental artifacts. In short, the correlation supports the validity of the measure of sharing. Second, when doing a laboratory task, friends do not behave in the same way as they say they would behave in real-life settings. At first glance, this conclusion casts doubt on the validity of the sharing measure.

The paradox can be easily resolved by a closer inspection of the concept of a natural setting. Critiques of laboratory research often depend on the implicit assumption that there is a single natural setting in which behavior should be observed or, perhaps, that behavior would be similar in all natural settings. This assumption is clearly false. In some natural settings, close friends probably share and help each other more than do children who are not close friends, but they do so in some laboratory settings as well (Berndt, 1981a; Newcomb & Brady, 1982). In other natural settings, friends probably share and help each other less than children who are not close friends. The recent research suggests that children are more likely to compete than share with friends when they believe sharing could result in their seeming inferior to the friend. That is, evidence for competition between friends should be sought in natural settings where there is a risk of losing to the friend.

In spontaneous conversations between young children who are friends, social comparisons that could be precursors to competitive behavior are common (Gottman & Parkhurst, 1980). Competition in the academic arena has been shown to affect friendships among school-aged children, although sometimes children prefer to do badly in school rather than competing with their friends (Ball, 1981). These findings support the claim that competition between friends is not merely a laboratory phenomenon.

Nevertheless, observations of behavior on laboratory-type tasks have certain limits (cf. Berkowitz & Donnerstein, 1982). Laboratory research can establish that friends compete with each other under certain conditions, but it cannot establish how often these conditions arise or how much they affect the stability of friendships. Therefore, an interplay between research with standardized tasks and research in natural settings is needed. For example, observations of friends' competition on structured tasks might be coordinated with observations of friends' interactions during an athletic or scholastic competition. Greatest understanding of a phenomenon can be achieved if it is examined both in settings controlled or arranged by an experimenter, and in natural settings.

Popularity and Research Settings

The research literature on popularity or social acceptance is biased in the opposite direction to that on friendship. There are numerous studies of the social behavior of popular and unpopular children in natural settings. In contrast, the social behavior of popular and un-popular children has rarely been examined in standardized or experi-mentally controlled conditions (Hartup, 1983).

The advantages of research on popularity in "unnatural" settings were demonstrated in several recent studies. Putallaz and Gottman (1981) observed popular and unpopular children who were trying to join a pair of classmates who were already engaged in playing a game. Unpopular children used several tactics that often led to their rejection by their classmates. This specific information about the unsuccessful tactics of unpopular children who are trying to enter a peer group clarifies why the children have trouble making friends and keeping friends (see also Dodge et al., 1983).

Coie and Kuperschmidt (1983) assessed the sociometric status of a sample of boys in their regular classrooms. Then they observed the social interactions in a laboratory playroom among four boys who dif-fered in their status. One boy in each group was popular in the regular classroom, another one was rejected, a third boy was neglected, and the fourth boy was average in his sociometric status. After each week's group interaction, a sociometric measure was completed by each boy. For this measure, boys indicated which other boys in their group they liked most and liked least. By the third week, boys' status in their ad hoc groups was significantly correlated with their status in the regular classroom. In other words, sociometric status remained consistent when boys moved to a new group of peers. These data demonstrate that children's sociometric status is partly due to stable characteristics of their personality and social behavior. More detailed analyses of the children's interactions illustrated the behaviors that apparently were responsible for their social position in the new groups. For example, popular children were less physically aggressive than children who were average or rejected.

The recent studies demonstrate one of the major advantages of research on sociometric status in a laboratory setting. When the tasks to be performed and the composition of the group are under an experi-menter's control, the relations between children's behavior and their sociometric status can be examined without the confounding influence of the children's reputations in their natural social environments. The research thus far has emphasized the behaviors of unpopular children that apparently contribute to their low status. Future research could be designed to examine the experimental arrangements that lead to changes in children's status. That is, techniques of structuring a social environment to improve the status of unpopular children could be explored. These techniques would be of great practical value for programs with handicapped children (cf. Ballard, Corman, Gottlieb, & Kaufman, 1977; Strain, this volume).

CONCLUSIONS

The three general methods for research that were discussed in this chapter can be characterized as focusing on three types of questions about friendship and popularity. First, best-friend nominations, ratings of liking for classmates, and other sociometric techniques are designed primarily to answer the questions, who are a child's close friends, and what is the child's position in the peer group. As a general rule, the techniques that yield the most reliable data require children to indicate their degree of liking (or relative preference) for all of their classmates.

In the past few years, researchers have revived and refined earlier systems for classifying children on the basis of sociometric data. Children may be classified as rejected if many of their classmates report that they dislike them. Children may be classified as neglected if most of their classmates do not mention them either as someone they like or someone they dislike. The new classification systems have been shown to reflect differences in children's social behavior and their reputations with peers. Therefore, they may be more useful than measures of sociometric status that simply contrast popular children with unpopular children.

Second, when the usual methods for examining children's conceptions of friendship are altered so that they focus on the features of an actual friendship, they provide an answer to the question, what are a child's friendships like. Measures of children's actual friendships have only been employed in a few recent studies, but these measures could be valuable in future research on the effects of friendships during childhood and adolescence.

In research on popularity or sociometric status, the related question is how children perceive their relationships with peers or are perceived by their peers. This question may be answered either in general or in specific terms. Standard peer-assessment techniques indicate children's reputations with their classmates, or their peers' impressions of their social behavior and personality. In contrast, measures of children's social problem-solving ability or social–cognitive skills provide information about a child's reactions in specific situations. The combination of the two methods would be a powerful one, because it would clarify how a child's reputation is created and maintained in a particular social environment.

Third, behavioral observations provide a direct answer to the question, how do friends interact with each other. When these observations are done in experimentally controlled settings, they can reveal features of friendship, such as their competitiveness, that are not obvious from children's verbal reports. Behavioral observations can also answer the more complex questions, how are friends' interactions affected by variations in their situational context.

A great deal of observational research has been done on the behavior of children who differ in their sociometric status. Most often, children have been observed in natural settings such as a preschool classroom or a school playground. The findings of this research provide suggestive evidence on the determinants of children's status, but because the research has been largely correlational, causal hypotheses have seldom been tested. A shift in research emphasis toward observations of popular, neglected, and rejected children in experimentally controlled settings is apparent in the recent literature. Therefore, more conclusive answers to questions about the origins of sociometric status can be expected in the future.

Taken together, the preceding questions constitute a very full agenda for research on friendships. They can be answered only if the current diversity in research methods is encouraged, and even increased. Furthermore, the most adequate answers are likely to come from research that relies not on a single method, but on an integration of the methods of sociometry, social cognition, and behavioral observation.

REFERENCES

Asher, S. R., & Gottman, J. M. (Eds.). (1981). *The development of children's friendships.* Cambridge, England: Cambridge University Press.

Asher, S. R., Markell, R. A., & Hymel, S. (1981). Identifying children at risk in peer relations: A critique of the rate-of-interaction approach to assessment. *Child Development 52,* 1239–1245.

Asher, S. R., & Renshaw, P. D. (1981). Children without friends: Social knowledge and social skill training. In S. R. Asher and J. M. Gottman (Eds.), *The development of children's friendships.* Cambridge, England: Cambridge University Press.

Asher, S. R., Singleton, L. C., Tinsley, B. R., & Hymel, S. (1979). A reliable sociometric measure for preschool children. *Developmental Psychology 15,* 443–444.

Ball, S. J. (1981). *Beachside comprehensive.* Cambridge, England: Cambridge University Press.

Ballard, M., Corman, L., Gottlieb, J., & Kaufman, M. J. (1977). Improving the social status of mainstreamed retarded children. *Journal of Educational Psychology 69,* 605–611.

Berndt, T. J. (1981). Age changes and changes over time in prosocial intentions and behavior between friends. *Developmental Psychology 17,* 406–416. (a)

Berndt, T. J. (1981). The effects of friendship on prosocial intentions and behavior. *Child Development 52*, 636–643. (b)

Berndt, T. J. (1981). Relations between social cognition, nonsocial cognition, and social behavior: The case of friendship. In J. H. Flavell and L. D. Ross (Eds.), *Social cognitive development: Frontiers and possible futures.* Cambridge, England: Cambridge University Press. (c)

Berndt, T. J. (1982). The features and effects of friendship in early adolescence. *Child Development 53*, 1447–1460. (a)

Berndt, T. J. (1982). Stability and change in childhood and adolescent friendship. Unpublished manuscript, University of Oklahoma. (b)

Berndt, T. J. (1983). Correlates and causes of sociometric status in childhood: A commentary on six current studies of popular, rejected, and neglected children. *Merrill-Palmer Quarterly, 29*, 439–448.

Berkowitz, L., & Donnerstein, E. (1982). External validity is more than skin deep: Some answers to criticisms of laboratory experiments. *American Psychologist 37*, 245–257.

Bigelow, B. J., & LaGaipa, J. J. (1980). The development of friendship values and choice. In H. C. Foot, A. J. Chapman, and J. R. Smith (Eds.), *Friendship and social relations in children.* New York: Wiley.

Bower, E. M. (1969). *Early identification of emotionally handicapped children in school* (2nd ed.). Springfield, IL: Charles C Thomas.

Cairns, R. B. (Ed.). (1979). *The analysis of social interactions: Methods, issues, and illustrations.* Hillsdale, NJ: Lawrence Erlbaum Associates.

Coie, J. D., & Dodge, K. A. (1983). Continuities and changes in children's social status: A five-year longitudinal study. *Merrill-Palmer Quarterly, 29*, 261–282.

Coie, J. D., Dodge, K. A., & Coppotelli, H. (1982). Dimensions and types of social status: A cross-age perspective. *Developmental Psychology, 18*, 557–570.

Coie, J. D., & Kupersmidt, J. B. (1983). A behavioral analysis of emerging social status in boys' groups. *Child Development, 54*, 1400–1416.

Conger, J. C., & Keane, S. P. (1981). Social skills intervention in the treatment of isolated or withdrawn children. *Psychological Bulletin, 90*, 478–495.

Damon, W. (1977). *The social world of the child.* San Francisco: Jossey-Bass.

Diaz, R. M., & Berndt, T. J. (1982). Children's knowledge of a best friend: Fact or fancy? *Developmental Psychology 18*, 787–794.

Dodge, K. A. (1980). Social cognition and children's aggressive behavior. *Child Development 51*, 162–170.

Dodge, K. A., & Frame, C. L. (1982). Social cognitive biases and deficits in aggressive boys. *Child Development 53*, 620–635.

Dodge, K. A., Schlundt, D. C., Schocken, I., & Delugach, J. D. (1983). Social competence and children's sociometric status: The role of peer group entry strategies. *Merrill-Palmer Quarterly 29*, 309–336.

Douvan, E., & Adelson, J. (1966). *The adolescent experience.* New York: Wiley.

Duck, S., & Gilmour, R. (Eds.). (1981). *Personal relationships. 2. Developing personal relationships.* New York: Academic.

Eder, D., & Hallinan, M. T. (1978). Sex differences in children's friendships. *American Sociological Review, 43*, 237–250.

Eisenberg, N. (Ed.). (1982). *The development of prosocial behavior.* New York: Academic Press.

Epstein, J. L. (1983). The influence of friends on achievement and affective outcomes. In J. L. Epstein & N. L. Karweit (Eds.), *Friends in school.* New York: Academic.

Furman, W., & Bierman, K. L. (in press). Children's conceptions of friendship: A multidimensional study of developmental changes. *Developmental Psychology.*

Foot, H. C., Chapman, A. J., & Smith, J. R. (Eds.). (1980). *Friendship and social relations in children.* New York: Wiley.

Gottlieb, B. H. (Ed.). (1981). *Social networks and social support.* Beverly Hills, CA: Sage, 1981.

Gottman, J. M., & Parkhurst, J. T. (1980). A developmental theory of friendship and acquaintanceship processes. In W. A. Collins (Ed.), *Minnesota Symposium on Child Psychology* (Vol. 13). Hillsdale, NJ: Erlbaum.

Green, K. D., Forehand, R., Beck, S. J., & Vosk, B. (1980). An assessment of the relationship among measures of children's social competence and children's academic achievement. *Child Development, 51,* 1149–1156.

Gresham, F. M. (1981). Validity of social skills measures for assessing social competence in low-status children: A multivariate investigation. *Developmental Psychology, 17,* 390–398.

Hallinan, M. T. Recent advances in sociometry. In S. R. Asher and J. M. Gottman (Eds.). (1981). *The development of children's friendships.* Cambridge, England: Cambridge University Press.

Hallinan, M. T., & Tuma, N. B. (1978). Classroom effects on changes in children's friendships. *Sociology of Education, 51,* 270–281.

Hartup, W. W. Peer relations (1983). In P. H. Mussen (Ed.), *Carmichael's manual of child psychology* (4th ed.). New York: Wiley.

Horrocks, J., & Buker, A. (1951). A study of friendship fluctuations of preadolescents. *Journal of Genetic Psychology, 78,* 131–144.

Hymel, S. (1983). Preschool children's peer relations: Issues in sociometric assessment. *Merrill-Palmer Quarterly, 29,* 237–260.

Kandel, D. B. (1978). Homophily, selection, and socialzation in adolescent friendships. *American Journal of Sociology, 84,* 427–436.

Ladd, G. W. (1983). Social networks of popular, average, and rejected children in school settings. *Merrill-Palmer Quarterly, 29,* 283–308.

Ladd, G. W., & Mize, J. (1983). A cognitive-social learning model of social-skill training. *Psychological Review, 90,* 127–157.

Lamb, M. E., Suomi, S. J., & Stephenson, G. R. (Eds.). (1979). *Social interaction analysis.* Madison, Wisconsin: University of Wisconsin Press.

Leinhardt, S. (1972). Developmental changes in the sentiment structure of children's groups. *American Sociological Review, 37,* 202–212.

Mannarino, A. P. (1976). Friendship patterns and altruistic behavior in preadolescent males. *Developmental Psychology, 12,* 555–556.

Mannarino, A. P. (1979). The relationship between friendship and altruism in preadolescent girls. *Psychiatry, 42,* 280–284.

Masters, J. C., & Furman, W. (1981). Popularity, individual friendship selection, and specific peer interaction among children. *Developmental Psychology, 17,* 344–350.

Newcomb, A. F., & Brady, J. E. (1982). Mutuality in boys' friendship relations. *Child Development, 53,* 392–395.

Newcomb, A. F., & Bukowski, W. M. (1983). Social impact and social preference as determinants of children's peer group status. *Developmental Psychology, 19,* 856–867.

Northway, M. L. (1944). Outsiders: A study of the personality patterns of children least acceptable to their age mates. *Sociometry, 7,* 10–25.

Peery, J. C. (1979). Popular, amiable, isolated, rejected: A reconceptualization of sociometric status in preschool children. *Child Development, 50,* 1231–1234.

Piaget, J. (1965). *The moral judgment of the child.* New York: Free Press. (Originally published, 1932.)

Putallaz, M., & Gottman, J. M. (1981). An interactional model of children's entry into peer groups. *Child Development, 52,* 986–994. (a)

Renshaw, P. D. (1981). The roots of peer interaction research: A historical analysis of the 1930s. In S. R. Asher and J. M. Gottman (Eds.), *The development of children's friendships.* Cambridge, England: Cambridge University Press.

Renshaw, P. D., & Asher, S. R. (1983). Children's goals and strategies for social interaction. *Merrill-Palmer Quarterly, 29,* 353–374.

Rubin, K. H., & Daniels-Beirness, T. (1983). Concurrent and predictive correlates of sociometric status in kindergarten and grade one children. *Merrill-Palmer Quarterly, 29,* 337–352.

Rubin, K. H., & Ross, H. S. (Eds.). (1982). *Peer relationships and social skills in childhood.* New York: Springer-Verlag.

Rubin, Z. (1980). *Children's friendships.* Cambridge, MA: Harvard University Press.

Sackett, G. P. (1978). *Observing behavior. Vol. 2. Data collection and analysis methods.* Baltimore: University Park Press.

Selman, R. L. (1981). The child as a friendship philosopher: A case study in the growth of interpersonal understanding. In S. R. Asher & J. M. Gottman (Eds.), *The development of children's friendships.* Cambridge, England: Cambridge University Press.

Sharabany, R., Gershoni, R., & Hofman, J. E. (1981). Girlfriend, boyfriend: Age and sex differences in intimate friendship. *Developmental Psychology, 17,* 800–808.

Staub, E., & Noerenberg, H. (1981). Property rights, deservingness, reciprocity, friendship: The transitional character of children's sharing behavior. *Journal of Personality and Social Psychology, 40,* 271–289.

Sullivan, H. S. (1953). *The interpersonal theory of psychiatry.* New York: Norton.

Urbain, E. S., & Kendall, P. C. (1980). Review of social-cognitive problem-solving interventions with children. *Psychological Bulletin, 88,* 109–143.

Vaughn, B. E., & Waters, E. (1981). Attention structure, sociometric status, and dominance: Interrelations, behavioral correlates, and relationships to social competence. *Developmental Psychology, 17,* 275–288.

Weisz, J. R. (1978). Transcontextual validity in developmental research. *Child Development, 49,* 1–12.

Youniss, J. (1980). *Parents and peers in social development.* Chicago: University of Chicago Press.

3

Children's Goals and Social Competence: Individual Differences in a Game-Playing Context

Angela R. Taylor
Steven R. Asher

The lack of social competence can be a major obstacle for mildly retarded children in mainstream school settings. Indeed, there is considerable evidence that educable mentally retarded (EMR) children fail in their interpersonal relationships with nonretarded peers (Corman & Gottlieb, 1978; Gottlieb & Leyser, 1981). For example, when nonretarded school children are asked on sociometric questionnaires to identify their best friends or preferred partners for play activities, EMR children are rarely chosen; rather, the retarded child is most likely to be identified as someone whom nonretarded children would prefer not to have as a friend or a playmate (e.g., Goodman, Gottlieb, & Harrison, 1972; Iano, Ayers, Heller, McGettigan, & Walker, 1974; Johnson, 1950). These findings are particularly significant, since sociometric status is generally recognized to be a strong criterion index of social competence (Asher & Hymel, 1981; Asher & Taylor, 1981; Greenspan, 1981; Putallaz & Gottman, 1982).

An initial approach to promoting peer acceptance of low-status EMR children was to pair them with higher status children in order to increase their visibility and acceptance in the classroom. Research on this type of intervention indicates that it promotes short-term gains, but that children do not maintain their social relationships once special interactional opportunities are terminated (Chennault, 1967; Lilly, 1971; Rucker & Vincenzo, 1970). This research suggests that EMR children lack skills in forming and maintaining relationships, and that more direct social skill training methods are needed.

This line of reasoning also suggests the need for research on the social skill deficits of EMR children. Indeed, over the past several decades, researchers have attempted to identify behavioral characteristics of EMR children which might contribute to their inferior social status in the regular classroom. Correlational studies have demonstrated a significant relationship between the EMR child's social rejection by nonretarded peers and peer perceptions of the EMR child's misbehavior (Baldwin, 1958; Gottlieb, Semmel, & Veldman, 1978; Johnson, 1950). These findings are consistent with the idea that EMR children are socially rejected because they engage in more inappropriate, antisocial behavior than their non-EMR classmates. However, comparative studies involving naturalistic observation in mainstream classrooms have not generally found marked differences in the behavior of EMR and non-EMR children (Gampel, Gottlieb, & Harrison, 1974; Gottlieb, Gampel, & Budoff, 1975). In fact, EMR children have been found to display a socially inactive but relatively prosocial behavior pattern as compared to their nonretarded classmates (see Taylor, 1982, for a review). As a result, the observational literature has provided limited guidance for the development of social intervention programs to promote social competence and peer acceptance of the EMR child.

Past observational research has had certain limitations for examining individual and group differences (Asher & Hymel, 1981; Taylor, 1982). Three factors are of particular concern. First, researchers have not collected adequate samples of behavior. Naturalistic observations, unless conducted over extended time periods, tend to be inadequate for capturing the kinds of low-frequency but highly salient events, such as aggression, which contribute significantly to social status and negative peer evaluations. Second, the highly structured elementary-school classroom may not always be the best setting for observing status-related social behavior. Informal social situations, as well as classrooms, should be observed to capture the important behavioral dimensions of children's peer relations. Finally, the fairly global categories of behavior examined in most observational studies are probably not sensitive to the diverse and more subtle kinds of behavior which may distinguish low- and high-status children as well as EMR and non-EMR children.

Clearly, there is a need for more sophisticated observational studies of the formation as well as maintenance of the EMR child's social status (see, for example, work with non-EMR children by Coie & Kupersmidt, 1983; Dodge, 1983; Putallaz, 1983). We believe that future progress in this area will also depend on the adoption of a more differentiated conceptual approach to social competence—one which focuses not only on children's behavioral characteristics but also on the social–cognitive and motivational processes that contribute to competent behavior and successful integration into the peer group. Furthermore, we suggest that such a process approach to defining social competence should be organized around the construct of children's goals.

Toward this end, we will advance the case that personal goals play a central role in the child's ability to interact competently with others. We will review research with both retarded and nonretarded children which demonstrates how attention to children's goals can help account for individual and group differences in social competence. In addition, we will suggest that game playing is a particularly salient context for the assessment of children's goals, and we will describe a framework for conceptualizing children's goals within game-playing situations with peers. Finally, we will suggest how a focus on goals can help account for the effects of social skill training with children and how a focus on children's goals may help us to design more effective intervention procedures for both retarded and nonretarded children.

DEFINING SOCIAL COMPETENCE

Traditional Approaches

There has generally been little consensus regarding how the construct of social competence should be defined and measured. In the field of mental retardation, the most widely adopted approach to defining social competence emphasizes adaptive behavior. Adaptive behavior is explicitly included in the American Association on Mental Deficiency (AAMD) definition of mental retardation (Grossman, 1973), and there has been a serious commitment to the development of measures of behavioral adaptation (e.g., Nihira, Foster, Shellhaas, & Leland, 1974).

Traditionally, the adaptive behavior approach has been oriented toward severely retarded, institutionalized populations, rather than mildly retarded children in school settings (Gottlieb, 1978). Measures of adaptation have focused primarily on fairly rudimentary self-help skills (e.g., toileting, dressing) and extreme forms of maladaptive behavior (e.g., self-abuse, stereotyped behavior). Although some modifications have been made for application to public school retarded populations (Lambert, Windmiller, Cole, & Figueroa, 1975), the adaptive behavior approach remains of limited usefulness for conceptualizing the kinds of abilities which might contribute to positive interpersonal relationships between less severely retarded school children and their nonretarded peers.

Among child development researchers, social competence has most often been defined in terms of some set of personality or behavior traits believed to be characteristic of socially competent persons (e.g., Anderson & Messick, 1974; Schaefer, 1975; Zigler & Trickett, 1978). These so-called "bag of virtues" approaches (Kleck, 1975) have involved the generation of a wide and varied range of skills and competencies. For example, Anderson and Messick (1974) identified 29 different facets of childhood social competence, ranging from social sensitivity and understanding to fine motor dexterity and quantitative skills. Such definitions are far too broad and diverse in scope to be practically or theoretically useful. Furthermore, many of the components included in these definitions are clearly nonsocial in content.

Process-Oriented Approaches: The Importance of Goal Construal

Recent writings on the topic of social competence have increasingly favored a process-oriented perspective over the more traditional approaches (e.g., Cicourel, 1975; Greenspan, 1979, 1981; Kleck, 1975; O'Malley, 1977; Schiefelbusch, 1981). Process-oriented definitions of social competence are concerned with delineating the nature of the social interaction process and the particular components that contribute to successful social transactions with others. This particular approach has its roots in the work of investigators such as Goffman (1959) and Weinstein (1969). However, it only has been relatively recently that researchers have recognized its relevance for conceptualizing social competence in retarded persons and the links with social–cognitive research in child development (Greenspan, 1979, 1981; Kleck, 1975; O'Malley, 1977).

Most process-oriented definitions of social competence highlight the fact that social competence involves the successful pursuit of interpersonal goals and purposes. For example, according to Weinstein's definition, social competence involves "the ability to accomplish interpersonal tasks . . . and to manipulate others' responses" (p. 755). O'Malley (1977) defined social competence in young children in terms of "productive and mutually satisfying social interactions with others." He suggested that interactions are productive and mutually satisfying when they attain personal goals of the child and when the child's goal-directed actions are received by others "in either a benign or positive manner" (p. 31). Likewise, Ford (1982) defined social competence as "the attainment of relevant social goals in specified social contexts, using appropriate means and resulting in positive developmental outcomes" (p. 324).

Renshaw and Asher (1982; Renshaw, 1981) have called attention to an important limitation of these conceptions of social competence. In defining competence as the ability to attain interpersonal goals, the existence of certain goals is taken for granted, and the focus for study becomes how children pursue these goals. This approach ignores the fact that the goal construal process itself is central to social behavior and the formation of social relationships. The importance of goal construal processes becomes readily apparent when we consider the fact that social situations are inherently ambiguous in nature (Greene, 1976). Unlike the social problem-solving tasks used in many research studies, real-life social situations often do not involve predetermined and explicitly specified goals for social behavior. On the contrary, a core task for children as well as adults is to figure out what is going on in particular social situations and what goals and lines of action to pursue. Consistent with this perspective, we propose that social competence involves the formulation and adoption of personal goals that are appropriate and adaptive to particular social situations and the implementation of effective behavioral strategies for achieving these goals. The process of goal formulation and adoption involves an interplay of social–cognitive and motivational factors, including the inferences and interpretations children make about social situations, the value or importance children attach to particular kinds of goals, and the degree of confidence children have in their ability to achieve particular goals.

As suggested by Renshaw and Asher (Asher & Renshaw, 1981; Renshaw & Asher, 1982), a major problem for unpopular children may be that they tend to define situations in terms of maladaptive goals that promote dysfunctional social behavior. Along similar lines, Taylor (1982) proposed that EMR children may have difficulties in their interpersonal relationships with nonretarded peers, not only because they have social–cognitive deficits but also because their motivational tendencies lead them to pursue maladaptive goals. Researchers recently have begun to directly examine children's goals and motivational aspects of interpersonal behavior.

In the following sections of this chapter, we will review recent social and motivational research on goal-related processes in nonretarded and retarded children's competence. We will then present a framework for conceptualizing children's goals within the context of game playing with peers. Finally, we will suggest how focusing on goals can help interpret social skill training effects with children, and how a focus on children's goals may help us to design even more effective intervention procedures for both retarded and nonretarded children.

DIMENSIONS OF CHILDREN'S SOCIAL GOALS

Social versus Nonsocial Orientations

Evers-Pasquale (1978) and Evers-Pasquale and Sherman (1975) have addressed the idea that children respond differently in social situations because of differences in the degree to which they value social interaction as compared to nonsocial experiences and activities. These investigators have attempted to account for individual differences in the effectiveness of a modeling film (O'Connor, 1969) designed to increase social interactions of isolated preschool children.[1] It was hypothesized that the isolated children who failed to benefit from the intervention were those for whom peer interaction held relatively little reward value. To assess the reward value of peers, Evers-Pasquale (1978) developed a pictorial test (The Peer Preference Test) on which children indicated their preference for engaging in various activities (e.g., playing ball) with a peer, an adult, or alone. Socially isolated preschool children were classified as peer-oriented or non-peer-oriented (i.e., preferring to be with adults or alone), and were then randomly assigned to either a modeling treatment or a control condition. Both peer-oriented and non-peer-oriented children in the treatment condition showed significantly higher levels of peer interaction than children in the control group. However, as hypothesized, the peer-oriented modeling subjects increased their social interaction significantly more than their non-peer-oriented counterparts.

The social–nonsocial goal dimension was also examined in a recent multivariate study by Ford (1982). Ford examined the relationship between several process variables and social competence on ninth- and twelfth-grade students. Among the variables examined were interest in social versus nonsocial goals and social and nonsocial goal capabilities. Interest in social versus nonsocial goals was based on students' rankings of the personal importance of social goals, such as "having a lot of close friends" or "helping other people with their problems," and nonsocial goals, such as "getting good grades in school" or "learning new skills and knowledge." Social and nonsocial goal capabilities pertained to students' self-ratings of their degree of skill in attaining different types of goals. Social competence was assessed by having peers, teachers, and the subjects themselves make judgments concerning the stu-

---

1. O'Connor's rate-of-interaction measure has been criticized as an index of social competence because it ignores the quality of children's social interaction. The Evers-Pasquale data suggest that the rate measure may index a child's desire to be with peers, although not the effectiveness with which the child interacts.

dent's competence in handling six hypothetical situations (e.g., serving as a peer counselor, organizing and coordinating a student activity group). Ford found that adolescents who were judged to be competent in these hypothetical situations tended to assign higher priority to interpersonal goals than to nonsocial, task-oriented kinds of goals, and also tended to perceive themselves as having the capabilities necessary to attain these goals.

Both Evers-Pasquale and Ford define the social orientation dimension in terms of the child's valuing of interpersonal interactions and relationships with others. A slightly different conceptualization of the social–nonsocial goal dimension is reflected in Nakamura and Finck's (1980) research. According to these investigators, the social orientation dimension refers to the child's sensitivity to social attention, recognition, and evaluation. This orientation is contrasted with a task orientation in which the child is primarily concerned with task-related achievement goals.

Nakamura and Finck (1980) propose that children's effectiveness in school situations can be described in terms of three main "perception–response" dimensions: social orientation, task orientation, and self-assurance. These dimensions are based on the following assumptions:

> that socially-oriented children are sensitive to social stimuli and to potential positive or negative evaluation; that task-oriented children are primarily interested in the task per se, are likely to be achievement oriented, and are less concerned with evaluation of their performance by others; and that self-assured children are generally confident, competent, and accepting of responsibility. (Nakamura & Finck, 1980, p. 14)

Nakamura and Finck developed the Hypothetical Situations Questionnaire (HSQ) to create child profiles corresponding to high (H) and low (L) scores on each of the three perception–response dimensions. Using this measure, the authors conducted a series of studies with elementary-school children to determine the relationship between the HSQ profile categories and various outcome measures of school effectiveness. They hypothesized that the more effective children would demonstrate one of two profile patterns on the HSQ: a socially oriented pattern characterized by high-social, high-task, and high-self-assurance scores (HHH), and a task-oriented pattern consisting of a low social orientation but high scores on task orientation and self-assurance (LHH). It was further predicted that the less effective children would either be primarily socially oriented, but low on task orientation and self-assurance (HLL), or low on all three dimensions (LLL).

The research findings tended to support the investigators' hypotheses. For example, children identified as most effective on the HSQ were found to be more socially independent (i.e., were less susceptible to external social influence on a preference-judgment task) than the less effective children. Likewise, on a laboratory team project, the more effective children exceeded their less effective counterparts in the extent to which they demonstrated leadership, responsibility, and initiative, as well as cooperation and helpfulness in working with their teammates.

It is noteworthy that the studies reviewed here tend to suggest that a nonsocial or task-focused goal orientation is not necessarily socially maladaptive. Also, it is apparent that an excessive focus on either social or nonsocial goals could be maladaptive. On the one hand, the child who is overly concerned with the social evaluations of others and has little concern with the task per se is likely to perform incompetently, particularly on tasks requiring the ability to make independent judgments. On the other hand, excessive attention to nonsocial, task-related goals can interfere with competent responding to the interpersonal demands of social situations (e.g., helping or cooperating with others). What seems to be important, then, is the child's ability to achieve an appropriate balance between social and nonsocial kinds of goals, dependent upon the requirements of the particular situation. This is particularly important in the school context, where effective performance depends on the ability to accomplish both social and nonsocial tasks and goals.

Cooperative versus Competitive or Individualistic Goals

There is an extensive line of developmental–descriptive research which has been concerned with the assessment of children's social motives (or goals) under conditions of social interdependence—that is, when the child's behavior has consequences not only for his or her own outcomes but also for those of others (e.g., Knight & Kagan, 1977; Madsen, 1967; McClintock & Moskowitz, 1976). Of particular interest has been the extent to which children prefer cooperative outcomes (that maximize one's own gains relative to others' gains) or individualistic outcomes (involving maximum absolute gains for self). The assumption underlying this work is that individuals come to prefer particular distributions of outcomes and that an individual's social motives can be inferred from his or her pattern of outcome preferences (Griesinger & Livingston, 1973; McCrimmon & Messick, 1976).

Research in this area has typically involved using experimental games to assess children's social motives with respect to this cooperative–competitive–individualistic framework. In such games, children choose between two or more alternatives which provide different outcomes for themselves and one or more other individuals. Recent research has demonstrated the validity of the social motives construct. For example, Knight (1981) found that children's choice patterns on a social motives game were consistently related to a sociometric measure in which peers were asked to predict the child's outcome preferences.

Research on children's social motives has primarily been concerned with the examination of cultural and developmental differences in children's outcome preferences. It has consistently been found that Anglo-American children tend to be more competitive and less cooperative than Mexican-American children and that children in both cultural groups tend to become more competitive with increasing age (Knight & Kagan, 1977). At the present time, however, there has been no research addressed to the relationship between children's social motives and their social competence with respect to peer relations. For example, it would be of interest to know whether sociometric status differences might be associated with individual differences in children's preferences for cooperative versus competitive or individualistic social goals.

Friendliness versus Hostility and Assertiveness versus Submissiveness

Children's goals for social interaction differ in the degree to which they reflect a positive, prosocial, and congenial orientation (friendliness) versus a negative, antisocial, and aggressive orientation (hostility). This particular dimension is the one most often emphasized in research and intervention with respect to children's social behavior. For example, research on the behavioral correlates of sociometric status of both retarded and nonretarded children has focused primarily on the friendly–hostile dimension of children's interactions and relationships (see Asher & Hymel, 1981, for a review).

Renshaw and Asher (1983; Renshaw, 1981), drawing upon personality theory and research (e.g., Schaefer, 1961; Wish, 1976; Wish, Deutsch, & Kaplan, 1976), combined the friendly–hostile dimension with an assertive–submissive dimension to develop a general framework for characterizing children's goals and strategies for peer interaction. The assertive–submissive dimension refers to the extent to which the child is outgoing, forthright, and self-confident versus passive, withdrawn, and avoidant in his or her approach to social situations. Renshaw and Asher hypothesized that children low in sociometric status would tend to adopt unfriendly, highly assertive goals involving aggressive and inappropriately hostile responses, or unfriendly, unassertive goals involving withdrawal and avoidance of social interaction.

To test these hypotheses, Renshaw and Asher had third- through sixth-grade children of high- and low-sociometric status indicate what they would do in four types of hypothetical situations—initiating interactions with peers, dealing with peer rejection, maintaining friendships, and handling interpersonal conflict. The situations were first presented in the form of a production task and then in the form of a recognition task. On the production task, the goal was not explicitly indicated, and children were simply asked to give reasons for their proposed actions in each situation. On the recognition task, children were presented with a set of four social goals relevant to each hypothetical situation and were asked to rank order them in terms of what they would most try to do.

The recognition task produced no significant differences; however, the production task revealed differences in children's social goals as a function of both age and sociometric status. The most consistent and striking differences were found in relation to age. Older children most often suggested friendly—assertive goals, while younger children were more likely than older children to suggest goals which were assertive but unfriendly. With respect to sociometric status, it was found the high-status children suggested significantly more friendly—assertive goals than low-status children. However, the hypothesized tendency for low-status children to adopt more unfriendly, highly assertive or more unfriendly, low assertive goals than high-status children was not supported by the research findings. Renshaw and Asher suggested that the sociometric status effects might have been stronger had an extreme-groups design been employed (rather than a mean split), and had the distinction been made between unpopular children who are neglected versus rejected (for important work on this distinction, see Coie & Dodge, 1983; Coie, Dodge, & Coppotelli, 1982; Coie & Kupersmidt, 1983; Dodge, 1983).

This study also highlights the fact that children's goals vary as a function of the situation (see Renshaw, 1981). For example, in the situation involving the possibility of initiation of relationships (a child new to the school goes out on the playground for recess), 50% of the children stated goals that were highly friendly and highly assertive. None of the children provided hostile goals (low on friendliness and high on assertiveness). In contrast, on the item involving interpersonal conflict (a visiting child suddenly changes the television to a different station), 43% of the children suggested goals that were unfriendly—assertive or hostile. Thus, it is important to keep in mind that situational factors strongly influence (or cue) children's goals and that research on individual differences within situations needs to be appreciated in this context.

GOALS AND CHILDREN'S SELF-PERCEPTIONS

The adoption and pursuit of adaptive social goals requires certain motivational resources on the part of the child. In particular, the child must have confidence in his or her ability to attain desired outcomes. For example, Ford (1982) and Nakamura and Finck (1980) found that social competence was associated not only with an orientation toward particular kinds of goals, but also with a high degree of self-assurance or perceived competence in one's ability to attain those goals.

Although there is an extensive literature on children's perceptions of their competence, this work has primarily been addressed to cognitive–intellectual performance rather than behavior within the social domain. However, there are a few notable exceptions. Wheeler and Ladd (1982) recently developed the Children's Self-Efficacy for Peer Interaction Scale to assess children's perceptions of their persuasive abilities in social interactions with peers. In their research with third-through fifth-grade children, the investigators found significant positive correlations between social self-efficacy and sociometric status in the peer group. Children also reported less confidence in their ability to handle conflict than nonconflict situations. In another recent study, Harter (1982) developed the Perceived Competence Scale for Children to assess children's perceptions of their ability in cognitive, social, and physical domains. Research by Thompson (cited in Harter, 1982) with fourth- through sixth-grade children demonstrated a significant correlation between the social subscale and an index of sociometric status.

Recent research on learned helplessness has also been addressed to children's social competence. Learned helplessness, a construct widely used in achievement motivation literature (e.g., Diener & Dweck, 1978; Dweck & Reppucci, 1973), refers to the tendency to give up or withdraw in the face of failure due to the belief that one is unable to control the outcome of one's problem-solving efforts. Alternatively, a mastery orientation involves the tendency to respond to problem-solving setbacks with increased effort and alternative problem-solving strategies. Studying these processes in the social domain, Goetz and Dweck (1980) found that fourth- and fifth-grade children who showed a learned helpless attributional pattern (i.e., attributed peer rejection to personal incompetence) were more likely than nonhelpless children to give up or repeat ineffective strategies for gaining peer acceptance following mild social rejection by a peer. This particular relationship between attributions and responses to rejection held regardless of the child's sociometric status; however, low-status children were somewhat more likely than high-status children to make helpless attributions. This latter finding is consistent with the idea that the learned helpless orientation can be acquired through a history of interpersonal failure.

The learned-helplessness construct is of particular relevance to the present discussion not only because it has been shown to apply to children's social behavior with peers but also because it has been interpreted in terms of children's goals. In their recent model of achievement motivation, Dweck and Elliott (1983) have suggested that the contrasting learned-helpless and mastery-oriented achievement patterns tend to be associated with differences in children's choice of goals. Some children focus on the "learning" goal of increasing competence, while others focus on "performance" goals—that is, on obtaining favorable judgments of competence or avoiding unfavorable judgments of competence. These learning and performance goals are much like the task and social orientation dimensions proposed by Nakamura and Finck (1980). In both cases, a distinction is made between children who are primarily concerned with mastery of the task itself versus those who are largely concerned with other persons' evaluations of their task performance.

As conceptualized by Dweck and Elliott, the learning goal and the performance goal of attaining a positive competence judgment represent approach orientations; both are associated with a high level of confidence in achieving the desired goal and a tendency to display mastery-oriented behavior on achievement tasks. In contrast, children who have a low level of confidence in being judged competent will tend to adopt the goal of avoiding a negative competence judgment and display a learned helpless behavior pattern in response to achievement tasks. Preliminary research by Elliott and Dweck provides support for the proposed relationships between children's goals, levels of confidence, and patterns of achievement behavior (see Dweck & Bempechat, 1983, for a summary of these studies). This work suggests, then, that children's feelings of helplessness in social situations might be associated with adoption of a goal of avoiding social rejection from peers.

Motivational Characteristics of the Retarded

The motivational literature with nonretarded children suggests that children who lack confidence in their ability to attain positive task-related goals are likely to adopt an avoidant goal orientation and to demonstrate withdrawal or performance deterioration in relation to the task. This particular pattern is particularly likely to occur when the child has experienced repeated failures in his or her goal-directed efforts. Consistent with this picture, there is considerable evidence indicating that the retarded child's history of failure experiences in dealing with the environment has debilitating effects on motivation and goal-directed behavior (see Balla & Zigler, 1979; Cromwell, 1963; Siegel, 1979, for reviews). For example, retarded children have lower expectancies of success, little sense of control over their own outcomes, and are failure avoidant rather than success striving (Cromwell, 1963). Mentally retarded school children are also more likely than non-retarded children to develop a learned helpless orientation (Weisz, 1979). These maladaptive motivational tendencies interfere with the retarded child's use of effective or optimal problem-solving strategies on learning tasks (e.g., Gruen & Zigler, 1968; Stevenson & Zigler, 1958; Weisz, 1981).

Like the work with nonretarded children, research on the motivational characteristics of the retarded has focused primarily on cognitive–intellectual performance. To date, there has been no research addressed to retarded children's goals or motivational orientations in the social domain. There is some indirect evidence, however, that the kinds of tendencies documented in relation to cognitive tasks may also influence the retarded child's goal orientation and behavior in social situations. For example, the behavior observation research reviewed earlier indicates that mainstreamed EMR children tend to assume a socially inactive but relatively prosocial behavior pattern in the regular classroom setting. This observed behavior pattern appears to be consistent with a passive–avoidant orientation on the part of EMR children. Indeed, Gampel et al. (1974) concluded that mainstreamed EMR children may try to avoid drawing attention to themselves in order to "conceal from their classmates the fact that they had previously been enrolled in a class for retarded pupils" (p. 20).

Along similar lines, pilot research that we have conducted suggests that EMR children adopt an avoidant orientation in relation to game-playing situations with peers. In this research, we presented main-streamed elementary school EMR children with pictorially illustrated story items representing various social situations and asked children what they would do in each situation. The EMR children's strategies were compared to those of similar-age non-EMR children who had been interviewed in an earlier study in the same school. In general, the EMR children as compared to their non-EMR counterparts suggested strategies which were rated by adult judges as less effective and less likely to maintain or enhance interpersonal relationships with peers.

Two items produced particularly striking differences between EMR and non-EMR children. Interestingly, these items tapped children's responses to personal failure in game-playing situations with peers. In one story, the child was shown a picture of two children playing a board game. The story was presented as follows: "Pretend that this is you playing a game with another child. You aren't having much fun because you are losing. What would you do?" In the second story, the child sees a picture of children playing in a dodgeball game. Here the story is—"You're playing dodgeball with some other kids at school and you get knocked out of the game. The other kids start teasing you and saying, 'You're as slow as a turtle.' What would you do?"

The most frequent strategy suggested by the EMR children to both situations involved quitting or leaving the game-playing situation. In contrast, non-EMR children suggested that they would keep on playing and try to win in the "losing a game" situation, and they suggested verbally assertive strategies, such as teasing or talking back, in the "teasing" situation. This pattern of responses by EMR and non-EMR children is consistent with the learned-helpless versus mastery-oriented patterns described in the motivational literature. The EMR children's response pattern is likely to be maladaptive, given the kinds of social situations children often face in school.

SITUATIONAL FACTORS AND THE EMR CHILD'S SOCIAL COMPETENCE

In the school setting, social interactions usually occur within the context of formal academic activities or less formal activities involving play and games. In general, the EMR child performs less competently than the non-EMR child in relation to both academic and nonacademic tasks, making him or her less desirable to peers as a work partner or playmate. Indeed, there is evidence that competence in performing academic and nonacademic tasks (e.g., sports, perceptual–motor games) is significantly related to peer acceptance. For example, Gottlieb et al. (1978) found that peer and teacher perceptions of the EMR child's academic incompetence were significant predictors of his or her social acceptance in the regular classroom; nonretarded children were more accepting of EMR children who showed adequate ability to handle academic tasks. Similarly, experimental studies by Aloia, Beaver, and Pettus (1978) and Strichart and Gottlieb (1975) showed that EMR children who were perceived as being highly competent game-players were more likely to be selected by non-EMR children as partners for game activities.

The above findings suggest that EMR children's task-related incompetence can have direct effects on peer-related social outcomes to the extent that other children are aware of their performance deficiencies and in turn come to perceive them as less socially desirable. More importantly, EMR children's cumulative history of activity-related failure and social rejection can undermine their ability to perform competently in subsequent social interactions (where task incompetence has not yet been demonstrated) through its debilitating effects on motivation and goal-orientation patterns. This can produce a negative social interaction cycle, involving inappropriate withdrawal and avoidance on the part of the EMR child. Specifically, the EMR child may approach activity-centered social situations with the expectation that he or she will perform less competently than others and that nonretarded peers will make negative judgments of competence and respond by rejecting them. As a result, the EMR child may try to avoid social situations in which there is a likelihood of exhibiting incompetence. Furthermore, when engaged in such activities, the retarded child is likely to respond to initial failures and difficulties by engaging in escape behaviors which are disruptive of ongoing social interactions (e.g., quitting a game). This in turn further reinforces the retarded child's expectations of failure and rejection as well as negative perceptions of the child on the part of nonretarded peers.

The relative freedom from adult surveillance provided by the game-playing context may make it a particularly salient one for the development of motivational and goal orientation patterns. Here, peers are likely to be more explicit and overt in relaying negative feedback about the retarded child's performance and competence—for example, by engaging in teasing and name calling. Thus, for the retarded child, the social game-playing situation may become associated with unpleasant failure and rejection experiences. In addition, the game-playing context is the most likely setting for social encounters between mainstreamed retarded and nonretarded children, since the mainstreaming of retarded children is usually implemented in relation to nonacademic and extracurricular activities (e.g., physical education, recess).

GAME PLAYING AS A CONTEXT FOR EXAMINING CHILDREN'S GOALS

The discussion of situational factors in social competence suggests that game-related activities are an important context for the development and demonstration of social goal orientations of both retarded and nonretarded school children. Because game-playing activities are usually less constrained by teacher supervision and formal rules of social conduct than are academic tasks, they provide greater opportunities for the initiation and maintenance of social interactions with peers and for the development of peer preference patterns. At the same time, game-playing activities are similar to intellectual achievement tasks in that there are opportunities for learning and skill mastery as well as evaluation of task performance and competence. Thus, within the game-playing context, children are likely to pursue a variety of social and task-oriented goals and to engage in a range of behaviors which contribute to peer acceptance and rejection.

The research on children's social and nonsocial goals suggests some useful dimensions for conceptualizing children's goals in the game-playing context. Table 1 outlines eight goal types which are organized around social versus task-oriented, approach versus avoidant, and friendly versus unfriendly goal dimensions.

The task mastery and performance (approach, avoidant) goal types generally correspond to the Dweck and Elliott (1983) learning and performance goal types. Thus, the task mastery goal focuses on the process (rather than the outcomes) of game playing. Here the child is concerned with developing and improving game-playing skills and with enjoying the physical and/or mental activity or challenge of the game (e.g., learning how to play the game, getting better at the game). Involvement in the task or activity itself is seen as more important than one's outcome in the game.

The performance goals focus on the outcomes of game playing,

Table 1
Children's Goals in the Game-Playing Context

Goal Type	Description
Task Mastery	To master and develop game-playing skills; to enjoy involvement in task for its own sake
Performance	
Approach	To attain positive performance outcomes and positive peer judgments of game-playing competence
Avoidant	To avoid negative performance outcomes and negative peer judgments of game-playing competence
Rule-oriented/Fairness	To make sure the game is played by the rules
Relationship	
Approach	To initiate and maintain positive or neutral interactions and relationships with peers
Avoidant	To avoid negative interactions and relationships with peers
Self-protection	To protect oneself or retaliate against peer hostility and aggression
Dominance	To control or dominate others

such as winning or losing, how one's performance is evaluated by others, and how one's performance compares with that of other game players. The approach-oriented performance goal reflects concerns with attaining positive performance outcomes and positive judgments of competence (e.g., winning the game, showing others you are a good game player). The avoidant performance goals, on the other hand, focus on avoiding negative performance outcomes and negative competence judgments (e.g., not making mistakes, not looking clumsy or dumb). The performance goals tend to parallel the individualistic and competitive orientations outlined in the research on childrens' social motives.

The rule-oriented/fairness goal has to do with concerns about participants' compliance with the rules of the game and issues of fairness (e.g., that children play by the rules, that kids play fair). This is consistent with the rule-oriented goal type identified by Renshaw and Asher (1983). For example, in response to their hypothetical conflict situation, a number of children stated goals related to the enforcement of rules and norms applicable to the particular situation. This suggested that these children were concerned that individuals comply with culturally given rules governing social behavior and rights of individuals in the situation.

The relationship goals focus on the social interactions and relationships among participants in the game-playing situation. The approach-oriented relationship goal involves concerns with the initiation and maintenance of positive (or neutral) social interactions and relationships (e.g., getting along well with the other kids, making friends). These goals are consistent with a cooperative social orientation. In contrast, the avoidant relationship goals focus on avoidance of negative interactions and relationships with peers (e.g., not being rejected, not getting into arguments).

Children may also have less friendly social goals. For example, Dodge's research (Dodge, 1980; Dodge & Frame, 1982) suggests that aggressive children may assume a defensive or self-protective orientation in relation to peers. Here, there is a focus on protecting oneself from anticipated peer hostility or retaliating against perceived aggression from peers (e.g., not letting other children push you around, getting back at another child who provokes you during the game). Other children may be concerned with social control or dominance over others. Here the focus is on having control over the game-playing activities and establishing and maintaining a dominant status position vis-à-vis the peer group (e.g., deciding the rules of the game, being the leader in the game).

During the course of game playing, a child is likely to adopt and pursue any one or all of the goals outlined. What is of interest is which goal types tend to be given priority by the child, and how children manage to reconcile or coordinate potentially conflicting goals (e.g., the goal of winning and the goal of maintaining a relationship with a partner).

GOALS AND SOCIAL INTERVENTION

Several interventions designed to facilitate peer acceptance of low-status children have been organized around game-playing situations. In this section, we will suggest that the success of these interventions may be due to their influence on the goals children adopt in game-playing interactions with peers.

Social Skill Training Research

Several investigators have examined whether unpopular non-EMR children's low status in the peer group can be improved by direct instruction in social skills (Bierman, 1981; Coie & Krehbiel, 1983; Gottman, Gonso, & Schuler, 1976; Gresham & Nagle, 1980; Hymel & Asher, 1977; Ladd, 1981; Oden, Asher, & Hymel, 1977; Siperstein & Gale, 1983). Most of these studies have found immediate and lasting changes in peer acceptance. This is an extremely important result because without intervention, low sociometric status, particularly rejected status, is a rather stable phenomenon (Coie & Dodge, 1983). Furthermore, longitudinal studies suggest that children with poor peer relations may be "at risk" for a variety of later adjustment difficulties (see Putallaz & Gottman, 1982, for a review).

Social skill training studies with unpopular children have involved teaching children social skills that previous descriptive research has found to correlate with sociometric status. However, the particular skills taught have varied across studies. For example, Oden and Asher (1977) taught four general concepts or principles concerning social interaction: participation, cooperation, communication, and validation-support. The purpose was to have children learn these general concepts and then use them as guidelines for generating behavior in specific situations. Ladd (1981), by contrast, taught three rather specific behaviors: asking questions, making suggestions, and offering supportive statements. Interestingly, these and other skill training procedures have been quite successful, despite varying content. In the Oden and Asher (1977) study, children made gains in acceptance that were maintained at one-year follow-up. Ladd (1981), Gresham and Nagle (1980), and Gottman, Gonso, and Schuler (1976) have all found significant gains that were maintained when one-month follow-up data were collected.

In a recent paper, Asher and Renshaw (1981) hypothesized that social skill training may be effective not only because it teaches new knowledge of how to interact but also because it affects the way children construe goals in social situations. This possibility is seen most clearly in a coaching study by Oden and Asher (1977) that produced maintenance at one-year follow-up. As part of the coaching, children were told repeatedly that trying out certain ideas would make games more fun to play. Thus, there was a constant emphasis on game playing as a vehicle for having fun and for making sure that the game partner had fun as well. No mention was made of winning, of demonstrating or improving skills, or other potential goals. Instead, the emphasis was on both partners having fun, and learning whether the ideas helped make games more enjoyable.

Coaching's effectiveness in this study, therefore, may have resulted not just from new knowledge about how to cooperate, communicate, etc., but from altering children's goals in social situations. This interpretation helps explain why a relatively brief intervention (six 25-minute sessions) had considerable and lasting impact. Surely, many of the ideas children were exposed to in the coaching were not new to them; what may have been most important was the provision of goals that were different from the goals they otherwise would have pursued in game situations.

Social Intervention with EMR Children

Most of the interventions designed to promote peer acceptance of retarded school children have focused on the manipulation of environmental or situational factors, rather than on direct training of social skills. One approach, as noted earlier, has involved the use of new grouping arrangements, such as pairing low-status and high-status children (Chennault, 1967; Lilly, 1971; Rucker & Vincenzo, 1970). As mentioned earlier, this approach has produced only short-term effects and has not been successful in producing maintenance of change. Another widely used approach involves the systematic structuring of classroom tasks and cooperative goals (Ballard, Corman, Gottlieb, & Kaufman, 1977; Marlowe, 1979, 1980; Rynders, Johnson, Johnson, & Schmidt, 1980). In cooperative goal structuring, learning or non-academic tasks are structured so that children's goals are positively or cooperatively interrelated; an individual child can achieve his or her goal only if other group members also achieve their goal. Here, then, children's goal orientations are manipulated by redefining the nature of the task or activity itself. Rynders et al. (1980) found that this type of procedure produced more positive verbal interactions and greater interpersonal attraction among Downs' Syndrome and nonretarded students participating in a bowling activity as compared to competitive and individualistically structured task conditions. Research within this tradition has not yet studied whether changes are long-lasting.

Two other task structuring interventions, one by Ballard et al. (1977) and the other by Marlowe (1979, 1980), are noteworthy because, unlike most other environmental manipulation studies, they have demonstrated maintenance of sociometric status gains of participating students. Ballard et al. (1977) had EMR and non-EMR elementary-school students participate in small-group cooperative tasks over an 8-week period. EMR students gained in peer acceptance and decreased in peer rejection. In addition, these students were found to be significantly higher in social acceptance than an untreated control group 2–4 weeks following the intervention.

Among the factors probably contributing to the success of the Ballard et al. study was that the group tasks were highly structured and nondemanding. This would reduce the possibility of failure on the part of the EMR students and likely reduce the possibility that the EMR students would engage in maladaptive motivational and performance patterns. In addition, teachers oriented the children toward cooperative goals by informing them of the "benefits of cooperative group work." They also instructed the children in social skills for working together cooperatively (e.g., listening, giving and accepting feedback). It is not possible to determine then, whether the positive and lasting effects are due to the promotion of cooperative goals, the acquisition of social skills by EMR children, or a combination of these.

The intervention employed by Marlowe (1979, 1980) was explicitly based on the idea that EMR and other low-status children often respond maladaptively because they are unable to perform competently at games, and thus experience social rejection from peers. The "games analysis" intervention employed by Marlowe involved children in a group problem-solving process to decide how traditional games could be modified so that all children could participate successfully regardless of motor abilities. Marlowe (1979) employed this procedure to improve the social behavior and social acceptance of an EMR boy in game-playing interactions with nonretarded peers. In a subsequent study, sociometric status gains were found with a group of low-status nonretarded children (Marlowe, 1980). Like the Ballard et al. intervention, the success of the games-analysis intervention can be attributed to the fact that it facilitated successful (rather than failure-oriented) game-playing experiences for the EMR child, and oriented both EMR and non-EMR children toward more prosocial, cooperative game-playing goals.

The findings of the cooperative task studies, together with the social skill training research, suggest that interventions which focus on children's goals can have significant and enduring effects on peer acceptance of low-status retarded and nonretarded children. The success of such interventions seems to be facilitated by orienting children toward positive interpersonal goals rather than competitive or individualistic performance goals and by directly instructing children in social skills for attaining these goals. In addition, making game-playing tasks less challenging decreases the likelihood that EMR children will adopt an avoidant orientation in response to the demands of the game-playing activity. This kind of task structuring may be particularly important in the initial stages of intervention with retarded children. However, more generalizable and long-term improvements will most likely be facilitated by also training EMR children to approach task situations of greater difficulty with more adaptive kinds of goals.

SUMMARY

In this chapter, we have reviewed research suggesting that goals play an important part in children's social competence. In addition, we discussed how maladaptive motivational and goal-orientation patterns of retarded children may contribute to the difficulties they experience in interpersonal relationships with nonretarded peers. We also proposed that game-playing situations serve as important contexts for the development and demonstration of goal orientation and social behavior patterns of retarded and nonretarded children. A framework was presented for conceptualizing children's goals in game-playing situations with peers which can be used as a basis for structuring research on children's goals and social interactions. Finally, we reviewed social intervention studies which have used the game-playing situation as a context for promoting social competence and peer acceptance of retarded and low-status nonretarded children. It appears that interventions directly or indirectly influencing children's goals have produced significant and enduring improvements in children's sociometric status in the peer group. Thus, intervention research, too, lends support to the hypothesis that a focus on goals and social competence will be productive.

REFERENCES

Aloia, G., Beaver, R., & Pettus, W. (1978). Increasing initial interactions among integrated EMR students and their nonretarded peers in a game-playing situation. *American Journal of Mental Deficiency, 82,* 573–579.

Anderson, S., & Messick, S. (1974). Social competency in young children. *Developmental Psychology, 10,* 282–293.

Asher, S. R., & Hymel, S. (1981). Children's social competence in peer relations: Sociometric and behavioral assessment. In J. D. Wine & M. D. Smye (Eds.), *Social competence* (pp. 125–157). New York: Guilford.

Asher, S. R., & Renshaw, P. D. (1981). Children without friends: Social knowledge and social skill training. In S. R. Asher & J. M. Gottman (Eds.), *The development of children's friendships* (pp. 273–296). New York: Cambridge University Press.

Asher, S. R. & Taylor, A. R. (1981). Social outcomes of mainstreaming: Sociometric assessment and beyond. *Exceptional Education Quarterly, 1,* 13–30.

Baldwin, W. K. (1958). The social position of the educable mentally retarded child in the regular grades in the public schools. *Exceptional Children, 25,* 106–108, 112.

Balla, D., & Zigler, E. (1979). Personality development in retarded persons. In N. R. Ellis (Ed.), *Handbook of mental deficiency, psychological theory and research* (2nd ed., pp. 143–168). Hillsdale, NJ: Erlbaum.

Ballard, M., Corman, L., Gottlieb, J., & Kaufman, M. T. (1977). Improving the social status of mainstreamed retarded children. *Journal of Educational Psychology, 69,* 605–611.

Bierman, K. L. (1981, April). *Enhancing the generalization of social skills training with peer involvement and superordinate goals.* Paper presented at the biennial meeting of the Society for Research in Child Development, Boston.

Chennault, M. (1967). Improving the social acceptance of unpopular educable mentally retarded pupils in special classes. *American Journal of Mental Deficiency, 72,* 455–458.

Cicourel, A. V. (1975). Oral and non-oral representations of communicative and social competence. In M. J. Begab & S. A. Richardson (Eds.), *The mentally retarded and society: A social science perspective* (pp. 229–243). Baltimore: University Park Press.

Coie, J. D., & Dodge, K. A. (1983). Continuities and changes in children's social status: A five-year longitudinal study. *Merrill-Palmer Quarterly, 29,* 261–282.

Coie, J. D., Dodge, K. A., & Coppotelli, H. (1982). Dimensions and types of status: A cross-age perspective. *Developmental Psychology, 18,* 557–570.

Coie, J. D., & Krehbiel, G. G. (1983). *Skill-based intervention strategies for socially rejected, low-achieving children.* Paper presented at biennial meeting of the Society for Research in Child Development, Detroit.

Coie, J. D., & Kupersmidt, J. (1983). A behavioral analysis of emerging social status in boys' groups. *Child Development, 54,* 1400–1416.

Corman, L., & Gottlieb, J. (1978). Mainstreaming mentally retarded children: A review of research. In N. R. Ellis (Ed.), *International review of research in mental retardation* (Vol. 9, pp. 251–275). New York: Academic Press.

Cromwell, R. (1963). A social learning approach to mental retardation. In N. R. Ellis (Ed.), *Handbook of mental deficiency* (pp. 41–91). New York: McGraw-Hill.

Diener, C. I., & Dweck, C. S. (1978). An analysis of learned helplessness: Continuous changes in performance, strategy, and achievement cognitions following failure. *Journal of Personality and Social Psychology, 36,* 451–462.

Dodge, K. A. (1980). Social cognition and children's aggressive behavior. *Child Development, 51,* 162–170.

Dodge, K. A. (1983). Behavioral antecedents of peer social status. *Child Development, 54,* 1386–1399.

Dodge, K. A., & Frame, C. L. (1982). Social cognitive biases and deficits in aggressive boys. *Child Development, 53,* 620–635.

Dweck, C. S., & Bempechat, J. (1983). Children's theories of intelligence: Consequences for learning. In S. G. Paris, G. M. Olson, & H. W. Stevenson (Eds.), *Learning and motivation in the classroom* (pp. 239–256). Hillsdale, NJ: Erlbaum.

Dweck, C. S., & Elliott, E. S. (1983). Achievement motivation. In P. Mussen (Ed.), *The handbook of child psychology* (4th ed., Vol. 4, pp. 643–691). New York: Wiley.

Dweck, C. S., & Reppucci, N. D. (1973). Learned helplessness and reinforcement responsibility in children. *Journal of Personality and Social Psychology, 25,* 109–116.

Evers-Pasquale, W. (1978). The peer preference test as a measure of reward value: Item analysis, cross-validation, concurrent validation, and replication. *Journal of Abnormal Child Psychology, 6,* 175–188.

Evers-Pasquale, W., & Sherman, M. (1975). The reward value of peers: A variable influencing the efficacy of filmed modeling in modifying social isolation in preschoolers. *Journal of Abnormal Child Psychology, 3,* 170–180.

Ford, M. E. (1982). Social cognition and social competence in adolescence. *Developmental Psychology, 18,* 323–340.

Gampel, D., Gottlieb, J., & Harrison, R. (1974). Comparison of classroom behavior of special class EMR, integrated EMR, low IQ, and nonretarded children. *American Journal of Mental Deficiency, 79,* 16–21.

Goetz, T. E., & Dweck, C. S. (1980). Learned helplessness in social situations. *Journal of Personality and Social Psychology, 39,* 246–255.

Goffman, E. (1959). *The presentation of self in everyday life.* New York: Doubleday.

Goodman, H., Gottlieb, J., & Harrison, R. H. (1972). Social acceptance of EMRs integrated into a nongraded elementary school. *American Journal of Mental Deficiency, 76,* 412–417.

Gottlieb, J. (1978). Observing social adaptation in schools. In G. Sackett (Ed.), *Observing behavior: Theory and applications in mental retardation* (pp. 285–309). Baltimore: University Park Press.

Gottlieb, J., Gampel, D. H., & Budoff, M. (1975). Classroom behavior of retarded children before and after integration into regular classes. *Journal of Special Education, 9,* 307–315.

Gottlieb, J., & Leyser, Y. (1981). Friendships between mentally retarded and nonretarded children. In S. R. Asher & J. M. Gottman (Eds.), *The development of children's friendships* (pp. 150–181). New York: Cambridge University Press.

Gottlieb, J., Semmel, M. I., & Veldman, D. J. (1978). Correlates of social status among mainstreamed mentally retarded children. *Journal of Educational Psychology, 70,* 396–405.

Gottman, J. M., Gonso, J., & Schuler, P. (1976). Teaching social skills to isolated children. *Journal of Abnormal Child Psychology, 4,* 179–197.

Greene, D. (1976). Social perception as problem solving. In J. S. Carroll & J. W. Payne (Eds.), *Cognition and social behavior* (pp. 155–161). Hillsdale, NJ: Erlbaum.

Greenspan, S. (1979). Social intelligence in the retarded. In N. R. Ellis (Ed.), *Handbook of mental deficiency, psychological theory and research* (2nd ed., pp. 483–531). Hillsdale, NJ: Erlbaum.

Greenspan, S. (1981). Defining childhood social competence: A proposed working model. In B. K. Keogh (Ed.), *Advances in special education (Vol. 3): Socialization influences on exceptionality* (pp. 1–39). Greenwich, CT: JAI Press.

Gresham, F. M., & Nagle, R. J. (1980). Social skills training with children: Responsiveness to modeling and coaching as a function of peer orientation. *Journal of Consulting and Clinical Psychology, 18,* 718–729.

Griesinger, D. W., & Livingston, J. W. (1973). Toward a model of interpersonal motivation in experimental games. *Behavioral Science, 18,* 173–188.

Grossman, H. (Ed.). (1973). *Manual on terminology and classification in mental retardation*. Washington, DC: American Association on Mental Deficiency.

Gruen, G., & Zigler, E. (1968). Expectancy of success and the probability learning of middle-class, lower-class, and retarded children. *Journal of Abnormal Psychology, 73*, 343–352.

Harter, S. (1982). The perceived competence scale for children. *Child Development, 53*, 87–97.

Hymel, S., & Asher, S. R. (1977). *Assessment and training of isolated children's social skills*. Paper presented at the biennial meeting of the Society for Research in Child Development, New Orleans (ERIC Document Reproduction Service No. ED 136 930).

Iano, R. P., Ayers, D., Heller, H. B., McGettigan, J. F., & Walker, V. S. (1974). Sociometric status of retarded children in an integrative program. *Exceptional Children, 40*, 267–271.

Johnson, G. O. (1950). A study of the social position of mentally handicapped children in the regular grades. *American Journal of Mental Deficiency, 55*, 60–89.

Kleck, R. E. (1975). Issues in social effectiveness: The case of the mentally retarded. In M. J. Begab & S. A. Richardson (Eds.), *The mentally retarded and society: A social science perspective* (pp. 181–195). Baltimore: University Park Press.

Knight, G. P. (1981). Behavioral and sociometric methods of identifying cooperators, competitors, and individualists: Support for the validity of the social orientation construct. *Developmental Psychology, 17*, 430–433.

Knight, G. P., & Kagan, S. (1977). Development of prosocial and competitive behavior in Anglo-American and Mexican-American children. *Child Development, 48*, 1385–1394.

Ladd, G. W. (1981). Effectiveness of a social learning method for enhancing children's social interaction and peer acceptance. *Child Development, 52*, 171–178.

Lambert, N., Windmiller, M., Cole, L. J., & Figueroa, R. (1975). *AAMD adaptive behavior scale manual* (rev. ed.). Washington, DC: American Association on Mental Deficiency.

Lilly, M. S. (1971). Improving social acceptance of low sociometric status, low-achieving students. *Exceptional Children, 37*, 341–347.

Madsen, M. C. (1967). Cooperative and competitive motivation of children in three Mexican sub-cultures. *Psychology Reports, 20*, 1307–1320.

Marlowe, M. (1979). The games analysis intervention: A procedure to increase the peer acceptance and social adjustment of a retarded child. *Education and Training of the Mentally Retarded, 14*, 262–268.

Marlowe, M. (1980). Games analysis intervention: A procedure to increase peer acceptance of socially isolated children. *Research Quarterly for Exercise and Sport, 51*, 422–426.

McClintock, C. G., & Moskowitz, J. M. (1976). Children's preferences for individualistic, cooperative, and competitive outcomes. *Journal of Personality and Social Psychology, 34*, 534–555.

McCrimmons, K. R., & Messick, D. M. (1976). A framework for social motives. *Behavioral Science, 21*, 86–100.

Nakamura, C. Y., & Finck, D. N. (1980). Relative effectiveness of socially-oriented and task-oriented children and predictability of their behaviors. *Monographs of the Society for Research in Child Development, 45* (3–4, Serial No. 185).

Nihira, K., Foster, R., Shellhaas, M., & Leland, H. (1974). *AAMD adaptive behavior scale*. Washington, DC: American Association on Mental Deficiency.

O'Connor, R. D. (1969). Modification of social withdrawal through symbolic modeling. *Journal of Applied Behavior Analysis, 2*, 15–22.

Oden, S., Asher, S. R., & Hymel, S. (1977). *Procedures for coaching socially isolated children in social skills.* Unpublished manuscript, University of Illinois, Urbana.

O'Malley, J. (1977). Research perspective on social competence. *Merrill-Palmer Quarterly, 23,* 29–44.

Putallaz, M. (1983). Predicting children's sociometric status from their behavior. *Child Development, 54,* 1417–1426.

Putallaz, M., & Gottman, J. M. (1982). Conceptualizing social competence in children. In P. Karoly & J. J. Steffen (Eds.), *Improving children's competence: Advances in child behavioral analysis and therapy* (pp. 1–33). Lexington, MA: D. C. Heath.

Renshaw, P. D. (1981). *Social knowledge and sociometric status: Children's goals and strategies for peer interaction.* Unpublished doctoral dissertation, University of Illinois, Urbana.

Renshaw, P. D., & Asher, S. R. (1982). Social competence and peer status: The distinction between goals and strategies. In K. H. Rubin & H. S. Ross (Eds.), *Peer relationships and social skills in childhood* (pp. 375–395). New York: Springer-Verlag.

Renshaw, P. D., & Asher, S. R. (1983). Children's goals and strategies for social interaction. *Merrill-Palmer Quarterly, 29,* 353–374.

Rucker, C. N., & Vincenzo, F. M. (1970). Maintaining social acceptance gains made by mentally retarded children. *Exceptional Children, 36,* 679–680.

Rynders, J., Johnson, R., Johnson, D., & Schmidt, B. (1980). Producing positive interaction among Downs Syndrome and nonhandicapped teenagers through cooperative goal structuring. *American Journal of Mental Deficiency, 85,* 268–273.

Schaefer, E. S. (1961). Converging conceptual model for maternal behavior and for child behavior. In J. C. Glidewell (Ed.), *Parental attitudes and child behavior* (pp. 124–146). Springfield, IL: Charles C Thomas.

Schaefer, E. S. (1975). Factors that impede the process of socialization. In M. J. Begab & S. A. Richardson (Eds.), *The mentally retarded and society: A social science perspective* (pp. 197–227). Baltimore: University Park Press.

Schiefelbusch, R. (1981). Development of social competence and incompetence. In M. J. Begab, H. C. Haywood, & H. L. Garber (Eds.), *Psychosocial influences in retarded performance (Vol. 1): Issues and theories in development* (pp. 179–195). Baltimore: University Park Press.

Siegel, P. (1979). Incentive motivation and the mentally retarded person. In N. R. Ellis (Ed.), *Handbook of mental deficiency, psychological theory and research* (2nd ed., pp. 1–61). Hillsdale, NJ: Erlbaum.

Siperstein, G. N., & Gale, M. E. (1983). *Improving peer relationships of rejected children.* Paper presented at the biennial meeting of the Society for Research in Child Development, Detroit.

Stevenson, H., & Zigler, E. (1958). Probability learning in children. *Journal of Experimental Psychology, 56,* 185–192.

Strichart, S., & Gottlieb, J. (1975). Imitation of retarded children by their nonretarded peers. *American Journal of Mental Deficiency, 78,* 506–512.

Taylor, A. R. (1982). Social competence and interpersonal relations between retarded and nonretarded children. In N. R. Ellis (Ed.), *International review of research in mental retardation* (Vol. 11, pp. 247–283). New York: Academic Press.

Weinstein, E. (1969). The development of interpersonal competence. In D. A. Goslin (Ed.), *Handbook of socialization theory and research* (pp. 753–775). Chicago: Rand McNally.

Weisz, J. (1979). Perceived control and learned helplessness among mentally retarded and nonretarded children: A developmental analysis. *Developmental Psychology, 15,* 311–319.

Weisz, J. (1981). Learned helplessness in black and white children identified by their schools as retarded and nonretarded: Performance deterioration in response to failure. *Developmental Psychology, 17,* 499–508.

Wheeler, V., & Ladd, G. (1982). Assessment of children's self-efficacy for social interactions with peers. *Developmental Psychology, 18,* 795–805.

Wish, M. (1976). Comparisons among multidimensional structures of interpersonal relations. *Multivariate Behavior Research, 11,* 297–324.

Wish, M., Deutsch, M., & Kaplan, S. (1976). Perceived dimensions of interpersonal relations. *Journal of Personality and Social Psychology, 33,* 409–420.

Zigler, E., & Trickett, P. K. (1978). IQ, social competence, and evaluation of early childhood intervention programs. *American Psychologist, 33,* 789–798.

II

RESEARCH STUDIES ON FRIENDSHIPS IN NORMAL CHILDREN

Becoming Acquainted with Peers in the Nursery Classroom*

Jaipaul L. Roopnarine

Researchers have attributed great importance to social competence with peers for personality development (e.g. Cowen, Babijian, Izzo, & Trost, 1973; Roff, Sells, & Golden, 1972). The increased realization of the importance of peer relationships has led to an upsurge of interest in young children's friendships (see, for instance, the recent volume by Asher and Gottman, 1981). Nonetheless, the process whereby children develop intimate interpersonal relationships has received little attention. More specifically, there is little data on the process of forming and maintaining friendship bonds. In this chapter, I will provide a selective review of previous research on one aspect of friendship formation— becoming acquainted—and I will present some of my own data on the social contacts of preschoolers during the early weeks of nursery school.

CONCEPTUAL FRAMEWORK

Several developmentalists and family researchers have proposed stages in the process of relationship formation (Furman, 1982; Gottman & Parkhurst, 1980; Huston & Burgess, 1979). The most commonly reported stages in the development of interpersonal relationships have

* This research was supported by grants from the College of Family Life at Utah State University, and the Western Regional Agricultural Experimental Station (Project W-144). The author extends his gratitude to Frank Ascione, Gerald Adams, Carla Seamons, and Soheila Shobani for their help on this manuscript.

been: (a) initial attraction, (b) becoming acquainted, (c) development of personal relationship, (d) maintenance of a relationship, and (e) deterioration and termination. Within this conceptual framework, Furman (1982) has further proposed four phases that are central to the process of acquaintanceship: (a) disclosure and self-discovery, (b) establishment of a mutual enterprise, (c) individuation of the relationship, and (d) development of an affective bond. Movement proceeds from disclosing information about the self to one another, which might lead to reinforcing interchanges and discovery of similarities and shared activities, to warm and more compatible exchanges that might become dyadic in nature and eventually lead to the formation of strong attachments (Furman, 1982). While few researchers have studied the process of acquaintanceship per se, some data exist on the interactions of familiar and unfamiliar children that might be related to the process of becoming acquainted.

BACKGROUND RESEARCH ON THE ACQUAINTANCESHIP PROCESS

The method most commonly used to study the acquaintanceship process has been to compare the interactions of dyads of familiar and unfamiliar children. Unfamiliar pairs of children tend to play together less frequently and in a less complex manner, make fewer social overtures, and are less successful when they do compared to more familiar pairs of children (Doyle, Connolly, & Rivest, 1980). By contrast, volunteering personal information and making inquiries about others are more frequently observed in unacquainted than in acquainted dyads (Jormakka, 1976).

Other work with preschool-aged children (Gottman & Parkhurst, 1980) has reported that behavioral differentiation occurs as children become increasingly familiar with one another. These researchers paired children with either a friend or a stranger. Interactions were audiotaped in the host child's home. Based on detailed sequential analyses of the children's interactions, Gottman and Parkhurst (1980) formulated an eight-stage process whereby children become acquainted. Initially, preschoolers appeared to engage in quite a bit of show and tell and social comparison before engaging in more extended fantasy play late in the acquaintanceship process. These results are congruent with those reported on dyads of third graders (Furman & Childs, 1981). While there was a high degree of participation among familiar children from the outset, unfamiliar children were noted to silently observe each other before more complex social interchanges, such as sharing information about themselves and mutual play, were evident.

Working with an adolescent sample at summer camp, Furman and Childs (1981) examined the relationships of individuals over a 7-day period. On the second, fifth, and seventh day of camp, each adolescent completed a questionnaire which assessed his or her relationships with his or her cabinmates on the following dimensions: (a) support, (b) intimacy, (c) companionship, (d) similarity, (e) affection, and (f) quarreling. The results indicated that quite a bit of differentiation occurred over the 7-day period. On all dimensions, the ratings were highest on the seventh day. Interestingly, children's ratings of "low" friendships decreased over time, whereas their ratings of "high" friendships remained stable over time.

In sum, then, existing data suggest that during the acquaintanceship process differentiation occurs in a sequential manner, and that during the latter stages in the acquaintanceship process relationships are characterized by more intimacy and involvement than at earlier stages. Nevertheless, the process of becoming acquainted remains relatively unexplored, and data to substantiate the more general stages of relationship formation are badly needed.

SOCIAL CONTACTS OF CHILDREN DURING THE EARLY WEEKS OF PRESCHOOL

The conceptual framework outlined earlier (Furman & Childs, 1981) suggests that differentiation occurs during the process of becoming acquainted. This conceptual framework, however, was formulated on the basis of brief observations of unacquainted children in a laboratory setting. It seems improbable that unacquainted children would really "hit it off" during a 30-minute encounter in a very strange environment. I believe that the formation of affective bonds between children may occur over a longer time span after children have had a great deal of meaningful social contacts. In this section, I will discuss the findings of a study I conducted on the social contacts of unacquainted children during the early weeks of nursery school. The intent was to test the differentiation process, reported in other studies (Furman & Childs 1981), among younger children in a group setting. At the outset, it should be stated that little attention has been paid to the process of becoming acquainted in group settings. Thus, the present study should be viewed as primarily inductive and hypothesis generating, rather than deductive and hypothesis testing.

To examine social contacts during the early weeks of preschool, 40 unacquainted 4-year-olds were observed on days 2, 7, 12, and 17 following enrollment in two classrooms at the Utah State University Laboratories. The children were primarily from middle- and lower-middle income backgrounds. Each child had at least one sibling. Because we were interested in how unacquainted children assort themselves into smaller playgroups, four behavioral measures that are commonly reported to be central to the interactions of preschoolers were observed: (a) *parallel play*, (b) *joint positive play*, (c) *negative interactions*, and (d) *general conversations*. Two primary issues were of interest: (a) overall patterns of changes in children's interactions and sex-typed preferences over the 17-day period, and (b) the nature and consistency with which children interacted with one another during the initial weeks of nursery school.

With respect to the first issue, there were significant changes in overall patterns of interactions over the 17-day period (see Figure 1). A

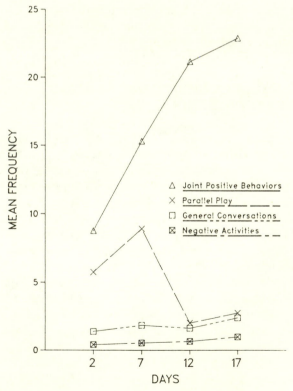

Figure 1. *Mean rates of interaction during preschool days 2, 7, 12, and 17 for all children (N = 40).*

Table 1

Sex Segregation: Percentage of Children Who Interacted with Same- And Opposite-Sex Peers Significantly Greater Than Chance Over the 17-Day Period

	Day 2		Day 7		Day 12		Day 17	
Sex	Same-Sex	Opposite-Sex	Same-Sex	Opposite-Sex	Same-Sex	Opposite-Sex	Same-Sex	Opposite-Sex
Boys	14	9	18	5	36	5	41	14
Girls	17		26	5	37		43	5

Note: Blanks indicate that no girl interacted with boys at a significantly greater than chance level.

To assess the prevalence of same-sex and opposite-sex interaction over the 17 days, a comparison was made between observed rates of interaction and "availability quotients." The observed rates at which each child engaged in each of the four behaviors with same- and opposite-sex peers during each time period were computed. The availability quotients represented the exact number of boys and girls who were available to each child, if playmate selection had occurred on a random basis. Because it could not be assumed that the behavior of any child was independent of other children in the peer group, it was necessary to analyze these data on an individual basis. For each child, then, the observed percentage of interaction with same- and opposite-sex peers was compared with the corresponding availability quotient. The resulting Z score indicated whether a child engaged in interaction with same- and opposite-sex peers significantly more or less than would be expected by chance. A Z score of at least 2 indicated a significant difference between proportions (see Bakeman, 1978).

significant increase occurred in joint positive play, whereas a significant decrease occurred in parallel play ($p < .01$). Although negative activities and general conversations showed a slight increase over the 17 days, both types of behaviors occurred very infrequently. Similarly, as can be seen in Table 1, children's choice of playmates became increasingly stereotyped over time. Both boys and girls showed an increasing preference for same-sex playmates over time, while interactions with cross-sex playmates remained relatively low and stable.

Since there was no clear-cut procedure to analyze the nature and consistency of children's interactions over time, the social contacts of 10 dyads (2 boy–boy pairs, 5 girl–girl pairs, and 3 boy–girl pairs) who interacted consistently over the four time periods were examined.[1] Interactions with the consistent partner, and those involving other children, were compared within and across time periods. The analyses failed to show differentiation in the focal children's interactions with

1. These analyses were performed by using a repeated measures MANOVA and matched t-tests. In addition, the social contacts the 10 dyads engaged in with one another, and with other children in the classroom, were mapped on a grid to examine whether certain configurations of playmate preferences were more prominent than others (see McGrew, 1972).

their consistent partners and those involving other children within or across time periods. However, the number of new playmates these children interacted with in nursery school decreased steadily after the second day.

The data failed to confirm the differentiation process observed by Furman and Childs (1981). Perhaps 17 days is not enough time for younger children to form strong affective bonds. While these data cannot be interpreted within the conceptual framework outlined by Furman and Childs (1981), they can be viewed within the framework discussed by Levinger and Snoek (1972). They argue that relationships between people can be interpreted as being in one of three phases: unilateral awareness, surface contacts, and mutuality. In the first phase, unilateral awareness, individuals are aware of one another but no interaction has occurred as yet. In the second phase, surface contact, individuals interact in a superficial manner. Individuals may be perceived as important, but the relationships are not very deep. Behavioral interactions are chiefly determined by the roles the individuals assume during social encounters. Finally, during mutuality a great deal of self-disclosure occurs, and individuals may form close relationships. The children in the present study were probably in the surface contact phase of Levinger and Snoek's (1972) notion of relationship formation. They engaged in quite a bit of interaction that could be termed associative play without revealing much about themselves to their peers. Furthermore, changes in the patterns of positive interactions and sex-typed preferences over the initial period in preschool would suggest that these children were becoming more involved with peers of the same sex, and perhaps that in group settings differentiation may occur at a much slower pace. Moreover, among preschool groups, strong dyadic relationships may take longer to develop than among preadolescent and adolescent groups.

CONCLUDING REMARKS

It is clear from the chapters presented in this book that a variety of approaches are being employed to study young children's friendships. However, the process whereby children form friendships requires far more attention. A process approach to the study of friendship formation might yield valuable data on the following: (a) the stability and/or the changing nature of young children's friendships, (b) the sequences and transitions during different phases in a relationship, and (c) the types of behaviors that are more conducive to relationship formation.

Finally, assessing young children's relationships with other members in a group is a complex task that might require more refined analyses than those employed in the author's study. For example, the sequential analyses used by Gottman and Parkhurst (1980) might be useful in our examination of relationship formation. Moreover, the changing dynamics of the nursery group may be explored within the perspective proposed by Levinger and Snoek (1972) as well. Whatever the approach, the process of becoming acquainted, and friendship formation in general, pose a number of important and intriguing questions.

REFERENCES

Bakeman, R. (1978). Untangling streams of behavior: Sequential analyses of observational data. In G. P. Sackett (Ed.), *Observing behavior, Volume II: Data collection and analysis methods.* Baltimore: University Park Press.

Cowen, E. L., Pederson, A., Babijain, J., Izzo, L. D., & Trost, M. A. (1973). Long-term follow-up of early detected vulnerable children. *Journal of Consulting and Clinical Psychology, 41,* 438–446.

Doyle, A., Connolly, J., & Rivest, L. (1980). The effect of playmate familiarity on the social interactions of young children. *Child Development, 51,* 217–223.

Furman, W. (1982). Children's friendships. In T. Field, A. Houston, H. Quay, L. Troll, & E. G. Finley (Eds.), *Review of human development.* New York: Wiley.

Furman, W., & Childs, M. K. (1981). *A temporal perspective on children's friendship.* Paper presented at meetings of the Society for Research in Child Development, Boston.

Gottman, J. M., & Parkhurst, J. (1980). A developmental theory of friendship and acquaintanceship. In A. Collins (Ed.), *Minnesota symposia on child psychology* (Vol. 13). Norwood, NJ: Lawrence Erlbaum.

Huston, T. L., & Burgess, R. L. (1979). Social exchange in developing relationships: An overview. In R. L. Burgess & T. L. Huston (Eds.), *Social exchange in developing relationships.* New York: Academic.

Jormakka, L. (1976). The behavior of children during a first encounter. *Scandinavian Journal of Psychology, 17,* 15–22.

Levinger, G., & Snoek, J. D. (1972). *Attraction in relationship: A new look at interpersonal attraction.* Morristown, NJ: General Learning Press.

Masters, J. C., & Furman, W. (1978). Popularity, individual friendship selection, and specific peer interactions among children. *Developmental Psychology, 17,* 344–350.

McGrew, W. C. (1972). Aspects of social development in nursery school children, with emphasis on introduction to the group. In N. Blurton Jones (Ed.), *Ethiological studies of child behavior.* London: Cambridge University Press.

Roff, M., Sells, S. B., & Golden, M. M. (1972). *Social adjustment and personality development in children.* Minneapolis: University of Minnesota Press.

Play Interactions of Friends and Acquaintances in Nursery School*

Jaipaul L. Roopnarine
Tiffany M. Field

Despite the current interest in young children's peer interactions (see Field & Roopnarine, 1982; Hartup, 1977, 1983; Lewis & Rosenblum, 1975; Mueller & Vandell, 1979), there is remarkably little information on interactions between close friends and on the behaviors of young children who do and do not have friends. This is surprising, given the correlations between early relationships and later development (Asher, Oden, & Gottman, 1977). Low peer acceptance is correlated with social problems (Cowen, Pederson, Babijian, Izzo, & Trost, 1973; Roff, 1963) and lower achievement scores (Austin & Draper, 1981). In view of the developmental significance attributed to early friendships, and given the paucity of data on the interactions between friends and between nonfriends, in this chapter we will present data on the interactions of children with friends and nonfriends.

Two studies have been reported in which the interactions of young acquaintances versus strangers were observed (Gottman & Parkhurst, 1980; Masters & Furman, 1981). Using home-based audiotape recordings, Gottman and Parkhurst (1980) coded the verbal interactions of 2- to 6-year-olds when they were playing with a close friend or stranger. Younger children were more respondent, compliant, more willing to resolve disagreements, and more likely to engage in fantasy play with

* We thank the teachers and children of the Mailman Center nurseries for their participation, and Kristen Comstock and Jenny Julien for assistance with the observations and coding. This research was supported by grant Nos. 90-CW-605 (1) and 90-CW-605 (2) from the Administration of Children, Youth, and Families to Tiffany Field.

friends than with strangers; older children were willing to resolve disagreements with strangers than with friends. Younger children differed from older children in their behavior toward friends as well; their friendships were marked by less conflict, more compliance, and more fantasy play than older children's friendships. Other work with preschoolers (Masters & Furman, 1981) has revealed that children who were friends were more likely to engage in reinforcing and neutral behaviors than children who were not friends.

While revealing, these studies are limited in several ways. First, Gottman and Parkhurst (1980) observed children in dyadic situations. Children's interactions in dyadic situations may differ from their interactions in group settings where they have a choice of interacting with friends and nonfriends. Moreover, while audiotape recordings permit detailed codings of verbal behavior, important nonverbal behaviors cannot be coded. Second, Masters and Furman (1981) failed to compare the behaviors of children who had friends when they were interacting with their friends and with nonfriends. As Gottman and Parkhurst (1980) have noted, children's interactions with friends and nonfriends are characteristically different.

Given the limitations of previous research, and the small data base on the interactions of children with friends and nonfriends, the research reported herein had two major objectives. The first objective was to identify, among groups of toddlers and preschoolers, those children who had at least one good friend. Then we examined behavioral differences in the interactions of children who did and did not have friends, and the behavior of children who had friends when interacting with their friends versus acquaintances in nursery school. Following speculations on the types of behaviors that might discriminate between the social interactions of friends and the social interactions of nonfriends (see Gottman & Parkhurst, 1980), we recorded the children's fantasy play, the nature of their verbal interactions, and a range of social behaviors.

A second goal of the research was to examine the relationships between a measure of extraversion–introversion (Buck, 1975), mental development scores, and peer interaction behaviors. Recent reviews (Shantz, 1975; 1983) suggest that the relationship between social competence with peers and social-cognition has been one of the most ignored areas in the study of children's development. Moreover, scattered evidence (Emmerich, Cocking, & Sigel, 1979) suggests that intellectual development might facilitate social adaptation in the preschool classroom. An extraversion–introversion measure was used because it has been empirically linked to children's nonverbal expressiveness (Buck, 1975; Field & Walden, 1982), and because expressiveness might be an important construct for friendship formation.

METHODS AND PROCEDURES

Subjects

Observations were conducted on 16 preschoolers (6 girls) ranging in age from 36 to 56 months (M=46 months), and 12 toddlers (7 girls) ranging in age from 18 to 32 months (M=25 months). The children were enrolled in two university nursery school classrooms.

Identifying Children with and without Friends

OBSERVATIONAL METHOD

Three observers assessed the frequency with which children played with one another in the different "activity areas" of their nursery room. The three observers systematically rotated through all of the play areas every 5 minutes, recording each child's name and the other children engaging in cooperative and associative play with them, and the area of the room in which the activity occurred (see Ellis, Rogoff, & Cromer, 1980). Seventy-two 5-minute observations were conducted 3 days per week, for a total of 108 hours over a 4-month period. Interobserver agreement assessed throughout the 4-month period averaged 90%. Those children who interacted with one another more than 66% of the total time observed were considered friends, while those who interacted with one another for less than 25% of the time observed were considered nonfriends. Based on these criteria, 16 children (8 pairs) had close friends (8 boys and 8 girls), and 12 children did not have close friends (7 boys and 5 girls).

TEACHER SELECTION METHOD

Given that most researchers advocate the use of a sociometric or nomination method in research on young children's friendships, and given the limitations of the "rate of interaction" method (see Asher, Markell, & Hymel, 1981), the head teachers of each classroom were asked to list children they thought were close friends. The teachers selected 14 (7 pairs) of the 16 children identified by the observational method as having close friends.

SOCIOMETRIC RATING METHOD.

Because 13 of the 28 children in our sample were below 32 months of age, sociometric ratings were only made on the 15 older children. Using a sociometric rating task adapted from Asher, Singleton, Tinsley, and Hymel (1979), the children sorted a randomly mixed pile of photos of their peers under stylized drawing cards of "happy," "sad," and "neutral" faces which were verbally labeled "liking to play with a whole bunch," "not at all," and "a little bit," respectively. Children who gave each other a rating of three ("happy face") were considered friends. Of the 15 children administered this task, 12 had been identified by the observational method as having friends, while 10 of the children had been identified by the teachers as having friends. The sociometric rating identified five pairs of close friends, or 10 of 12 children previously identified by the observational method, and all 10 of the children previously identified by the teacher selection method.

Observations

Subsequent to identifying children who had friends and friend pairs, each child in our sample was observed for six 5-minute sessions during free play in their nursery setting over a 6-week period. Using a time-sampling technique, an observer watched for 10 seconds and then recorded the behaviors for the next 10 seconds, for a total of 30 time-sampling units per observation period (180 10-second units per child). The observer noted the target child's behavior, and with whom he or she was engaging in play interaction. The following behaviors were coded:

A. *Domestic Fantasy*—Doctor, house, food preparation, baby, making a phone call, hairdresser, boy and girl friend, family, pets, going on a trip, and school.
B. *Adventure Fantasy*—monsters, superheroes, cops and robbers, TV characters, and other adventures.
C. *Social Behaviors*—directing, submitting, giving, taking, sharing, helping (verbal or instrumental), imitating, watching, and fighting.
D. *Verbal Interaction*—positive, negative, and neutral; observer also noted whether these were in the form of a question, imperative or "command," request, or general statement.

Interobserver Agreement

Interobserver agreement was assessed by having two independent observers record children's behaviors simultaneously throughout the study. Percentage of agreement was calculated by dividing the number of agreements by agreements plus disagreements. These percentages are presented in Table 1. Cohen's Kappa was used to correct for chance agreements (see Hollenbeck, 1978). These calculations revealed that all coefficients were greater than .80.

Extraversion/Introversion and Mental Development Assessment

Extraversion–introversion was assessed by the children's version of the Buck Affect Rating Scale (Buck, 1975). This scale is comprised of 37 items yielding a summary rating of children's extraversion–introversion and is based on a likert-type scale. Examples of items are: "Is quiet and reserved," "Is warm and friendly toward other children." Student observers who had known the children for 6 months made this assessment. Mental development of the toddlers was assessed by the Bayley Scales of Infant Development (Bayley, 1969). The McCarthy Scale was used to assess the mental development of older children (McCarthy, 1972).

RESULTS

Characteristics of Friendship Pairs

As noted earlier, 16 of the 28 children we observed had a close friend. Of the 16, there were only two cross-sex pairs of friends. Thus, there was a marked tendency to form friendships with children of the same sex. There was also a marked tendency to form friendships with children of the same age and the same height. This was evidenced by the between pair correlations performed on friends' ages ($r=.75$, $p<.01$) and heights ($r=.79$, $p<.01$). Similar analyses performed on friends' extraversion–introversion scores and mental development scores failed to yield significant correlations.

Social Behaviors of Children Who Had and Did Not Have Close Friends

Since we were interested in the behaviors of children who did and did not have friends, one-way analyses of variance were conducted on the measures listed in Table 1.[1] As can be seen in Table 1, children who had a close friend were more likely to engage in domestic fantasy play,

---

1. These data were also analyzed using a 2 (Sex) × 2 (Friend/Nonfriend) multivariate analysis of variance. There was no significant main effect for Sex, and the univariate tests for sex differences that were significant could be due to chance alone. There was a significant main effect for friend/nonfriend status, and the 10 measures that yielded significant differences between the two groups in the one-way analysis also yielded significant differences in the multivariate analysis. There were no significant interaction effects.

Table 1
Percentage of Observation Time Behaviors Were Observed For Children Who
Did and Did Not Have Close Friends

Behaviors	Children With Friends	Children Without Friends	F
Domestic Fantasy (88)	25.25	6.83	8.16*
Adventure Fantasy (85)	7.81	4.16	
Positive Verbal Interaction (96)	24.88	10.00	10.21***
Negative Verbal Interaction (90)	16.62	3.58	10.17***
Neutral Verbal Interaction (86)	50.69	29.17	9.57***
Statements (93)	61.86	33.58	11.65***
Requests (100)	2.37	.00	3.09*
Imperatives (96)	19.44	8.08	7.06*
Questions (96)	6.62	4.17	
Directing (99)	28.31	12.33	5.64**
Submitting (100)	4.25	1.16	4.25**
Giving (99)	3.06	5.00	
Taking (99)	1.69	3.67	1.73
Sharing (98)	12.44	6.83	2.48
Helping (100)	1.94	1.83	
Imitating (100)	6.56	4.08	
Watching (88)	12.13	35.67	18.54***
Fighting (95)	12.06	11.08	

Note: Blanks indicate F less than 1.
***p < .005.
**p < .01.
*p < .05.

verbalize in a positive, negative, and neutral manner to peers, direct
their peers' activities and submit to them, and make statements, imper-
atives (or "commands"), and requests to their peers than children who
did not have friends. By contrast, children who did not have friends
were more likely to watch the activities of their peers than children
who had friends.

Similar analyses performed on the behaviors of younger and older
children who had a close friend revealed few significant age differences. Older children who had friends were more likely to direct
their peers' activities (F [1,14] = 6.84, p<.05) and engage in positive
verbal interactions than younger children who had friends (F [1,14] =
6.51, p<.05). Younger children who had friends were more willing to
share than older children who had friends (F [1,14] = 5.41, p<.05).
Children who had friends scored significantly higher on the Buck scale,
suggesting they were more extraverted than children who did not have
friends (M=46.25; M=22.0, t (26)=5.26, p<.001). However, children
who had friends did not differ from children who did not have friends
on sociometric ratings.

Social Behavior toward Friends and Nonfriends

As noted previously, we were interested in determining how children with close friends differed in their behaviors directed toward friends and nonfriends. Matched t-tests performed on the fantasy play and social behavior measures revealed that the children who had a close friend were more likely to engage in domestic fantasy ($M = 29.37$; $M = .25$; t [15] = 3.45, p<.01) and adventure fantasy ($M = 8.75$; $M = .00$; t [15] = 1.92, p<.10) with their friends than with nonfriends. On the other hand, children who did not have friends were more likely to watch the activities of those who had friends ($M = 47.16$; $M = 25.42$; t [11] = 3.58, p<.01) but showed a tendency to fight with other children who did not have friends ($M = 8.25$, $M = 18.00$, t [11] = 2.06, p<.10).

Relationship between Behaviors toward Peers and Social–Cognitive Measures

Pearson correlations were performed on the percentage of observation time spent in fantasy play, verbal interaction, and social behaviors, and the mental development scores and extraversion–introversion scores, partialing for age. The analyses revealed no significant relationships between mental development scores and the behavioral measures. However, extraversion–introversion scores were significantly related to fantasy play ($r = .37$, p<.05), verbal interaction ($r = .53$, p<.01), and social behavior ($r = .38$, p<.05).

DISCUSSION

The selection of friends among these toddlers and preschoolers corresponds to the selection factors reported for older children. These children developed friendships with peers of the same age (Hartup, 1983), of the same sex (Asher, Oden, & Gottman, 1977; Challman, 1933; Masters & Furman, 1981), and of the same height. However, friends' mental development and extraversion–introversion scores were not significantly related. The importance of similarity on factors such as age, sex, and height may developmentally precede friendship formation based on more abstract factors such as intellectual and personality characteristics.

The free play behaviors of children who had close friends were significantly different from those of children who did not have close friends. Those who had close friends were more verbal, more likely to take turns directing and submitting during interactions, more likely to engage in fantasy play, and less likely to watch the activities of their peers than children who did not have friends. Few age differences were noted between the behaviors of younger and the behaviors of older children who had close friends. Older children who had friends were more likely to direct their peers' activities and engage in more positive verbal interaction than younger children who had friends. Younger children who had friends were more likely to share with peers than older children who had friends. Although these findings tend to match those of Gottman and Parkhurst (1980), the amount of fantasy play did not vary with age in our study. However, our preschoolers averaged 4 years of age while the children in their sample averaged 6 years of age, a time when fantasy play is noted to decline (Field, DeStefano, & Koewler, 1982).

Children who had close friends were significantly more extraverted, as assessed by the Buck Affect Rating Scale (Buck, 1977). On the other hand, they were not necessarily more popular among their peers than children who did not have friends. As Hartup (1983) and Furman (1982) have noted, one does not need to be popular to have friends: in fact, the determinants of popularity and individual friendship selection may not be isomorphic. It is not clear, however, that popularity is best judged by children, since sociometrics are frequently unreliable among this very young population. Even the procedure used in this study, while previously reported to be reliable for very young children (Asher et al., 1979), has been notably unreliable in other studies (Walden & Field, 1983). The children's ratings in this study seemed to reflect the group of children they happened to play with on the day of the rating procedure, rather than their preferred playmates.

Interactions with close friends versus interactions with acquaintances were noticeably different. When children were playing with their close friends, they engaged in domestic and adventure fantasy a greater proportion of the time than when they were playing with acquaintances or nonfriends. The greater amount of fantasy play, both in this study and that of Gottman and Parkhurst (1980), suggests that this measure may be one of the more salient discriminators of play among friends and nonfriends. On the other hand, children who did not have friends in our study tended to watch the activities of those who had friends, and fight with those who did not have friends. Social overtures of rejected children are rebuffed at much higher rates than the overtures of popular children, and rejected children engage in more verbal and physical aggression than popular children (Dodge & Coie, 1978). Children who did not have friends in this study may have been in that position because of their own behaviors and because of rejection/exclusion by others.

Finally, the correlation analyses support the idea that extraversion might facilitate peer interactions among young children. Children who had high scores on the extraversion–introversion measure were more likely to engage in fantasy play, verbal interaction, and social behaviors. On the other hand, children's mental scores did not relate to peer social behaviors. Why mental development did not relate to the behavioral measures is not clear. While the data on the importance of intellectual abilities for social competence are contradictory (Hartup, 1970), it appears that extraversion might be an important construct in social relations with peers.

Whether children who have friends engage in more verbal interactions, fantasy play, and take turns directing and submitting during social activities more often because they have friends, or whether these behaviors contribute to their having friends in the first place, cannot be answered by these data. Nonetheless, the data suggest that children who had close friends engaged in more of those behaviors which appear to be conducive to friendship formation, whether they were playing with their close friends or with acquaintances. Children who did not have friends appeared to display behavioral characteristics that are similar to those reported for rejected children (see Dodge & Coie, 1978). Their aggressive displays may be perceived as highly inappropriate, and therefore maximized the likelihood of exclusion by children who had friends. Moreover, their high levels of "watching" may be characteristic of entry skill deficits. That is, they are probably unable to ease into the play activities of other children, and consequently engage in quite a bit of watching. The issues addressed by this research will require more prolonged observations of young children over longer periods of time, using coding and data analysis techniques that preserve sequential relationships. To understand why some children have friends and others do not, and how interactions between friends are gradually differentiated from interactions between acquaintances, requires a careful examination of the developmental process of making friends and remaining friends.

REFERENCES

Asher, S., Markell, R., & Hymel, S. (1981). Identifying children at risk in peer relations: A critique of the rate-of-interaction approach to assessment. *Child Development, 52,* 1239–1245.

Asher, S., Oden, S., & Gottman, J. (1977). Children's friendship in school setting. In L. G. Katz (Ed.), *Current topics in early childhood education* (Vol. 1). Norwood, NJ: Ablex.

Asher, S., Singleton, L., Tinsley B., & Hymel, S. (1971). A reliable sociometric measure of preschool children. *Developmental Psychology, 15,* 443–444.

Austin, A., & Draper, D. (1981, April). *Peer acceptance, visibility and academic achievement in middle childhood.* Paper presented at the biennial meeting of the Society for Research in Child Development, Boston, MA.

Bayley, N. (1969). *Manual for the Bayley Scales of Infant Development*. New York: Psychological Corporation.

Buck, R. (1975). Nonverbal communication of affect in children. *Journal of Personality and Social Psychology, 31*, 4, 644–653.

Challman, R. (1933). Factors influencing friendships among preschool children. *Child Development, 3*, 146–158.

Cowen, R., Pederson, A., Babijian, H., Izzo, L., & Trost, M. (1973). Long-term follow-up of early detected vulnerable children. *Journal of Consulting and Clinical Psychology, 41*, 438–446.

Dodge, K., & Coie, J. (1978). *Behavioral patterns among socially rejected, average, and popular fifth graders*. Paper presented at the Fifth Biennial Southeastern Conference on Human Development, Atlanta, GA.

Ellis, S., Rogoff, B., & Cromer, C. (1981). Age segregation in children's social interaction. *Developmental Psychology, 17*, 399–407.

Emmerich, W., Cocking, R., & Sigel, I. (1979). Relationship between cognitive and social functioning in preschool children. *Developmental Psychology, 15*, 495–504.

Field, T., DeStefano, L., & Koewler, J. (1982). Fantasy play of toddlers and preschoolers. *Developmental Psychology, 18*, 503–508.

Field, T., & Roopnarine, J. L. (1982). Infant peer interactions. In T. Field, A. Huston, H. Quay, L. Troll, & G. Finley (Eds.), *Review of human development*. New York: John Wiley & Sons.

Field, T., & Walden, T. (1982). Production and discrimination of facial expressions by preschool children. *Child Development, 53*, 1299–1311.

Furman, W. (1982). Children's friendships. In T. Field, A. Houston, H. Quay, L. Troll, & G. Finley (Eds.), *Review of Human Development*. New York: John Wiley & Sons.

Gottman, J., & Parkhurst, J., (1980). A developmental theory of friendship and acquaintanceship process. In A. Collins (Ed.), *Minnesota Symposium on Child Psychology* (Vol 13). Hillsdale, NJ: Lawrence Erlbaum.

Hartup, W. (1977). *Peer intervention and the integration of handicapped and nonhandicapped children*. Baltimore: University Park Press.

Hartup, W. (1983). The peer system. In E. M. Hetherington (Ed.), *Carmichael's manual of child psychology: Social development*. New York: Wiley.

Hollenbeck, A. R. (1978). Problems of reliability in observational research. In G. P. Sackett (Ed.), *Observing behavior* (Vol. 2). Baltimore: University Park Press.

Lewis, M., & Rosenblum, L. A. (Eds.) (1975). *Friendship and peer relations*. New York: John Wiley & Sons.

McCarthy, D. (1972). *McCarthy scales of children's abilities*. New York: Psychological Corporation.

Masters, J., & Furman, W. (1981). Popularity, individual friendship selection, and specific peer interaction among children. *Developmental Psychology, 17*, 344–350.

Mueller, E., & Vandell, D. (1979). Infant-infant interaction. In J. D. Osofsky (Ed.), *Handbook of infant development*. New York: Wiley.

Roff, J. (1963). Childhood social interaction and adult psychosis. *Journal of Clinical Psychology, 19*, 152–157.

Shantz, C. (1983). Social cognition. In J. Flavell & E. Markman (Eds.), *Carmichael's manual of child psychology: Cognitive development*. New York: Wiley.

Shantz, C. (1975). The development of social cognition. In E. M. Hetherington (Ed.), *Review of child development research*, (Vol. 5), Chicago: University of Chicago Press.

Walden, T., & Field, T. (1983). *Sociometric ratings of preschool children*. Unpublished manuscript, University of Miami.

Children's Fantasies of Interaction with Same and Opposite Sex Peers

Judith Rubenstein
Carol Rubin

One of the most consistently documented sex differences in early social behavior is the tendency for boys and girls to segregate themselves by sex during play. Children are more socially active with members of their own sex as early as the second year of life (Jacklin & Maccoby, 1978; Rubin, 1980) and perhaps earlier (Dunn & Kendrick, 1979). The preference for same sex playmates begins early and intensifies during elementary school years, when girls develop more intimate friendships with a few girls, and boys play with larger, less intimate groups of boys (Rubin, 1980). Along with these behavioral patterns, many children begin to derogate members of the opposite sex, verbally labelling them as undesirable. The intensity of many of these verbal comments, and the very active avoidance of opposite sex children, indicate more than a casual preference for same-sex peers. An active psychological process, highly reinforced by the behavior and attitudes of the peer group, is suggested, a process which has been widely observed, but not well understood.

When we look at friendships, as opposed to merely peer interaction, the salience of gender is even more striking. By early adolescence, the attributes most extensively shared by friends are age, gender, and race (Kandel, 1978). Since age can be explained by age-grouping in school, and since gender concordance between friends outweighs racial concordance, gender emerges as the single most potent psychological determinant of friendship choice. Behavioral and attitudinal similarities between best friends lag behind similarity in gender, age, and race.

These data raise two questions: What is the basis for the striking tendency to associate with and form friendships with like-sex peers; and, what are the social and affective consequences of this practice?

In addition to possible biological determinants, different social factors have been proposed to account for children's preferences for like-sex playmates (Hartup, 1983; Jacklin & Maccoby, 1978):

(1) A child may prefer same-sex playmates, because perceived similarity to the self enhances interpersonal attraction (Kohlberg, 1966; Lewis & Brooks-Gunn, 1979).

(2) There may be adult reinforcement (by parents and teachers) of children's tendency to play with same-sex peers.

(3) A child may prefer same-sex playmates because social and play patterns are more like his or her own—the "behavioral compatibility" notion.

(4) There may be sex role stereotypes within the peer group which maintain and strengthen sex-linked preferences.

To these explanations, we propose to add another, one derived from psychoanalytic theory. (It should be noted that these explanations are not mutually exclusive and can in fact reinforce each other.)

(5) It may be that same-sex preference, particularly in boys, is influenced by a need to disengage from early female (maternal) identification, and to consolidate a sense of oneself as male. The first and primary attachment figure for both boys and girls is usually the mother, who is the powerful figure in domains central to the toddler. The preschool age boy, unlike his female counterpart, is faced with the task of disengaging from this primary identification. His responses to the ambivalent feelings evoked by disengagement from the maternal figure may include avoiding and devaluing females and things feminine, including female peers. His need for alternative models for his own growth may lead him to search out other boys, often slightly more developmentally advanced than he is in the male stereotyped characteristics of size, strength, and motor skill. Preschool age girls are not confronted with ambivalent feelings generated by de-identification, nor with the need to find alternative models for their own development. They are thus not impelled by the intense need noted in boys to avoid or devalue members of the opposite sex, nor to seek out same sex playmates to establish their gender identity with quite the same intensity that boys may be. This hypothesis predicts that boys, more than girls, will be more rejecting of social initiations by

opposite sex peers, and will more actively seek out other boys to the exclusion of girls as playmates. This explanation would also account for Greif's findings (1977) of a higher proportion of initiations to same sex playmates by preschool age boys than girls.

Evidence supporting the notion that during the preschool years boys more than girls seek out models for their own growth is found in a study by Edwards and Lewis (1979). In a doll play interview, boys had a tendency to select as playmates the older child figure, whereas girls tended to select peers or younger social objects. The authors interpreted this and their previous findings to suggest that boys more than girls want to conceive of themselves as, and to associate themselves with, "big" children in the age group one up from their own. The question is whether, in their search for models for their own growth, boys also tend to select same-sex playmates more than girls do.

A second question concerns the different significance same- and opposite-sex peers have as agents of socialization. Via interacting with peers in general, the child develops for use in later life skills as well as behavioral and motivational patterns in the instrumental, affective, and interpersonal domains (Hartup, 1983). Unlike adult–child interaction, which is characterized largely by dominance–nurturance relations, peer interaction is noted for reciprocity and assertiveness. Same-age socialization is a context for acquiring skills needed in "give and take" in both prosocial and aggressive exchanges between "equals." Mixed-age child–child interaction provides more of a context for the development of assertiveness (on the part of the older child) and the use of the other as a resource (directed by the younger to the older) (Hartup, 1983). Both contexts develop aspects of social competence in ways which complement adult–child socialization.

In addition to social skills, play with peers fosters motor skills and the mastery of the inanimate environment. Through games, sports, and the manipulation of toys and objects, the child develops control over his or her body and over the inanimate world. Via friendships and selective affective ties, the child extends his or her attachments beyond the family and explores extrafamilial emotional relationships (Rubenstein & Howes, 1976, 1979).

These functions of peer relations have been well documented, but the differential impact of male versus female peers is largely unexplored. We wonder if the affiliation with the same-sex peers mediates, and perhaps limits, the nature of the child's learning about the world and his or her affective responses to it. If boys and girls tend to play with different children, different toys, and to use toys in different ways, then they may eventually evolve different styles of interacting, different approaches to the inanimate environment, and different ways of viewing and seeing themselves in the world. Later competencies and interests may be enhanced or limited by the kinds of social learning and experiences young children have with the same-sex peers, and do not have with opposite-sex peers.

The learning attendant upon associating with members of one's own sex has been called the "gender curriculum" (Luria & Herzog, 1983). Examples include the greater reluctance of adult women, compared to men, to speak in front of large groups and the lesser propensity of adult men, as compared to women, for intimate conversation or self-disclosure (Rubenstein, 1972). Both these sex differences may have their origins in the tendency of young girls to play and converse in dyads, while their male counterparts are associating in larger, less intimate groups.

Do boys and girls socialize different social skills, different patterns of emotional response, or different instrumental behaviors in their peers? For example, are problem solving strategies different in boys' and girls' groups? Do male and female friends rely on different modes of communication, self disclosure versus one-upmanship, for example? These are questions about "first order" (Bronfenbrenner, 1979) or direct effects of same-sex peer socialization. One might also ask about indirect, "second order" effects, that is, the effect of one person on the relationships between two others, or about the relation between the peer group and other social systems in which the child participates. An example of social importance is the effect of the peer group in mediating the effects of maternal employment. We have proposed that boys and girls respond differently to maternal employment, in part because of differences in the nature of the support systems provided by male and female peers in the mother's absence (Rubenstein, in press).

The present study was designed to explore sex of peer as a schema for organizing the child's fantasies about interaction with peers. Previous studies of peer relations have focused largely on observations of behavior from which conclusions have been drawn about the differential socializing effects of male and female peers. Our goal in this study was to focus on the children's own view of their interaction with peers, with particular reference to sex of peer as a mediating factor. Assuming that children tend to choose same sex peers as play partners and friends, we focused on children's fantasies to understand what they view as different about the social environments created by a same versus opposite sex peer. Knowing how they view these play partners differently should give us some understanding about the basis for their choice and the social experience that evolves as a result of the choice.

We noted that existing observational studies (e.g., Jacklin & Maccoby, 1978) did not uncover the basis for the tendency to prefer like-sex playmates, and so we turned to fantasy as a potential source of information. We chose children's drawings of social interaction as a vehicle for assessing their fantasies about what might go on in different kinds of social situations. The expressive modality of children's drawings was chosen since drawings provide an opportunity to express different elements of fantasy and ideation which are not necessarily accessible at the level of verbal conceptualization and communication.

Method

We asked 125 children drawn from several public schools to draw two pictures, each on a separate occasion about 1 week apart. Forty-five children were in first grade, 44 in fifth grade, and 36 in junior high school. Each grade level had approximately 50% boys and 50% girls. On one occasion, the children were asked to draw "a boy and a girl doing something together." On the other occasion, boys were asked to draw "two boys doing something together," and girls "two girls doing something together." Same- and opposite-sex instructions were counterbalanced for order. When we collected the pictures, we asked the child to describe the picture briefly, to be sure we could identify each activity correctly.

We then developed a coding scheme for a content analysis of the drawings. The content analysis was designed to assess the children's perceptions of peer interaction along several dimensions. Observations of boys' and girls' interaction have raised the issue of sex differences in the extent to which children focus on activities versus relationships (Block, 1982; Lever, 1976). Moreover, previous studies have discussed the extent to which aggression, competition, cooperation, and struggles over dominance differentially characterize boys' versus girls' play (Maccoby & Jacklin, 1974). With these issues as the starting point, we generated codes for describing the focus of the activities portrayed in the drawings as well as the nature of the interaction between the two figures portrayed. A variety of codes were piloted. Those which could not be scored reliably were dropped, leaving codes tapping focus of activity, nature of the peer interaction, and physical characteristics of the figures. Each drawing was coded by two people, one male and one female. Intercoder reliability was .89 or better for all codes.

Focus of Activity

There are two codes that deal with the focus of the activity portrayed in the drawings. *Skill and Mastery* is a 4-point (0–3) rating of the extent to which the primary focus of the activity concerns development of a skill, manifestations of competence, producing a product, or mastery of the inanimate environment. Diving, tennis, climbing a pole, gardening, and reading a book were scored 3; "in transit," nonspecific talking, standing and looking at an object, etc., were scored "0." (See Illustrations 1 and 2 for drawings scored 3, and Illustrations 3 and 4 for drawings scored 0.)

Primacy of Social Interaction (scale 1–4) reflects the extent to which the social aspects of the peer interaction are primary. A high score reflects an activity focused on being together with a high degree of social interaction. Examples are a birthday party, going to the movies, and a dating or kissing scene. Examples of low points on the scale include a scene where one child is climbing and the other swinging, or two children are skiing separately and independently. (See Illustrations 3 and 5 for a high degree of social interaction, and Illustration 4 for a low score on this variable.)

Nature of Peer Interaction

The presence or absence of *Aggression* and *Competition* were coded. Competition referred to an activity which is explicitly or implicitly competitive, for example, chess, football (see Illustrations 1 and 7). Aggression referred to physical and/or verbal expression of hostility or inflicting physical harm, including subtle manifestations, for example, a bee sting, punching, throwing tomatoes at each other, arguing angrily (see Illustration 6).

The presence or absence of a *Power–Dominance* distinction was coded. Here, we were interested in whether the two figures were equally powerful or equally dominant. A power–dominance distinction was coded present if one figure was an actor and the other acted upon; if one was central and one subordinate; if one was a winner and one a loser; if one was a victimizer and one a victim; if one was active and one was passive; and if one was more competent than the other. If none of these distinctions was portrayed, the figures were considered egalitarian in their relationship, and no power–dominance distinction was coded.

Illustrations 7 and 8 portray scenes in which power–dominance distinctions were present. In the race, one child was described as winning. Batman is the more central, important figure, accompanied by a smaller, less ornamented version of himself, Batgirl. Illustrations 2 and 4 illustrate egalitarian relationships.

Cooperation is rated on a 3-point scale (1–3), with the high point involving a prosocial behavior with an inherently cooperative focus.

ILLUSTRATION 1
"Football"

ILLUSTRATION 2
"Pairs Ice Skating"

ILLUSTRATION 3
"Walking and Talking"

ILLUSTRATION 4 "Standing and Looking"

ILLUSTRATION 5
"Birthday Party"

ILLUSTRATION 6 "Killing"

ILLUSTRATION 7
"A race—he's winning"

ILLUSTRATION 8
"Batman and Batgirl"

ILLUSTRATION 9
"Playing Candyland"

The children drew these pictures in color, using pencils with crayons or colored markers. Many of the distinctions scored are more obvious in the originals than in the black-and-white reproductions, for example, pink cheeks indicating rouge and yellow lines at the neck indicating necklaces.

The highest score goes to peers engaged in the same activity, where one's behavior must be adjusted to the other's behavior on a continuing basis (e.g., pairs ice-skating or building a structure together, see Illustration 2). The lowest score is given to primarily individual, parallel, or minimally related activities, such as flying kites or practicing gymnastics.

Note that cooperation and competition are not mutually exclusive or opposites in this coding scheme. Team sports, for example, require both competition with the opposing team and cooperation with one's teammates. A drawing of a team game, therefore, might be given a high score on both competition and cooperation.

Physical Features of the Figures

Distance between Figures reflects how far apart the figures are drawn in millimeters. The distance was measured between the two points at which the figures were closest together, including clothing but excluding any object held in the hand.

Sexual Markers are physical features of the figures which differentiate male from female gender. Here we coded adornments, certain aspects of clothing, and aspects of the body itself. Only figures the same sex as the subject were coded for sexual markers. That is, we coded girls drawn by girls and boys drawn by boys. The score (with a possible maximum of 17) is the total number of markers present on the figure. The girl in Illustration 9 was coded "6" (feminine hair, eyelashes, bows, necklace, puffed sleeves, high heels) and the boy "1" (masculine hair).

Data Analysis

We were interested in the main effects of sex of subject, sex of peer partner, and grade level. Thus, variables were analyzed using a 2 (Sex of Subject) × 3 (Grade Level) × 2 (Sex of Partner) analysis of variance. Our N was large enough for the analysis of dichotomous as well as continuous variables (Glass & Stanley, 1970, p. 124). For variables with a significant F, subcomparisons were analyzed with a Duncan Multiple Range Test and F tests for Simple Effects (Winer, 1962).

Results

Intercorrelations of the eight variables with each other reveal primarily low (i.e., $r < .25$) or no statistically significant relationships. Of the 28 correlation coefficients, three were higher than .25: Skill–Mastery and Competition ($r = .37$, $p < .01$); Skill–Mastery and Cooperation ($r = .40$, $p < .01$); Cooperation and Primacy of Social Interaction ($r = .46$, $p < .01$). On the whole, then, the eight variables seem to be measuring quite different aspects of peer relationships.

The first three tables present the means and significant Fs for the main effects of grade level of subject, gender of subject and gender of peer partner (same or opposite). Table 1 presents developmental changes between first grade and junior high school on the coded variables. For variables with significant Fs, subcomparisons between grade levels were performed using the Duncan Multiple Range Test, with a significance level of .05 or less. The developmental changes are consistent with what one might expect from other descriptions of the developmental course of children's psychological organization. Orientation toward skill and mastery increases significantly from first to fifth grade, with no significant change thereafter, reflecting the increasing focus on competence in children in the early elementary school years.

Table 1
Mean Scores for Peer Interaction Variables at Different Grade Levels

	Grade Levels			
	First	*Fifth*	*Jr. High*	F^a
Focus of activity				
Skill and mastery[b]	1.62	2.16	1.92	4.37*
Social interaction[c]	2.43	2.63	3.22	7.92**
Nature of peer interaction				
Aggression[d]	.13	.11	.15	.16
Competition[d]	.11	.31	.28	5.36*
Power/Dominance[d]	.31	.39	.33	.66
Cooperation[e]	1.93	2.13	2.13	1.21
Physical features of figures				
Distance between figures[f]	45.13	46.94	28.86	3.56*
Sexual markers[g]	1.76	1.47	1.38	.99

*p < .05.
**p < .01.
[a]$df = 1, 119$.
[b]Rating Scale (0–3).
[c]Rating Scale (1–4).
[d]Presence/Absence (1–0).
[e]Rating Scales (1–3).
[f]In millimeters.
[g]Number of indicators (0–17).

Competitive imagery also increases significantly between first and fifth grade, suggesting that, in our culture, increased emphasis on mastery is reflected in competitive situations in school and on the playground.

Social interaction as the primary focus of activity increases with age. The significant increase occurs between fifth grade and junior high, in early adolescence. However, further analysis indicates that the increase is significant only for the boys. Boys' and girls' scores begin at the same level, but the girls demonstrate a more gradual increase, with boys increasing dramatically between fifth grade and junior high.

The pattern for physical proximity of the two figures is similar to that of the social interaction scale. That is, the two figures in the pictures are drawn, on the average, about the same distance apart in first and fifth grade, but the distance decreases significantly in junior high. Thus, heightened focus on social interaction appears to be reflected in the figures being drawn closer together.

Thus, our data suggest that the peer culture in middle childhood provides a context in which developmentally expected changes are rehearsed and perfected. The focus on mastery of the inanimate world, and on competence via competition, reaches a maximum in middle childhood. Following this peak, we see an increased concern with social activities, a focus characteristic of early adolescence.

Table 2 presents the main effects for gender of subject. Boys and girls differ on several dimensions in their fantasies about peer relations. Boys are significantly higher in the extent to which their fantasies contain themes of mastery of the environment and the development of personal skills. Boys are more likely to have aggression and competition themes in their fantasies, and they are more likely to imagine peer relations in hierarchical terms; that is, they are more likely to imagine distinctions in power and dominance between the two figures drawn in their pictures. In contrast, girls are significantly higher than boys in one variable only: They are more likely to depict sexual markers on the figures in their drawings. Girls tend to draw the figures in somewhat closer proximity, but this difference does not quite reach the usual significance level ($p \leq .07$).[1]

We would like to emphasize that these differences between boys and girls are present by first grade and are stable thereafter. There are no Gender of Subject × Age interactions which would indicate that

1. The sizes of the figures in the opposite sex drawings were measured in millimeters and compared via a 2(Sex of S) × 3(Grade Level) × 2(Gender of Figure) ANOVA. The only significant finding was that both boys and girls drew figures of their own gender as larger. There were no significant interaction effects. These data will not be reported further.

Table 2
Mean Scores for Peer Interaction Variables for Boys and Girls

	Gender of Subject		
	Boys	Girls	F^a
Focus of activity			
Skill and mastery[b]	2.05	1.72	4.15*
Social interaction[c]	2.72	2.74	.06
Nature of peer interaction			
Aggression[d]	.22	.03	20.11**
Competition[d]	.32	.13	13.41**
Power/Dominance[d]	.47	.20	22.14**
Cooperation[e]	2.06	2.05	.01
Physical features of figures			
Distance between figures[f]	45.90	35.69	3.23
Sexual markers[g]	.82	2.36	94.22**

*$p < .05$.
**$p < .01$.
[a]$df = 1, 119$.
[b]Rating Scale (0–3).
[c]Rating Scale (1–4).
[d]Presence/Absence (1–0).
[e]Rating Scales (1–3).
[f]In millimeters.
[g]Number of indicators (0–17).

these differences drop out at any age.[2] They are consistent across the age groups we studied.

Thus, the drawings suggest that, by age 6 and through early adolescence, boys more than girls are concerned with achieving control over the inanimate environment and dominance over peers. Girls are more concerned with identifying and demarking their sexual identity via their physical appearance and via sexually relevant adornments. It is notable that most gender differences are present by age 6, and stable thereafter through early adolescence.

2. The data on sexual markers in Tables 1, 2, and 3 represent the number of markers drawn by the children on the figure which is the same-sex as the subject in the opposite-sex drawing, and the mean number of markers drawn on the two figures in the same sex drawing. That is, sexual markers in this study reflect those drawn on figures which are the same sex as the subject. While girls at every age draw significantly more markers than do boys, they tend to draw fewer markers as they get older, while boys draw more markers as they get older. Specifically, first grade girls draw more markers than fifth or junior high girls ($p < .02$), who do not differ from each other. First grade boys draw fewer markers ($p < .03$) than older boys, who do not differ from each other.

Main Effects of Figure

Table 3 presents the main effects of gender of peer on the children's fantasies of peer interaction. For each of the variables showing a significant difference, the higher score is found in the drawing where a boy and girl are depicted together. The opposite-sex condition, as compared to the same-sex condition, elicits a greater focus on social interaction, more power dominance distinctions between the two figures, more focus on cooperative activities, and more sexual markers. Although some of these differences make intuitive sense, others seem a little more surprising. Perhaps it is to be expected that drawings in which children portray their own sex with an opposite-sex peer contain more of a focus on interaction which is primarily social than do same-sex drawings. When thinking of interacting with the opposite sex, children are more likely to imagine parties, dinners at restaurants, social greetings, and highly social games. Similarly, it makes some intuitive sense that one's membership in the class of boys or girls, denoted by sexual markers on one's person, becomes more salient when one interacts with a member of the opposite sex. While we note that the

Table 3
Mean Scores for Peer Interaction Variables in Same and Opposite Sex Conditions

	Gender of Partner		
	Same	Opposite	F[a]
Focus of activity			
Skill and mastery[b]	1.99	1.80	2.19
Social interaction[c]	2.50	2.96	18.93**
Nature of peer interaction			
Aggression[d]	.17	.10	2.57
Competition[d]	.24	.22	.16
Power/Dominance[d]	.26	.43	8.94**
Cooperation[e]	1.95	2.16	4.52*
Physical features of figures			
Distance between figures[f]	41.01	38.16	1.00
Sexual markers[g]	1.46	1.68	4.09*

*p < .05.
**p < .01.
[a]df = 1, 119.
[b]Rating Scale (0–3).
[c]Rating Scale (1–4).
[d]Presence/Absence (1–0).
[e]Rating Scales (1–3).
[f]In millimeters.
[g]Number of indicators (0–17).

opposite-sex condition also evokes more cooperation between the figures than does the same-sex condition, this finding was less expected. We will explore it in more detail later.

Also surprising was the finding that children fantasied more distinctions in the power or dominance of the figures vis-à-vis each other when drawing interaction with opposite-sex peers. It seems that hierarchical rather than egalitarian peer relations are more likely to be evoked in male–female interaction in the fantasies of these children than they are in same-sex peer interaction. It is important to note that competition and the distinctions between figures in power–dominance are quite different. Competition is equally frequent in same-sex and in opposite-sex peer interaction. In this study, this variable reflected structured competitive games where competitive elements were explicit and where rules governed the activities of the competitors. Children were as likely to imagine themselves competing with opposite-sex peers as with same-sex peers. In contrast, the distinction in power and dominance was found more frequently in the opposite-sex condition. Thus, in boy–girl relations it is more likely that one figure is seen as more central, more active, or more competent than the other. An example is the drawing of Batman and his helper, the less ornamented and smaller Batgirl, standing to the side.

In sum, the opposite-sex condition elicited more focus on social activities, more cooperative activity, more sexual differentiation, and, finally, more hierarchical relationships. It is notable that every significant finding in Table 3 is qualified by an interaction with sex of subject. Our conclusion is that the sex of the peer is an extremely salient cue, which affects boys and girls differently. It is to these interactions that we now turn our attention.

Gender × Figure Interactions

One central question addressed by this study is whether peers serve different functions for boys and girls. This issue has two components—whether boys and girls respond differentially to the peer system and whether boys and girls respond differentially to same and opposite sex peers. For most variables we studied, the gender of the peer was a salient cue modifying the children's fantasies of interaction with that partner; however, it operates differently for boys and girls. We will now turn to a consideration of the peer variables in which boys and girls were affected differently, depending on the gender of the imagined partner. The relevant data are presented in Table 4 and described in Figures 1–5.

Figure 1 presents the mean ratings on skill and mastery as the focus

Table 4
*Mean Scores for Boys' and Girls' Interaction Variable with Male
and Female Partners*

	Sex of Subject			
	Boys		Girls	
Variables	Boy Partner	Girl Partner	Boy Partner	Girl Partner
Skill and Mastery	2.32	1.79	1.81	1.63
Social Interaction	2.58	2.86	3.07	2.41
Aggression	.29	.15	.03	.03
Competition	.38	.26	.17	.09
Power/Dominance	.38	.56	.29	.12
Cooperation	2.06	2.02	2.27	1.98
Distance between figures	55.95	35.85	40.75	30.64
Sexual Markers	.75	.89	2.58	2.25

of activity depicted for boys' and girls' opposite- and same-sex drawings. This figure indicates that sex of the partner makes a difference for
boys but not for girls. The arrows in the figure indicate the significant
differences. Boys imagine activities which are more highly focused on
mastery with same- than with an opposite-sex peer. Recall that boys'
scores on skill and mastery are higher overall than girls' (see Table 2).
Analysis of the interaction displayed here shows that this finding is

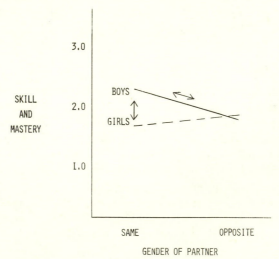

Figure 1. *Gender of partner and skill and mastery.*

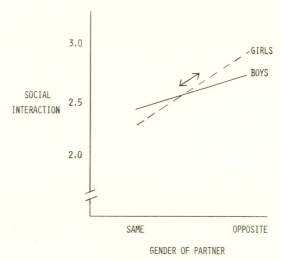

Figure 2. *Gender of partner and social interaction.*

accounted for primarily by the heightening of mastery imagery in boys by the presence of a male peer.

In contrast, social interaction as the focus of the activity does not differ overall between boys and girls (see Table 2). Boys and girls depicted equal frequencies of socially focused activities. Figure 2 indicates, however, that sex of the partner makes a difference, but for girls only. Girls imagine more socially oriented activities in fantasies of interactions with boys than in fantasies of interactions with other girls. Boys are equally likely to fantasize socially oriented activities in the presence of either sex partner.

Figure 3, which portrays results for competition, indicates a similar pattern to that seen for skill and mastery. Recall that boys had higher overall competition scores than did girls (see Table 2). Again, however, boys are more competitive than girls only in the presence of a male peer. Thus, the sex difference is primarily accounted for by the heightened competition imagery in boys imagining themselves playing with other boys. For girls, gender of partner does not matter.

Figure 4 shows the pattern of results for cooperation. Cooperation imagery shows a pattern similar to that of social interaction as the primary focus of the activity. The sex of the partner matters significantly for girls only. Girls imagine themselves in more cooperative activities when interacting with boys than when interacting with other girls.

The interaction between gender of subject and gender of partner approached significance for aggression ($F = 3.09$; $p \leq .08$). Subcom-

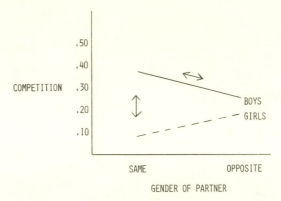

Figure 3. *Gender of partner and competition.*

parisons indicated that sex of the partner made a difference for boys, but not for girls. Boys had much higher levels of aggressive imagery overall, and were significantly more likely to imagine aggressive themes in the presence of boy partners ($M = .29$) than in the presence of girl partners ($M = .15$; $p \leq .05$). Girls had very little aggressive imagery with partners of either sex ($M = .03$ for both).

As we noted earlier, hierarchical peer relations were more often drawn by boys than by girls, and were significantly more frequent in pictures of boy–girl interaction than in pictures of same-sex interaction. This predominance of hierarchical peer relations held true for both boys' and girls' drawings in boy–girl conditions. Thus, boys and girls agree that same sex peer relations are more egalitarian than are opposite sex peer relations. However, boys and girls disagree about

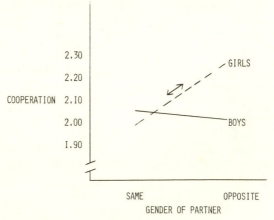

Figure 4. *Gender of partner and cooperation.*

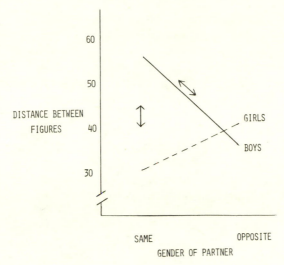

Figure 5. *Gender of partner and distance between figures.*

who is dominant in hierarchical relationships. In the opposite sex drawings in which a Power-Dominance distinction was coded, the gender of the more dominant figure was noted. A chi-square analysis indicated that, when hierarchical relationships are depicted between boys and girls, boys usually depict the boy as dominant over the girl; girls are as likely to depict the girl as dominant over the boy as vice versa. Seventy-eight percent of the boys, as compared to 53% of the girls, designated the boy as the dominant member of the pair ($\chi^2 = 11.9$; $p <$ .01).

Figure 5 depicts the Gender of Subject × Gender of Partner interaction for distance between figures. These data indicate that boys distinguish by sex of partner, but girls do not. Girls maintain approximately the same distance from same and opposite-sex peer partners. Boys and girls maintain the same distance from opposite-sex partners, but boys draw two boys much further apart at all ages.

Finally, girls drew more sexual markers overall than did boys. Opposite-sex drawings had more markers overall than did same-sex drawings, and this was true for both boys and girls. The Gender of Subject × Gender of Partner interaction was not significant.

Discussion

This study is concerned with three general issues: (1) sex differences in children's perceptions of the nature of peer relations; (2) the differential impact of male and female peers on boys and girls; and (3) developmental changes both in children's perceptions of peer relations and in the differential impact of male and female peers.

We found several sex differences in the children's perceptions of peer interaction. Boys' drawings contained scenes portraying more skill oriented activities, more competition, more aggression, and more hierarchical relationships, reflecting boys' greater concern with control over the environment and dominance over peers. These differences correspond to behavioral differences noted by previous researchers (e.g., Block, 1982). Girls portrayed more sexual markers on their figures, reflecting their greater concern with identifying their sexual identity via their physical appearance and gender-relevant adornments. This sex difference, too, has been noted in previous studies of children's drawings (Harris, 1963). Of notable interest is how stable these sex differences were in the age range between 6 and 13 years. We wonder if the stability of these differences carries forward into adult life and influences differences in men and women's career choices, attitudes, and behaviors. Does their stronger orientation toward competition and mastery lead men more than women to choose certain occupations, or give men an advantage over women in certain occupations?

It is often implied that girls are more "social" in their orientation toward friends than are boys (e.g., Block, 1982). Our data indicate that this distinction is perhaps oversimplified. We found no difference between boys and girls in the extent to which the activities they portrayed were socially oriented. Rather, boys were as socially oriented as girls, but often in a different context. Competitive games, for example, which were scored "3" on the primacy of social interaction scale, represent a highly social activity, where one must pay close attention to the subtleties of the behavior of one's opponents and one's teammates in order to be successful, but the focus of the activity is very different than sitting and listening to records, or going to the movies with another person. In social activities, boys were more likely than girls to emphasize mastery and skill development, competition, and being in control. Our data suggest that boys are as likely as girls to be interested in spending time in social situations, but their attention in these situations is more likely to be focused on the use of skills or on winning versus losing.

These data raise questions about the particular focus of girls' activities. Since drawings portray activity better than conversation, we lack information on the content of the potential verbal exchanges in the relationships portrayed. Perhaps the girls' focus is more on the verbal exchange of information, a focus to which our methodology was less sensitive. If so, we would be interested in the content of such information; for example, to what extent is it oriented toward social knowledge, or to the disclosure of feelings, or toward developing strategies for solving problems or undertaking tasks?

More interesting than overall boy–girl differences is the fact that the gender of the imagined peer modified the children's perceptions of interaction with that partner. Moreover, gender of peer significantly qualified most of the overall male–female differences discussed above. Thus gender of peer operates differently for boys and girls.

Male peers stimulate the fantasies of boys and girls differently. Boys respond to other boys (more than to girls) with a heightened focus on mastery, competition, and aggression. Why should this be so? Put differently, why do boys temper their interest in skill development, competition, and aggression in the presence of girls? As a result of parental socialization, do boys perceive girls as more fragile, less competent, or less worthy of their best efforts? If so, are these perceptions limited to recreational settings, which our sample of children spontaneously drew, or do they appear as well in task-oriented or school settings? To explore the question further, one might obtain a set of children's drawings with a more explicitly task-focused instruction, such as "Draw a picture of a boy and a girl working on something together."

Boys' responsiveness to other boys with an increased emphasis on mastery and competition, together with their responsiveness to girls in terms of hierarchical relationships in which they tend to be dominant, suggests that stereotypic adult sex roles are operating in boys in middle childhood. That is, traditionally, adult males needed to use their skills to compete with other men at work, while their wives were more likely to be engaged in non-competitive work situations at home. Furthermore, in more traditional times, it was expected that men would be dominant over women. The relationships in our sample of boys' drawings seem to conform to these stereotypic ones, despite the recent social changes in adult roles. We wonder why the recent changes in maternal employment, and the less stereotyped role differentiation in many families, have not done more to change children's perceptions of peer relationships.

Girls respond to male peers (more than to female peers) with a heightened focus on purely social activities and with an increased emphasis on cooperative interaction. That is, girls, with boys, imagine participating in activities which are more mutually engaging, more organized and cooperative, rather than parallel or minimally related. Thus, girls imagine themselves sitting and listening to music with another girl, or building two individual towers side by side. With a boy, girls imagine themselves pairs-skating or building a single tower cooperatively. The data suggest that girls may be more spontaneous, less vigilant, less mutually contingent, and more apt to engage in individual or parallel activities in the presence of a female than a male peer. With two girls, just companionship or proximity may at times be sufficient to sustain interaction in either structured (e.g., skiing or gymnastics) or unstructured activities (e.g., walking or eating). Girls appear to feel that interaction with boys requires a more mutually engaging activity to sustain the interaction.

We have speculated about the reasons girls may see themselves so differently when with boys than with other girls. It may be that what they see boys doing simply looks like fun, and girls want to participate. Others have speculated that girls are fearful of aggression in interaction with boys. It may be that the highly structured nature of the activities girls imagine with boys represents a strategy for managing boys' aggression. Girls may see boys' play as involving too much rough physical contact, in which case a structured activity would minimize the danger of being pushed or hurt. A third possibility is that girls may feel activities with boys are not likely to persist without a mutually engaging task. A planned activity may be perceived by girls as required to maintain the continued involvement and interest of boys. Girl–girl pairs may imagine themselves in situations where the verbal exchange is the most central feature of the interaction, whereas girl–boy pairs may rely less on verbal exchange and more on activity. If this is the case, our speculation is that girls are saying they have to *act* or *do* with boys, and *talk* with girls.

In sum, male and female peers impact differentially on boys and girls. We wonder whether these gender-related expectations in the peer system represent another factor which may contribute to the preference children have for same sex playmates, and, if so, how this process might work.

This study highlights the utility of children's drawings as a method for studying children's perceptions of interpersonal relations. While drawings have been interpreted in various ways, in this study we have viewed them as conveying the child's social perceptions or expectations about peer relations. The drawings reflect psychological reality, that is, peer relationships as perceived or experienced subjectively by the child artist. For example, boys tended to portray hierarchical rather than egalitarian relationships more frequently than girls did, which parallels observations by others that power/dominance is a relevant dimension ordering relationships more frequently for males than for females (Rubin, 1980). However, in hierarchical relationships involving opposite-sex figures, the boys in our sample viewed themselves as usually dominant over the girls, while the girls viewed the division in dominance as more nearly 50–50. Observations of social structure among nursery school children (Strayer, 1979) find boys more often than girls near the top of the dominance hierarchies, and observations of elementary school children on the playground find boys dominant over girls in mixed groups (Luria & Herzog, 1983). Boys and girls in our study obviously perceived this aspect of reality somewhat differently. We wonder how this differential perception affects the child's subsequent behavior.

Differing perceptions of social structure of this sort may underlie some of the sex segregation that is such a notable characteristic of children's peer groups in middle childhood. That is, if boys and girls view rules governing social interaction and social structure differently, it may be easier for them to interact with same rather than opposite sex children, partially because social expectations, social structure, and phasing of social behavior may function more smoothly or more predictably with same sex peers.

Finally, although there are some developmental changes in our data, we found that the differential responses of boys and girls to same and opposite sex peers are largely in place by first grade, and are stable through junior high. Thus, for example, girls emphasize more social and more cooperative activities with boys than with other girls as early as first grade, and this phenomenon does not change through junior high. Thus, it is not a purely preadolescent phenomenon. Similarly, boys tend to see themselves as dominant over girls from first grade on. What we are seeing seems to be an early anticipation of traditional stereotypic adult sex roles. Here we have a paradox. If we observe children in middle childhood, we find that the occurrence of sustained, elective social interactions between boys and girls is relatively rare. However, when we look at their fantasies of peer interaction with members of the opposite sex, we find that they think about interacting with one another in ways which approximate stereotyped adult heterosexual interaction. The pictures we collected depict children engaged in children's activities such as soccer, not adult activities such as the board room, but the relationships reflect the social roles commonly reported in adult life.

It has been widely assumed that children's relationships with same and opposite peers begin to diverge most dramatically with the onset of puberty and adolescence. Our data indicate, however, that peer relationships are influenced by gender role considerations much earlier. In fantasy, the appearance of the social aspects of adult heterosexual role behavior precedes the child's secondary sexual development and precedes by several years the time the culture expects this behavior. The larger issue our study raises is whether children's friendships can be studied as an encapsulated phenomenon developmentally specific to childhood, or whether they need be considered within the larger context of culturally determined role expectations, encompassing not only gender but many other aspects of social interaction.

REFERENCES

Block, J. (1982). Gender differences in the nature of premises developed about the world. In E. Shapiro & E. Weber (Eds.), *Cognitive and affective processes in development: A developmental-interaction point of view*. Hillsdale, NJ: Erlbaum.

Bronfenbrenner, U. (1979). *The ecology of human development*. Cambridge: Harvard University Press.

Dunn, J., & Kendrick, C. (1979). Interaction between young siblings in the context of family relationships. In M. Lewis & L. Rosenblum (Eds.), *The child and its family: Genesis of behavior* (Vol. 2). New York: Plenum.

Edwards, C., & Lewis, M. (1979). Young children's concepts of social relations: Social functions and social objects. In M. Lewis & L. Rosenblum (Eds.), *The child and its family: The genesis of behavior* (Vol. 2). New York: Plenum.

Glass, G., & Stanley, S. (1970). *Statistical methods in education and psychology*. Englewood Cliffs, NJ: Prentice-Hall.

Greif, E. (1977, April). *Initiation of peer interaction in preschool children*. Paper presented at the meeting of the Eastern Psychological Association, Boston.

Harris, D. (1963). *Children's drawings as measures of intellectual maturity*. New York: Harcourt, Brace & World.

Hartup, W. (1983). The peer system. In P. Mussen & E. Hetherington (Eds.), *Handbook of child psychology*, (Vol. 4). New York: Wiley.

Jacklin, C., & Maccoby, E. (1978). Social behavior at 33 months in same-sex and mixed-sex dyads. *Child Development, 49*, 557–569.

Kandel, D. (1978). Similarity in real-life adolescent friendship pairs. *Journal of Personal and Social Psychology, 36*, 306–312.

Kohlberg, L. (1966). A cognitive-developmental analysis of children's sex role concepts and attitudes. In E. Maccoby (Ed.), *The Development of Sex Differences*. Stanford: Stanford University Press.

Lever, J. (1976). Sex Differences in the Games Children Play. *Social Problems, 23*, 478–487.

Lewis, M., & Brooks-Gunn, J. (1979). *Social cognition and the acquisition of self*. New York: Plenum.

Luria, Z., & Herzog, E. (1983, April 21–24). *Gender segregation in play groups: A matter of where and when*. Paper presented at the Biennial Meeting of the Society for Research in Child Development, Detroit, MI.

Maccoby, E., & Jacklin, C. (1974). *The psychology of sex differences*. Stanford: Stanford University Press.

Rubenstein, J. (1972). Sex differences in patterns of adult verbalization. [Letter]. *Commentary, 54* (2), 14–16.

Rubenstein, J., & Howes, C. (1976). The effect of peers on toddler interaction with mother and toys. *Child Development, 47*, 597–605.

Rubenstein, J., & Howes, C. (1979). Caregiving and infant behavior in day care and in homes. *Developmental Psychology, 15*, 1–24.

Rubenstein, J. (in press). The effect of maternal employment on young children. In F. Morrison, C. Lord, & D. Keating (Eds.), *Advances in Applied Developmental Psychology* (Vol. 2). New York: Academic Press.

Rubin, Z. (1980). *Children's friendships.* Cambridge MA: Harvard University Press.

Strayer, F. F. (1979). Social ecology of the preschool peer-group. In W. Collins (Ed.), *Proceedings of the 12th Minnesota Symposium on Child Psychology.* New York: Erlbaum.

Winer, B. J. (1962). *Statistical principles in experimental design.* New York: McGraw-Hill.

Friendship Development in Normal Children: A Commentary

Judith Rubenstein

In the presentations at the 1982 Miami Conference on Friendship, several issues or themes emerged. The purpose of this commentary is to highlight some of these major issues and to add some personal comments on the themes raised by this conference.

DEFINING FRIENDSHIP

A central issue for research in this area is how to conceptualize friendship to distinguish it from other types of peer relationships. While the terms "friendship" and "peer relations" are often used interchangeably in the literature, their antecedents and consequences are not the same. Berndt's review (this volume) points out that a friend has been defined variously by various writers, the criteria ranging from the most minimal to very exclusive:

- *Simple designation:* a person a child designates as a friend
- *Reciprocal choice:* children who so designate each other
- *Stability of choice:* designation as a friend on at least two occasions
- *Preference:* the friend is preferred over others (alternative criteria: liking; affection)

- *Exclusiveness:* preference for spending time with the friend alone rather than in a group
- *Prosocial behavior manifested toward the friend*
- *Intimacy*

The criteria of reciprocity and some aspect of positive affective tie (either preference or affection) seem critical to the definition of friendship. While some degree of stability is required, how much is problematic, since the capacity for sustaining stable relationships may increase with age. Thus Howes (this volume) defined infant and toddler friends in terms of mutual preference, mutual enjoyment, and the ability to engage in skillful interaction; but stability of the relationship was a dependent variable rather than a defining characteristic. The nature of the prosocial behavior between friends and issues of exclusiveness and intimacy seem better cenceptualized as features of a friendship, not as defining characteristics.

Further issues concern popularity, the role of conflict, and attachment. Berndt distinguishes between friendship as relationship, implying reciprocity, and popularity, which is a status measure indicating social acceptance. Howes points out a related distinction in showing that social skill with a given peer and sociability (the tendency to interact with many peers) are statistically independent. Both Howes and Berndt report data suggesting that affection and conflict may vary independently, and that the presence of conflict does not necessarily imply the absence of friendship.

The concept of attachment raises the broader issue of the role of emotions and affect in friendship, about which there is not a great deal of substantive information. While friends are assumed to share a mutual preference for each other, the nature of the affective bond between them is unclear. Existing measures of friendship (e.g., sociometric ratings) tend to be status measures, not process measures. Bonding implies a process, as do questions about how children's friendships relate to other aspects of their emotional adjustment. Field's report of depressive symptomatology in young children separating from their friends in preschool implied the presence of attachments between peers, attachments inferred from reactions commonly seen in individuals experiencing loss of love objects.

In sum, it seems that friendship involves a higher order of affective involvement than does a peer relationship. There is a more enduring quality to friendship involving a higher order of consistent preference, mutual involvement, and positive feelings. Peer relationships can be transitory or enduring, superficial or meaningful, opportunistic or sought out, limited to one social setting or generalized across settings.

There is no obvious easy way to distinguish peer relationships from friendship, and some children would call a given relationship a friendship while others would not. Clearly, the more the relationship is mutual, enduring, consistent across settings, and positive in emotional tone, the closer it approaches being a friendship.

We need to refine the ways in which we operationalize our concepts to reflect the distinction between different levels of peer relationships, with friendship on one end of the continuum. Some children may be capable of forming transitory peer relationships, but not friends; yet they themselves may refer to their peers as "friends." It is likely that the social skills and affective factors involved in friendship are different from those involved in less intense and less enduring peer relationships; and the functions peer relationships perform may not be identical to the functions of friendships. The distinction is important, because the study of peer relations may essentially be the study of a smoothly functioning social system, while the study of peer friendships may center on the understanding of affective bonds.

THE FUNCTIONS OF FRIENDSHIP

Of central importance is the issue of functions served by childhood friendships, and the emotional consequences of having or not having these functions fulfilled. As most participants noted, having few or no friends is an important predictor of emotional maladjustment. Having no friends may contribute to future maladjustment, or may simply reflect emotional problems that both preclude the formation of friendships and cause the subsequent maladjustment.

There is some truth to both these interpretations: The lack of friends can be both a cause and an effect, but the relative importance of each varies with different children at different times. For the child who is basically emotionally healthy, who feels appreciated by his family, whose self esteem is reasonably high and who has a reasonable sense of self worth, peers and peer friendship provide the opportunity to learn how to influence age mates who are equal in power and status to the child. Unlike parents, peers do not have more influence and power than the child. Peers thus provide a unique opportunity for the child to expand his or her repertoire of skills in influencing others. Via peer interaction children learn to negotiate getting from others and giving to others, to their mutual satisfaction. Peers provide the opportunity to assert oneself in ways one cannot always do with parents, and to learn to negotiate terms and conditions that facilitate social relationships among equals. The social skills thus developed may contribute to later success in both personal and work relationships.

Another function of peers is to facilitate separation from mother and the development of autonomy. For toddlers, peers provide a source of social stimulation that is an alternative to mother. Rubenstein and Howes (1979, 1982) observed that when a toddler peer was visiting the subject's home the subject made fewer instrumental demands on his mother and directed fewer verbalizations to her. Toddlers in day care were observed to manifest more positive affect and to play better with their toys when interacting with a familiar peer than in other contexts in the day care centers. Thus, adaptation in a setting away from mother was facilitated by positive peer relationships.

Rubenstein and Rubin (this volume) pointed out that peers in middle childhood provide a context in which to develop a variety of nonsocial competencies, as well as a context in which to anticipate and rehearse adult sex roles. In adolescence, peers provide a sounding board against which to check out challenges to parental ideas and authority. It seems that children who lack close peer relations find it more difficult to separate from home and family, to set their own goals, to establish a sense of personal identity and ultimately a sense of self that is more than an extension of parental expectations and behaviors.

For the child with conflicted family relationships, peer relationships may provide a buffer against feeling completely isolated and unworthy. Freud and Dann's account is the classic example of the restorative role of peers. They reported on wartime orphans whose attachments to each other were so strong that subsequent adjustment was reasonably good.

But, for the child whose sense of self is so depleted that he or she cannot enter into friendships, the lack of friendship is both a reflection of serious emotional disorder and a contributor to maintaining that disorder. This child cannot make use of the affection, support, companionship and instrumental help that friends might provide. In Furman's model there is a deficit in the feedback loop which modulates the child's capacity to engage in peer relations. The child's self-evaluation and evaluation of others may be so distorted as to preclude peer relationships.

In clinical work we often see children reject or ignore bids for social interaction from their peers because of internal emotional difficulties that make the child unable to utilize the skills he or she has demonstrated during earlier periods. An example is an adolescent girl who came from a small parochial high school, where she had many friends, to a large public high school, recognized that her new peers wanted to get to know her, but declined their invitations because she felt uncomfortable and out of place in her new surroundings.

In designing intervention programs to improve the child's social skills and peer relationships, it is often advisable to focus on the family network, not just on the child. Families often influence their children's friendships in very subtle ways. One should consider the family's rules about friends, how often the child is encouraged to see them, and under what conditions. Who exercises control over the child's choice of friends—the child or the parent? What models does the child have in the household for having and keeping friends? Do the parents have friends? How often do they talk to their friends? How often do friends come to the house? What sort of attitude is expressed by the parents toward people outside the family? Some families have the implicit belief that the only important relationships are those inside the family, and that relationships outside the family don't matter. One informal measure of whether or not the child has permission to have friends is to ask the parents about the child's friends. If they recite a long list of negatives, we suspect not so much that the child's friends are actually undesirable, but rather that the parents do not like the idea of the child having friends. They may not want the child to leave the family, or they themselves may be uncomfortable with people outside the family.

The role of the family in developing the capacity for friendship is particularly important in the very early years. Howes' data on normal toddlers illustrate the generalization of skills developed in the context of mother–infant interaction to toddler–peer interaction in the day care center. Moreover, her data on abused toddlers imply that toddlers' behavior toward peers reflect the ways in which they themselves were treated by their parents. These data raise the following question: How much can intervention programs improve the peer relations and peer friendships of isolated, unpopular, or otherwise handicapped children without addressing the basic modes of interacting within the families in which the children live?

SEX DIFFERENCES

While the tendency for boys and girls to prefer same-sex peers is well established by the elementary school years, little is known about the basis for this preference. Rubenstein and Rubin point out that there are differences between boys and girls in their perceptions of peer interactions, perceptions involving both the nature of the activity which serves as the context for the interaction, and the ways in which peers relate to each other. Their data suggest that much of children's peer interaction serves to anticipate and rehearse traditional, culturally prescribed adult sex roles. Their data raise several unresolved questions: For example, does friendship serve different functions for boys versus girls? Are there modes of relating, such as the use of self disclosure, which are more characteristic of one sex or the other? The area of sex differences in childrens' friendships is one in which there are tantalizing leads but little coherence.

THE INFLUENCE OF SETTINGS

Consistency of friendship behavior across settings is a topic that needs more theoretical as well as empirical work. It is clear that minor variations in setting may be very influential. For example, class size, school size and organization, and absentees on a given day affect the number and stability of friend nominations (Berndt). The behavior of teachers affects the extent and nature of toddler–peer interaction (Howes). Laboratory versus natural settings may reveal different features of friendship patterns, but lab–natural setting differences are probably not more striking than differences revealed by comparing different natural settings. Friendship behavior can be very situation specific, because of implicit norms or demand characteristics of various settings.

DEVELOPMENTAL CHANGES

Developmental changes concerned most conference participants, for example, change in friendship, in perspective taking, and in friends' concern about equality (Berndt); in the goals children adopt in peer-oriented situations (Taylor & Asher); in the focus of peer oriented activities (Rubenstein & Rubin). However, in most studies, Sex × Age interactions receive less analysis than they merit, and, when they are examined, they are often statistically significant (e.g., Rubenstein & Rubin, this volume). The developmental course of friendship formation may be more different for the two sexes than we now suppose.

Developmental changes in the way friends relate to each other are likely to be related to other developmental tasks that characterize each period of development. Thus, for example, competition between friends peaks between 9 and 11 years, when the child is focused on skill development and on exhibiting competence. A greater emphasis on equality, on intimacy, and on loyalty appears in adolescence, when the individual is concerned with establishing strong extra-familial ties as he or she begins the process of separating from the family.

ISSUES OF ASSESSMENT

Berndt (this volume) provides a very thoughtful overview of the common methods (with their advantages and disadvantages) used in friendship research. Asher and Taylor propose the useful distinction between assessing goals versus assessing strategies; at times, the same measure can be interpreted to reflect either goals or strategies. Two additional methodological problems merit some consideration. One has to do with difficulties in operationalizing skill or competence. In observational research, the problem of units is still not solved, despite many attempts to do so. For purposes of illustration, assume that social skill is defined in terms of the number of positive responses elicited from a peer. This in turn is defined in terms of the ratio of positive responses to the number of approaches. Please consider the following vignette.

A approaches B shooting baskets and eyes the ball.
B smiles, but does not include A in the game.
A hovers nearby.
B smiles again, and then resumes playing.

Q: *How many approaches did A make?*
Q: *Does B's smile count as a positive response? Was A's goal to elicit a smile or join the game?*
Q: *Does not including A in the game count as a rejection?*
Q: *Finally, was A rejected with a smile?*

In studying social perceptions and social knowledge, we often rely on verbal responses from children. However, there are response biases in verbal responses which are difficult to resolve. Diaz and Berndt (1982) pointed out that when asked to describe B's attributes, in the absence of knowledge, A tends to guess, and the guess is in the direction of attributing to B qualities that A has. To the extent that A and B are similar, A will appear to be right more often, that is, to have more social knowledge as a result of this response bias. Diaz and Berndt propose that, if one controls statistically for the similarity between A and B, one pulls out the effects of similarity. However, friends tend in fact to be similar. They have common interests and common backgrounds. Moreover, friends have more real knowledge of each other than nonfriends do. If one controls similarities well, one may over-control what may be actual social knowledge and partial it out, when in fact one is trying to assess it.

Focusing on levels of perception and ideation that are not accessible at the level of verbal conceptualization and communication, Rubenstein and Rubin used drawings to assess children's ideas and fantasies about peer relations. While this technique avoids the problem of verbal response biases noted above, it has other disadvantages. The most notable of these is the confounding of wish with perception of fact; that is, the drawing may reflect the child's perception of how peers actually relate, or his wish about how peers should relate.

Overall, it appears that measures of status (e.g., peer nominations reflecting popularity, social impact, number of friends) are more reliable and definitive than are measures of process. The gap in our methods parallels the gap in our theory with respect to the process of friendship formation, development, and maintenance.

ON CONCEPTUALIZING SOCIAL COMPETENCE

Social competence may be defined in terms of the ability to interact with others in ways which are mutually satisfying, which further developmental growth, and which facilitate the attainment of other-than-social goals. Within this broad rubric, various participants emphasize various components of competence. In discussing behavioral styles that lead to peer acceptance or rejection, Taylor and Asher distinguish between the construal of goals and the adoption of effective strategies. Less socially competent children may choose goals which are at odds with maintaining a social relationship, rather than merely adopting maladaptive strategies to attain socially oriented goals.

Differentiating further popular versus unpopular children, Taylor and Asher distinguish between unpopular–rejected and unpopular–neglected. Berndt discusses a fourfold classification of popular, amiable, rejected, and isolated children. These concepts advance the field beyond a simple social skill deficit model, and encourage us to identify particular behavioral styles that lead to one of a number of possible social results.

Howes notes that, in normal toddlers, social skill with a given peer is independent of overall sociability (the tendency to interact with many peers). She suggests that skills which are perfected in a one-to-one relationship with a particular partner may be different from the skills needed to engage with many different peers. Furman makes the critical distinction between a skills deficit and a performance deficit. The child may have the skill, but is unable or unwilling to use it. He raises the intriguing question of the barriers to skill utilization, or the factors that facilitate skill utilization. What conditions do different children at different ages need to engage in peer relationships or in peer friendships?

Furman further distinguishes two different sets of social skills: those involved in initiating peer relationships, and those involved in maintaining them. He notes that more research attention has been given to relationship initiation skills (see Roopnarine, this volume) than to relationship maintaining skills—for example, capacity for intimacy, self-disclosure, or conflict resolution.

Initiating a relationship and maintaining it may involve very different skills and perhaps different motivations. Initiating interaction requires first establishing the self vis-à-vis the other as a potential partner in the eyes of both participants. This involves a whole set of perceptions, motivations, and feedback having to do with interpersonal attraction. The skills and motivational factors involved in maintaining the interaction may be quite different. Moreover, certain groups of children may favor certain friendship maintenance strategies, while other groups of children may rely on other strategies. For example, we wonder if boys rely on self-disclosure as much as do girls in the maintaining of friendships, and how the intimacy of their friendships is different as a result. Some unpopular children may lack skills in attracting and making friends, others in keeping them. For example, the abused toddlers studied by Howes had more trouble forming friendships than did normal toddlers, but their friendships once formed were similar in character to friendships between nonabused children.

Furman notes that teaching unpopular children skills used by popular ones may not necessarily make unpopular children more popular, because this intervention strategy does not address perceptions others have of the unpopular children. If there is a stigma of being disliked, possessing new skills may not be sufficient. This raises the issue of the moderating effect of status (i.e., handicapped, nonhandicapped, nonpopular, and popular, etc.) on the effectiveness of various social skills or behaviors. This issue has been studied most frequently in the context of relationship initiating skills, but it may also be relevant in the context of relationship maintaining skills.

MOTIVATIONAL FACTORS

We know some, but not a great deal, about the factors that motivate a child to choose another for a playmate, and less about the factors that mediate actual friendship choices. Age is one relevant factor. Edwards and Lewis (1979) report that preschool age boys prefer to interact with a boy slightly older than themselves, whereas preschool-age girls choose age mates. Perhaps boys' heightened focus on skill and mastery, especially in the presence of male peers, has something to do with their preference for older male peers who are presumably slightly more skillful than themselves. Gender is certainly a well-documented mediator of playmate choice. As young as 20 months of age, children tend to interact more with peers of their own gender (Howes, Rubenstein, & Eldredge, in press; Roopnarine, this volume).

A major determinant of peer interaction seems to be perceived similarity. Young children interact more with peers who are perceived to be like themselves. Moreover, this tendency is more consistent in higher status or majority group children. This fact is one of the major limitations on the integrative effects of mainstreaming. Similarity on a variety of dimensions influences selection of a playmate. These dimensions include sex, race, linguistic background, and majority–minority status, of which presence or absence of physical handicap often constitutes a subcategory.

Doyle (1982) reported a fascinating study of mixed classes containing English and French speaking preschoolers in Montreal. In the schools studied, the majority of each class was either fluent in French or English, but the minority group was bilingual in both languages. Nevertheless, the majority children initiated interaction primarily with their own group, while the minority children initiated equally to peers in both groups.

One implication, then, is that teaching nonhandicapped children to communicate with handicapped ones will not necessarily facilitate interaction or friendship unless the nonimpaired children are motivated to use those skills.

A second implication is that it may require different strategies and different skills to initiate a relationship with a peer who is predisposed to respond positively because of the similarities just noted, than with a peer who is predisposed to react less favorably because of differences in these characteristics. Thus, in assessing an individual's social skill in initiating a relationship, we need to take into account the difficulty presented by the potential partner, not only in his actual behavior, but in the child's perceptions and expectations of that partner's probable response.

In conclusion, the conference highlighted the fact that research on childrens' friendships is a relatively young endeavor. There is far more known about mother–child attachment, for example, than about peer–peer attachment. Hopefully, we are in the process of catching up. There is little of more consistent importance across the life span than the capacity for friendship.

REFERENCES

Diaz, R., & Berndt, T. (1982). Children's knowledge of a best friend: Fact or fancy? *Developmental Psychology, 18*, 787–794.

Doyle, A. (1982). Friends, acquaintances and strangers: The influence of familiarity and ethnolinguistic background on social interaction. In K. Rubin & H. Ross (Eds.), *Peer relationships and social skills in childhood*. New York: Springer-Verlag.

Edward, C., & Lewis, M. (1979). Young children's concepts of social relations: Social functions and social objects. In M. Lewis & L. Rosenblum (Eds.), *The child and its family*. New York: Plenum Press.

Howes, C., Rubenstein, J., & Eldredge, R. (In press). Early gender segregation in the peer group. *Acta Paedologica*.

Rubenstein, J., & Howes, C. (1979). Caregiving and infant behavior in day care and in homes. *Developmental Psychology, 15*, 1–24.

Rubenstein, J., & Howes, C. (1982). Second order effects of peers on mother–toddler interaction. *Infant Behavior and Development, 5*, 185–194.

III

RESEARCH STUDIES ON FRIENDSHIPS IN NORMAL AND HANDICAPPED CHILDREN

8

The Peer Interactions of Young Developmentally Delayed Children in Specialized and Integrated Settings

Michael J. Guralnick

Recent interest in the early peer relations of handicapped children has been prompted as much by the practical issues that have emerged from efforts to mainstream or integrate these children as by a growing interest in the topic itself. This is especially the case for that group of handicapped children considered developmentally (cognitively) delayed. In fact, mainstreaming developmentally delayed children has been an especially controversial practice, one in which the issues of appropriate peer relationships have figured prominently.

In the first sections of this chapter, a series of studies that focus on the relationships between mainstreaming and the peer relations of developmentally delayed children at the early childhood level will be reviewed. Many of these studies are part of a comprehensive ongoing research program seeking to understand these issues at many levels (Guralnick, in press). The pathways this research has taken have led to investigations of the development of the peer interactions of delayed children in specialized settings, efforts to modify peer related social interactions through participation in integrated settings, process studies focusing on the extent to which delayed children are actually socially integrated, and analyses of the linguistic and communicative adjustments that nonhandicapped children make when interacting with delayed companions. Following this review, the findings and themes of this research will be used to provide a basis for establishing an intervention framework designed to improve the peer relations of young handicapped children.

It is important to note at the outset the major dimensions around which this research has been organized, and some limitations. Developmentally delayed children are, of course, a particularly heterogeneous group with widely varying etiologies. For example, in a study to be described briefly below (Guralnick & Weinhouse, in press), the etiological distribution of the sample was as follows: 12% chromosomal disorders; 14% prenatal infections and intoxications, congenital anomalies and disorders of unknown origin, and inborn errors of metabolism; 14% perinatal disorders and trauma; 32% congenital neuromotor dysfunction; and 14% postnatal trauma or other environmental causes. The cause or presumed cause for the remaining 14% was unknown. Although etiology is likely to correlate with aspects of social behavior, especially when physical anomalies are present, etiology per se has not been a useful dimension for organizing data in this field. In contrast, the more typical approach and the one taken here has been to use a severity of developmental delay dimension, primarily following guidelines established by the American Association on Mental Deficiency's manual on terminology and classification (Grossman, 1977). As such, children have been classified in accordance with intelligence test scores into categories of severe (35 or below), moderate (36–51), and mild (52–67) developmental delay. As a first approximation, this has been especially helpful, but of course it is important to recognize the limitations of such arbitrary classification systems. Problems with this approach, especially in relation to mildly delayed children, will be considered in a later section of this chapter.

PEER INTERACTION DEFICITS
IN SPECIALIZED SETTINGS

In view of the well-documented problems in caregiver–child relations that are associated with the birth of a handicapped child (Farber, 1975; Robinson & Robinson, 1976; Stone & Chesney, 1978; Ulrey, 1981), especially problems related to social interactions (Cunningham, Reuler, Blackwell, & Deck, 1981; Terdal, Jackson, & Garner, 1976), it would not be surprising to find that many young delayed children exhibit substantial deficits in their peer relations. In fact, when these factors are combined with unusual expressive language difficulties that are characteristic of this group of handicapped children (Mahoney, Glover, & Finger, 1981; Miller, Chapman, & Bedrosian, 1977), the conditions for creating marked deficits in peer relations—deficits well beyond those expected on the basis of a child's cognitive development—appear to exist.

A number of recent studies of children enrolled in specialized programs serving only handicapped children have indeed confirmed the existence of these peer interaction deficits. For example, Field (1980) observed that developmentally delayed 4- and 5-year-olds were considerably less socially interactive with their peers in comparison to a developmentally equivalent group of 3- and 4-year-old normally developing children. Guralnick and Weinhouse (in press), in an extensive short-term longitudinal study of the peer relations of 52 moderately and mildly delayed children (mean chronological age 54.4 months), found marked discrepancies from typical developmental patterns. For the most part, only a small subset of their sample (about 20%) was able to turn simple two-unit initiation—response encounters into longer social exchanges. Solitary and parallel play remained the dominant forms of social participation (see Parten, 1932), with the frequency of occurrence of more advanced forms (i.e., associative and cooperative play) lagging far behind that which would be expected on the basis of the children's developmental levels. Of perhaps greatest concern was the finding that a cross-sectional analysis across chronological age (3 to 5½ years) failed to reveal any developmental changes, as evaluated by a wide range of peer related measures. This highly atypical pattern suggests that a majority of developmentally delayed children enrolled in specialized settings reach an asymptotic level of interacting with their peers during the early preschool period, a level which appears to be maintained at least until they enter their elementary school years.

These findings have now been corroborated in a number of other studies, such as the one by Crawley and Chan (1982), who observed groups of moderately and mildly delayed children in an outdoor playground setting. In this study, there was a strong trend for both delayed groups to reduce their involvement in unoccupied and onlooker activities with increasing chronological age. In contrast, participation in solitary or parallel play tended to increase with chronological age. However, despite a tendency for the mildly delayed older group to engage in peer interactions to a greater extent than the younger or moderately delayed group, both groups exhibited highly similar social participation patterns. On the average, they failed to engage in peer interactions in any form, even being the recipients of a simple initiation, in over 90% of the intervals observed. Significant deficits of this nature for a group of mildly delayed 5-year-olds enrolled in noncategorical special education preschool classes have also been observed (Mindes, 1982).

PEER INTERACTIONS IN MAINSTREAMED SETTINGS

Many proponents of mainstreaming argue that the participation of handicapped and nonhandicapped children in the same educational setting has the potential for improving the peer related social interactions of handicapped children (see Guralnick, 1978). There are, in fact, many developmental principles that can be invoked to support this position. For example, it has been well established that children tend to observe and imitate more competent classmates (Akamatsu & Thelen, 1974; Grusec & Abramovitch, 1982; Peterson, Peterson, & Scriven, 1977; Vaughn & Waters, 1981). Moreover, it is likely that classroom settings containing nonhandicapped children will be richer and more varied from a linguistic and communicative perspective, conditions which are associated with fostering social competence with one's peers (Guralnick, 1981a; Prutting, 1982). Similarly, the principle of reciprocity (Cairns, 1979) suggests that less interactive children may be encouraged to engage in more frequent social exchanges through their involvement with classmates more interactive than themselves. There are, of course, important humanistic and legal considerations which also argue for the availability of mainstreamed programs, but these issues are not considered in this chapter (see Guralnick, 1982, for a detailed discussion).

Despite the fact that numerous investigations have demonstrated that nonhandicapped children can be used successfully to alter a wide range of peer related social behaviors of handicapped children, as part of a carefully orchestrated educational or therapeutic program for selected children (see Strain, this volume), it is worthwhile examining the hypothesis that positive effects might occur through the more typical day-to-day participation of handicapped children in mainstreamed settings. Unfortunately, perhaps as a result of practical difficulties in sampling, in establishing fair comparison groups, and in maintaining control over potentially confounding variables, only two studies have addressed this problem to date (Field, Roseman, DeStefano, & Koewler, 1981; Guralnick, 1981b). In both studies, arrangements were made so that diverse groups of handicapped and nonhandicapped children were available to interact in one condition, whereas in another, children were restricted to playmates who were similar to themselves in terms of developmental level. Apart from this systematic difference, the play settings and other relevant factors were similar in the two conditions. The results indicate that despite the fact that handicapped children had ample opportunities to interact with nonhandicapped children, the availability of different playmates had very little effect on social and play interactions in either study. In neither case was any substantial change noted, although there was evidence suggesting that the presence of nonhandicapped playmates could reduce the level of inappropriate play of severely delayed children (Guralnick, 1981b), and that the frequency of certain specific but isolated social behaviors could be increased for both the handicapped and nonhandicapped children during the integration condition (Field et al., 1981). It is important to note that there were no adverse effects for any group in any condition; either small gains were observed, or play and social interactions continued as usual. Other reports, although sampling from intact groups, thereby making direct comparisons difficult (e.g., Cooke, Ruskus, Apolloni, & Peck, 1981; Novak, Olley, & Kearney, 1980), have nevertheless tended to confirm these conclusions.

It is possible that other experimental designs capable of addressing the difficult issues of sampling and subject assignment, as well as longer term follow-up studies, may yield outcomes different from those suggested by the initial studies. Nevertheless, at this time a closer examination of the nature of the interactions actually occurring between nonhandicapped and handicapped children in mainstreamed settings may be especially useful in suggesting explanations for existing results, as well as suggesting possible intervention strategies that may help realize any potential mainstreamed programs may have for improving the early peer relations of handicapped children.

POSSIBLE EXPLANATIONS FOR
THE MINIMAL EFFECTS OF MAINSTREAMING

It is possible that delayed and nondelayed children actually fail to interact with one another; that is, subgroups form on the basis of handicap. Indeed, this may well be the case for children who are moderately and severely delayed (Guralnick, 1980; Porter, Ramsey, Tremblay, Iancobo, & Crawley, 1978; Sinson & Wetherick, 1981). In contrast, children classified as mildly delayed appear to be socially well integrated with their nonhandicapped classmates (Guralnick, 1980; Ispa, 1981; Ispa & Matz, 1978; Dunlop, Stoneman, & Cantrell, 1980). Moreover, these studies have found consistently that delayed children have ample opportunities for observational learning (proximity and parallel play measures) and are not the recipients of any unusual negative interactions from the normally developing children in the setting.

Alternatively, it is possible that, when interacting with delayed children, nonhandicapped children are unable to adjust their communicative interactions to their companion's cognitive and linguistic level, thereby providing an array of confusing and unsatisfying social–communicative exchanges. However, this does not appear to be the case, as revealed in a series of studies focusing on this issue (Guralnick & Paul-Brown, 1977, 1980). These studies have demonstrated that the syntactic complexity, productivity, and semantic diversity of speech of normally developing children is reduced when addressing less developmentally advanced companions. Moreover, assessments of certain functional and discourse characteristics of their communicative interactions revealed that nonhandicapped children provided information less often, made fewer requests for information, but used more directive interactions and repeated more often when addressing children at lower developmental levels. Taken together, and utilizing adult–child, mixed-age child–child, and clinician–child interactions as a framework for interpreting the meaning of these differential patterns, these studies suggested that the communicative adjustments were appropriate (Guralnick, 1981a). For the most part, nonhandicapped children appeared to be effectively pursuing their communicative goals in relation to task demands and social and situational constraints, while using a wide range of strategies to maintain contact and to facilitate communication. At the same time, diverse and progressive linguistic input was being provided.

In fact, it is not just the surface-type measures that reveal these adjustments. In a study by Guralnick and Paul-Brown (in press), a large number of communicative episodes in which nonhandicapped children were attempting to gain compliance with their requests from children at different developmental levels were identified (nonhandicapped children randomly paired with mildly, moderately, and severely delayed as well as with other nonhandicapped children in a playroom setting). These behavior request episodes were then tracked until some resolution occurred. Resolution could occur by obtaining full and complete compliance, by switching the topic, and by obtaining some form of modified compliance (such as by assisting the companion or by accepting an alternative suggestion). Episodes could also end if a speaker completed the request independently (e.g., obtaining the toy in question).

A key objective of this investigation was to evaluate each communicative exchange in terms of its adaptiveness; adaptiveness being defined as a communication that attempted to clarify the behavior request to better enable the companion to comprehend the nature of the request, to clarify its basis, to encourage compliance, or to assist the companion in carrying out the request. If the communication was adaptive, a determination was made of the specific adaptive strategies employed (such as demonstration, motivation, attentionals, guides, repetition, and adds relevant information).

The results revealed that nonhandicapped children were indeed highly adaptive in their efforts to obtain compliance, not only from other nonhandicapped peers but from all groups (about 80% of the time). Moreover, they were reasonably effective in actually gaining compliance (overall mean of approximately 50%), although there was a strong tendency to fail more frequently when their companions belonged to the severely delayed group. Perhaps the most interesting finding, however, was the creativity displayed by the nonhandicapped children as they sought compliance with their requests. Even though they employed basically ten types of specific adaptive strategies, virtually all children combined these different strategies most of the time within a single communication (i.e., they would justify their request and provide guidance at the same time). In fact, 62 different combinations of these strategies were observed. Nonhandicapped children were also very flexible, as seen by the fact that, when a strategy failed, they altered that strategy or combination of strategies about 80% of the time on their next effort. Similarly, type–token ratios were calculated relating the total number of different specific adaptive behaviors to the total number of behaviors that were employed during each episode. The overall ratio was .67, a ratio which remained high to all groups, again providing evidence for considerable diversity of use of specific adaptive strategies.

Clearly, then, nonhandicapped children's communicative interactions during these behavior request episodes appear to be highly adaptive, flexible, and persistent, irrespective of the developmental level of their companion. However, as noted earlier for certain structural and discourse measures, some specific adaptations varying with the developmental level of the listener would be appropriate during these episodes. Such differential adjustments did in fact occur. Not only did the nonhandicapped children demonstrate and exemplify more often to the less advanced children, they tended to combine strategies more frequently to them as well. That is, nonhandicapped children didn't simply repeat a behavior request as they might have to a nonhandicapped child, but they also demonstrated or guided their less advanced companions at the same time. Furthermore, they tended to ask the more delayed children fewer questions and justified or mitigated their requests almost exclusively to other nonhandicapped companions, a point that will be discussed in more detail in what follows.

Taken together, if handicapped children appear reasonably well integrated, especially the mildly delayed children, do not receive an extensive or unusual number of negative interactions, have well documented opportunities for observational learning, and are the beneficiaries of rather impressive communicative adjustments by their nonhandicapped classmates, why are there only minimal effects from mainstreaming? As noted above, it is of course possible that undetected, delayed, or deferred effects may in fact be occurring, or that other experimental designs not forced to evaluate efficacy through repeated and immediate changes in group composition would yield different outcomes. Moreover, many severely and moderately delayed children may have inadequately developed observational skills, or the barriers of limited expressive language and related problems may be simply too severe to overcome, in any significant way, merely through interacting with normally developing children.

A SECOND LOOK

Yet, before appealing to these and other alternatives, a closer examination of the research relating to the more intuitive and more face valid explanations considered earlier are in order. In particular, despite an extensive literature to the contrary, it is important to consider the possibility that even mildly delayed children are not really as socially well-integrated as was first thought. In fact, looking closely at the different types of assessments that were utilized in the studies to evaluate the extent of social integration, a trend is apparent. Those investigations emphasizing more interactive measures (i.e., mutual or cooperative play) have suggested greater separation than those using more passive measures (i.e., parallel play—see Guralnick, 1981c). It is quite possible that rather extensive social separation occurs during the more elaborate, and perhas more important, forms of social play. This possibility is supported by a detailed analysis of the specific adaptive strategies used by nonhandicapped children when interacting with mildly delayed, as compared to other nondelayed, children in the behavior request episodes described above (Guralnick & Paul-Brown, in press). Specifically, nonhandicapped children chose to justify or mitigate their behavior requests almost exclusively to other nonhandicapped children, and rarely asked questions of their mildly delayed companions. This differentiation may well suggest differences in perceived social status (Ervin-Tripp & Mitchell-Kernan, 1977), a circumstance likely to correspond to some forms of social separation (see Rubin & Borwick, in press). Finally, it should be noted that the mildly delayed children selected for participation in mainstreamed programs, and observed as part of a research project, may not at all be representative of the general population of mildly delayed children. In fact, for many of the studies, these children appeared to be at the upper end of the mildly delayed range. Many displayed well developed and highly sophisticated social play and peer related skills, even prior to involvement in a mainstreamed program (e.g., Dunlop et al., 1980; Ispa & Matz, 1978). As noted earlier, the peer interaction skills of mildly delayed children tend to be characterized by substantial deficits for a large segment of that population.

Even the nature of the communicative adjustments of nonhandicapped children described earlier requires close scrutiny. It is important to note that, especially when addressing severely and moderately delayed children, the style of the nonhandicapped children's interactions can be characterized as more "adultlike" or "older sibling" than "peerlike." That is, nonhandicapped children tend to be dominating and controlling in their interactions, and the communicative adjustments that they make more closely resemble those adjustments parents make to their normally developing children (Broen, 1972; Gleason & Weintraub, 1978) or those made by older to younger children (Shatz & Gelman, 1973; Gelman & Shatz, 1977). In fact, extrapolating from research on mixed age child–child interactions to children at similar chronological but different developmental ages suggests that substantial discrepancies in developmental level may even lead to suppression of verbal exchanges in the less developmentally advanced children (Langlois, Gottfried, Barnes, & Hendricks, 1978). Although this style may appear less frequently when interacting with mildly delayed children, co-equal interactions, a condition which is apparently necessary for promoting peer relations (e.g., Hartup, 1978), may not be obtained in mainstreamed programs.

ASSESSMENT AND INTERVENTION
IN PEER RELATIONS

In a real sense, we are faced with a dilemma with regard to promoting the peer interactions of developmentally delayed children as they enter their preschool years. Specialized settings for the most part do not seem supportive of the development of peer interactions; deficits appear to be widespread. Yet participation of delayed children in mainstreamed or integrated programs generates strong tendencies for both social separation and for nonhandicapped children to behave "as if" they were adults or older siblings. Even when interacting with older mildly delayed children, social status issues appear to limit equality of interaction. The inequality in these handicapped-child–nonhandicapped-child interactions, although having other possible educational or developmental advantages, is unfortunately not compatible with promoting peer interaction skills—skills which require partners to interact on a more reciprocal, balanced basis.

Despite these concerns, there is probably no substitute for the richness, diversity, and responsivity found in mainstreamed programs. It is not possible, however, to rely simply on the placement of handicapped children in integrated settings to achieve a beneficial effect since, as we have seen, the forces governing the frequency, form, and function of child–child interactions are too variable to assure that whatever benefits are inherent in this integrated setting will be realized. It appears that, in order to take advantage of the potential educational and therapeutic resources, special arrangements and systematic programming must occur. The value of such systematic approaches directed toward individual children in highly structured situations has been well documented (Strain, 1981). What remains to be accomplished is a more general application of these and other principles and techniques into the daily flow of classroom interactions.

Historically, however, this aspect of a handicapped child's developing social competence has been severely neglected. Extensive research and corresponding intervention programs have focused on the cognitive, motor, and language development of young handicapped children, treating social development in general and peer related social interactions in particular as by-products of these more primary developmental domains. In fact, the general absence of systematic efforts in this regard may well be the most important factor to date limiting the effects of mainstreaming on peer related social behaviors.

Nowhere is the lack of attention to peer-related social interactions more apparent than in the assessment instruments that are currently available. A recently conducted analysis of all available tests for the 0–6-year age group containing peer-related items revealed widespread inadequacies (Guralnick & Weinhouse, 1983). Drawing items from general early childhood, primarily social, criterion-referenced, and clinical tests, it was apparent that test developers placed little emphasis on the development of peer relations. Specifically, the frequency of content domains (e.g., social participation, friendship, initiation–response) and the number of test items per domain were extremely low, chronological age equivalents for apparently the same item varied widely from test to test, sequences of items were often not compatible with existing developmental knowledge, and the psychometric properties of many of the tests failed to reach conventional standards of acceptability. If developmentalists, teachers, or clinicians expect to utilize existing tests to identify or confirm suspected peer social deficits, to estimate the severity of any deficit that has been identified, and to provide a developmental framework to guide the development of broad goals for intervention and identify areas requiring additional information and observation—reasonable expectations for intervention-oriented assessments—then clearly they are likely to be disappointed.

Beyond these difficulties, no protocol or system appears to have been developed that reflects the cross-disciplinary aspects of deficits in peer relations. Specific features of language and communicative development, especially those related to the fields of pragmatics and child sociolinguistics (Ervin-Tripp & Mitchell-Kernan, 1977; Ochs & Schieffelin, 1979), motivational—interpersonal characteristics, the level of a child's constructive play, and the nature of play themes, combined with information from a range of peer related behaviors, all converge to provide an essential informational base to develop and then implement successful peer interaction strategies (Guralnick, in press).

It is in this broader context that the value of the availability of a mainstreamed program can be placed in perspective. When linked to specific intervention strategies derived from a comprehensive peer relations assessment, small developmental or therapeutic playgroups can be formed within larger classes for specific purposes at specific times. In some instances, it may be important to capitalize on the adultlike characteristics of developmentally more advanced children in order to stimulate certain forms of peer related social behaviors, or to create a richer and more responsive social environment for the handicapped child. In other instances, it may be necessary to arrange for the availability of responsive playmates by selecting those that are likely to establish more co-equal relationships. In yet other instances, arrangements may be made to involve a handicapped child with less advanced playmates, or those who are less assertive, to provide opportunities for taking leadership and for exploring and establishing relationships in which they are more dominant (Furman, Rahe, & Hartup, 1979). What distinguishes these efforts is that they are seen as part of a more comprehensive plan to foster the development of peer relations. Within that framework, our expectations with regard to the impact of mainstreaming on peer relations are likely to be more realistic and represent a more accurate view of the forces that influence the development and modification of child—child social interactions.

REFERENCES

Akamatsu, T., & Thelen, M. (1974). A review of the literature on observer characteristics and imitation. *Developmental Psychology, 10*, 38—47.

Broen, P. A. (1972). The verbal environment of the language-learning child. *American Speech and Hearing Association Monograph, 17.*

Cairns, R. B. (1979). *Social development: The origins and plasticity of interchanges.* San Francisco: W. H. Freeman and Company.

Cooke, T. P., Ruskus, J. A., Apolloni, T., & Peck, C. A. (1981). Handicapped preschool children in the mainstream: Background, outcomes, and clinical suggestions. *Topics in Early Childhood Special Education, 1*, 73—83.

Crawley, S. B., & Chan, K. S. (1982). Developmental changes in the free play behavior of mildly and moderately retarded preschool-aged children. *Education and Training of the Mentally Retarded, 17*, 234—239.

Cunningham, C. E., Reuler, E., Blackwell, J., & Deck, J. (1981). Behavioral and linguistic development in the interactions of normal and retarded children with their mothers. *Child Development, 52,* 62–70.

Dunlop, K. H., Stoneman, Z., & Cantrell, M. L. (1980). Social interaction of exceptional and other children in a mainstreamed preschool classroom. *Exceptional Children, 47,* 132–141.

Ervin-Tripp, S., & Mitchell-Kernan, C. (Eds.). (1977). *Child discourse.* New York: Academic Press.

Farber, B. (1975). Family adaptations to severely mentally retarded children. In M. J. Begab & S. A. Richardson (Eds.), *The mentally retarded and society: A social science perspective.* Baltimore: University Park Press.

Field, T. M. (1980). Self, teacher, toy, and peer-directed behaviors of handicapped preschool children. In T. M. Field, S. Goldberg, D. Stern, & A. M. Sostek (Eds.), *High-risk infants and children: Adult and peer interactions.* New York: Academic Press.

Field, T., Roseman, S., DeStefano, L., & Koewler, J. H. III. (1981). Play behaviors of handicapped preschool children in the presence and absence of nonhandicapped peers. *Journal of Applied Developmental Psychology, 2,* 49–58.

Furman, W., Rahe, D. F., & Hartup, W. W. (1979). Rehabilitation of socially withdrawn preschool children through mixed-age and same-age socialization. *Child Development, 50,* 915–922.

Gelman, R., & Shatz, M. (1977). Appropriate speech adjustments: The operation of conversational constraints on talk to two-year-olds. In M. Lewis & L. A. Rosenblum (Eds.), *Interaction, conversation, and the development of language.* New York: John Wiley & Sons.

Gleason, J. B., & Weintraub, S. (1978). Input language and the acquisition of communicative competence. In K. Nelson (Ed.), *Children's language* (Vol. 1). New York: Gardner Press.

Grossman, H. J. (Ed.). (1977). *Manual on terminology and classification in mental retardation.* Washington, DC: American Association on Mental Deficiency.

Grusec, J. E., & Abramovitch, R. (1982). Imitation of peers and adults in a natural setting: A functional analysis. *Child Development, 53,* 636–642.

Guralnick, M. J. (Ed.). (1978). *Early intervention and the integration of handicapped and nonhandicapped children.* Baltimore: University Park Press.

Guralnick, M. J. (1980). Social interactions among preschool children. *Exceptional Children, 46,* 248–253.

Guralnick, M. J. (1981). Peer influences on the development of communicative competence. In P. Strain (Ed.), *The utilization of classroom peers as behavior change agents.* New York: Plenum Press. (a)

Guralnick, M. J. (1981). The social behavior of preschool children at different developmental levels: Effects of group composition. *Journal of Experimental Child Psychology, 31,* 115–130. (b)

Guralnick, M. J. (1981). The efficacy of integrating handicapped children in early education settings: Research implications. *Topics in Early Childhood Special Education, 1,* 57–71. (c)

Guralnick, M. J. (1982). Mainstreaming young handicapped children: A public policy and ecological systems analysis. In B. Spodek (Ed.), *Handbook of research on early childhood education.* New York: The Free Press/Macmillan.

Guralnick, M. J. (in press). The peer relations of young handicapped and nonhandicapped children. In P. S. Strain, M. J. Guralnick, & H. M. Walker (Eds.), *Children's social behavior: Development, assessment, and modification.* New York: Academic Press.

Guralnick, M. J., & Paul-Brown, D. (1977). The nature of verbal interactions among handicapped and nonhandicapped preschool children. *Child Development, 48,* 254–260.

Guralnick, M. J., & Paul-Brown, D. (1980). Functional and discourse analyses of nonhandicapped preschool children's speech to handicapped children. *American Journal of Mental Deficiency, 84,* 444–454.

Guralnick, M. J., & Paul-Brown, D. (in press). Communicative adjustments during behavior request episodes among children at different developmental levels. *Child Development.*

Guralnick, M. J., & Weinhouse, E. M. (1983). Child-child social interactions: An analysis of assessment instruments for young children. *Exceptional Children, 50,* 268–271.

Guralnick, M. J., & Weinhouse, E. M. (in press). Peer related social interactions of developmentally delayed young children: Their development and characteristics. *Developmental Psychology.*

Hartup, W. W. (1978). Peer interaction and the process of socialization. In M. J. Guralnick (Ed.), *Early intervention and the integration of handicapped and nonhandicapped children.* Baltimore: University Park Press.

Ispa, J. (1981). Social interactions among teachers, handicapped children, and nonhandicapped children in a mainstreamed preschool. *Journal of Applied Developmental Psychology, 1,* 231–250.

Ispa, J., & Matz, R. D. (1978). Integrating handicapped preschool children within a cognitively oriented program. In M. J. Guralnick (Ed.), *Early intervention and the integration of handicapped and nonhandicapped children.* Baltimore: University Park Press.

Langlois, J. H., Gottfried, N. W., Barnes, B. M., & Hendricks, D. E. (1978). The effect of peer age on the social behavior of preschool children. *The Journal of Genetic Psychology, 132,* 11–19.

Mahoney, G., Glover, A., & Finger, I. (1981). Relationship between language and sensorimotor development of Down syndrome and nonretarded children. *American Journal of Mental Deficiency, 86,* 21–27.

Miller, J. F., Chapman, R. S., & Bedrosian, J. L. (1977). *Defining developmentally disabled subjects for research: The relationship between etiology, cognitive development, and language and communicative performance.* Unpublished manuscript, University of Wisconsin–Madison.

Mindes, G. (1982). Social and cognitive aspects of play in young handicapped children. *Topics in Early Childhood Special Education, 2,* 39–52.

Novak, M. A., Olley, J. G., & Kearney, D. S. (1980). Social skills of children with special needs in integrated and separate preschools. In T. M. Field, S. Goldberg, D. Stern, & A. M. Sostek (Eds.), *High-risk infants and children: Adult and peer interactions.* New York: Academic Press.

Ochs, E., & Schieffelin, B. B. (Eds.). (1979). *Developmental pragmatics.* New York: Academic Press.

Parten, M. B. (1932). Social participation among preschool children. *Journal of Abnormal Social Psychology, 27,* 243–269.

Peterson, C., Peterson, J., & Scriven, G. (1977). Peer imitation by nonhandicapped and handicapped preschoolers. *Exceptional Children, 43,* 223–224.

Porter, R. H., Ramsey, B., Tremblay, A., Iancobo, M., & Crawley, S. (1978). Social interactions in heterogeneous groups of retarded and normally developing children: An observational study. In G. P. Sackett (Ed.), *Observing behavior* (Vol. 1). Baltimore: University Park Press.

Prutting, C. A. (1982). Pragmatics as social competence. *Journal of Speech and Hearing Disorders, 47,* 123–134.

Robinson, N. M., & Robinson, H. B. (1976). *The mentally retarded child: A psychological approach*. New York: McGraw-Hill Book Company.

Rubin, K. H., & Borwick, D. (in press). The communicative skills of children who vary with regard to sociability. In H. E. Sypher & J. L. Applegate (Eds.), *Social cognition and communication*. Hillsdale, NJ: Lawrence Erlbaum & Associates.

Shatz, M., & Gelman, R. (1973). The development of communication skills: Modification in the speech of young children as a function of listener. *Monographs of the Society for Research in Child Development, 38*, No. 5, Serial No. 152.

Sinson, J. C., & Wetherick, N. E. (1981). The behaviour of children with Down syndrome in normal playgroups. *Journal of Mental Deficiency Research, 25*, 113–120.

Stone, N. W., & Chesney, B. H. (1978). Attachment behaviors in handicapped infants. *Mental Retardation, 16*, 8–12.

Strain, P. S. (Ed.). (1981). *The utilization of classroom peers as behavior change agents*. New York: Plenum Press.

Terdal, L., Jackson, R. H., & Garner, A. M. (1976). Mother-child interactions: A comparison between normal and developmentally delayed groups. In E. J. Mash, L. A. Hamerlynck, & L. C. Handy (Eds.), *Behavior modification and families*. New York: Brunner/Mazel.

Ulrey, G. (1981). Emotional development of the young handicapped child. In N. Anastasiow (Ed.), *New directions for exceptional children: Socioemotional development*. San Francisco: Jossey-Bass, Inc.

Vaughn, B. E., & Waters, E. (1981). Attention structure, sociometric status, and dominance: Interrelations, behavior correlates, and relationships to social competence. *Developmental Psychology, 17*, 275–288.

9

Play Behaviors of Handicapped Children Who Have Friends

Tiffany Field

The importance of understanding the differences between the behaviors of children who have close friends versus those who do not is underscored by the fact that having no friends in the early years is correlated with later social problems such as juvenile delinquency and psychoses (Cowen, Pederson, Babijian, Izzo, & Trost, 1973; Roff, 1963). Determining how the play and interaction behaviors of children who have friends differ from those who do not have friends may enable us to design interventions to facilitate the behaviors of children who do not have friends.

In a study of normal preschool children who have close friends (i.e., played with one child 66% of the time) versus those who do not (Roopnarine & Field, this volume), a number of differences in play and social behavior were noted. Children who had friends scored significantly higher on the Buck affect rating scale, suggesting they were rated more extraverted than children who did not have friends. During free play, children who had close friends were more verbal, more facially expressive, more likely to take turns directing and submitting during play interaction, more likely to engage in fantasy play, and less likely to merely watch the activities of their peers. Thus, children who had close friends were generally "more engaging" in their social encounters, and children who did not have close friends were "more watchful." In a subsequent study, Roopnarine and Field (this volume) examined the behaviors of children who did not have close friends when paired with children who did have close friends in a laboratory setting. Of primary interest in this study was whether, in a dyadic play situation, children who did not have close friends would adopt some of those behaviors of children who had close friends. Only minimal changes were noted in the children who did not have friends, namely, an increase in positive verbal behavior and a decrease in fighting behavior. While it is conceivable that the modeling of behaviors by children who have friends may facilitate the behaviors of those who do not have friends, the time spent together in this dyadic laboratory situation may have been too brief, or this form of intervention may not be optimal.

Evidence that children's social behaviors can be facilitated by the modeling of social behaviors by their more sociable peers is provided by a preschool mainstream study (Field, Roseman, DeStefano, & Koewler, 1982). In this study, handicapped children were mainstreamed with normal children for a series of free play sessions. The handicapped children were observed playing alone as a group, and together with a group of normal preschool children. In the integrated situation, the handicapped preschoolers spent more time looking at other children and being proximal to them, and less time relating to their teachers and to play objects. Equivalent amounts of time were spent looking, smiling, vocalizing, and being proximal to their own handicapped classmates and to their normal preschool peers, and touching of their own classmates occurred with much greater frequency. These results suggest that more prosocial, child-directed, and less teacher-directed, as well as less teacher-initiated, behaviors occurred for handicapped children who were playing with normal preschool children. The handicapped children appeared to watch and make as many social overtures to their normal peers as to their own classmates. Thus, the handicapped children appeared to become more sociable in the presence of children who had more developed social skills.

The purpose of the present study was to compare the social play behaviors of handicapped children who have close friends with those who do not have close friends. Based on our previous studies with normal preschool children, we expected to observe more sociable behavior among those children who had close friends (Roopnarine & Field, this volume). For the purpose of this study, the handicapped children were mainstreamed with normal children of equivalent developmental age, inasmuch as our previous study on mainstreamed handicapped children had suggested that play behaviors may be facilitated in this situation (Field et al., 1982). In addition, we were interested in whether the play context might affect friendship formation and social behavior. Thus, the mainstreamed sessions were held both inside the handicapped children's classroom, and outside on a shared playground.

METHOD

Subjects

Sixteen handicapped preschoolers (ten boys, six girls) and sixteen normal preschoolers (nine boys, seven girls) who attended an all day nursery were participants in this study. Their parents represented a variety of ethnic groups and were lower to middle socioeconomic status. At the beginning of the study, the handicapped preschoolers ranged in age from 23 to 39 months ($M = 29$), and the normal preschoolers from 15 to 30 months ($M = 21$). Developmental age in months averaged 20 for the handicapped preschoolers and 21 for the normal preschoolers. The developmental quotients averaged 116 for the normal and 73 for the handicapped preschoolers. The handicapping conditions included minimal cerebral palsy, Down's syndrome, and developmental delays due to perinatal complications.

Procedure

Although the handicapped and normal preschool children attended different classrooms, the preschool programs in both classes were oriented toward free play and preschool readiness curricula. The handicapped classroom in which these observations were conducted was a rectangular room (9 × 15 m) which featured a number of special play areas partitioned by child height walls, including a block area, a store, a kitchen, reading, art–science, and manipulative play areas, and gross motor structures. The teacher/child ratio in this classroom was 1 : 8. The teachers were females and were oriented toward facilitating free play. The large playground (approximately 27 × 32 m) featured a number of climbing structures, tree swings, crawling tunnels, sand box, and wading pool.

Children were observed over one semester for 1 hour per day, 2 days per week. One-half hour was scheduled inside of the classroom, and one-half hour on the playground, with indoor–outdoor play sessions being counterbalanced. Although two teachers from each of the normal and handicapped classrooms were present, the play period was designated as "free play." The observations were made by psychology graduate students who were unaware of the purpose of the study or the developmental and chronological ages of the children at the time of the observations.

Two separate recording systems were used by separate observers. One system assessed the frequency with which children played with one another in the different activity areas of their nursery and in the different areas on the playground. In the second system, play behaviors were coded using a time sampling technique. In the first observation system, sociograms were made by an observer who rotated through all of the play areas every 5 minutes and recorded the child's name and the other child(ren) engaging in the same activity or parallel activity, and the area of the room in which the activity occurred. This system was used to determine which children had friends versus which children did not have friends. The children who had friends were defined for the purpose of this study as those who were observed playing with a particular peer during more than 66% of the sociogram time sample units. Children who did not have friends were defined as those who played with a particular peer less than 33% of the time sample units. The second recording system provided information about the child's fantasy play, verbal interaction, social behaviors, and facial expressions. Each child was observed for twenty 5-minute sessions during free play in the nursery classroom and twenty 5-minute sessions during free play on the playground. Using a time sampling technique, the observer watched for 10 seconds and then recorded the presence/absence of behaviors in the next 10-second period for a total of 30 time sample units per observation. The observer noted the target child's behaviors and with whom he or she was engaging in play interaction. The behaviors that were coded were selected on the basis of their frequent occurrence in running record descriptions written during 10 pilot sessions. These behaviors are listed in Table 1. Interobserver reliability was assessed by two independent observers recording simultaneously 10% of the observations. Reliability was expressed as a percentage of time. Both observers recorded the same activity within each time sample unit. The reliability coefficients were calculated by Kappa, a chance-corrected percent agreement measure with a statistical base and ranged from .78 to .97. ($M = .93$).

Extraversion-introversion was assessed by the children's version of the Buck affect rating scale (Buck, 1977). This scale is comprised of 37 items on the child's extraversion–introversion, and is rated on a Likert-type scale by independent observers. The observers who rated the children on this scale were comprised of one of the classroom teachers and one of the researchers conducting the observations. In the case of disagreement, an average of the two observers' ratings was used. Each of these observers had known the children for at least 6 months prior to rating them.

RESULTS

Based on the sociogram data, seven of the handicapped children were noted to have close friends, that is, to engage in play with a

Table 1
Play Behaviors of Handicapped Children with and without Friends
(df = 15)

Behavior	With Friends	Without Friends	p Level
Wandering	10.2	14.8	.05
Watching—children	4.6	8.2	.01
Watching—teachers	3.1	6.4	.05
Approaching—children	5.3	2.1	.001
Approaching—teachers	2.1	2.8	N.S.
Leading activity	2.3	.5	.005
Leaving activity	4.1	1.7	.001
Giving toys	.6	.3	N.S.
Taking toys	1.8	.5	.05
Touching child	2.6	1.6	N.S.
Hugging child	1.6	.1	.05
Aggressing against child	1.1	.8	N.S.
Imitation	3.0	2.0	N.S.
Fantasy play	1.6	1.1	N.S.
Vocalizing	4.3	1.6	.005
Laughing	2.7	.4	.005
Fussing	.7	.3	.005
Eye contact	8.4	7.4	N.S.
Happy face	3.9	.9	.001
Sad face	.1	.1	N.S.
Mad face	.5	.1	.05

particular peer at least 66% of the time, and nine handicapped children were noted to have no particular friend, based on their playing less than 33% of the time with a particular peer. Of the seven children who had a friend, one handicapped child's friend was a normal preschool peer, one handicapped child had both a handicapped classmate and a normal preschool peer as friends, and five children had handicapped classmates as friends. The sex distribution of those children who had friends was slightly skewed, with five males and two females having friends. Same-sex and cross-sex friendship pairs were evenly distributed.

Analyses of variance were then conducted on a number of background factors and play behaviors with the friend versus no friend group, and inside versus outside play as between groups measures. The children with friends did not differ from those without friends on height (M = 36 in. for children with friends versus 35 in. for children without friends), on chronological age (M = 29 months for children with friends versus 28 months for children without friends), developmental age (M = 20 months for both children with friends and without friends), developmental quotient ($M = 72$ for children with friends versus 74 for children without friends), or type of developmental delay. One background measure on which these two groups significantly differed was the extraversion–introversion rating on the Buck affect scale. Children who had friends were assigned significantly higher scores, indicative of their being more extraverted than children who did not have friends ($M = 46$ for children with friends versus 20 for children without friends, $p < .001$).

Analyses of the group differences on play behaviors suggested that the handicapped children who had close friends were generally more assertive in initiating, leading, and terminating play interactions than the handicapped children who did not have close friends. This was manifested by the greater percentage of time sample units they were noted to approach other children, to lead other children in dyadic or group activity, and to terminate their involvement by leaving the play activity. This greater assertiveness was also manifested in a greater frequency of hugging other children and of taking toys from other children. As a group they were more verbal, and their verbal behavior was more frequently reciprocated by their play partner than was the case for children who did not have friends. Affective displays occurred more frequently for children who had friends than for children who did not have friends—both in the positive mode, that is, more frequent happy expressions, and in the negative mode, more frequent angry expressions. In turn, both their happy and their angry expressions were more often reciprocated by other children with whom they were playing than was the case for children who did not have friends. Finally, they were more frequently observed to laugh and to be responded to by laughing in return, than the children who did not have friends. In contrast, the children who did not have friends were noted to spend more time wandering around, watching their teachers and the other children, than was noted for children who had friends. Fewer main effects were noted for the inside versus outside play factor. Observations of the play which occurred inside the classroom were characterized by more frequent approaches to the teacher (2% versus 1%, $p < .05$), more frequent vocalizations (4% versus 2%, $p < .05$), less frequent imitation (2% versus 4%, $p < .05$), more frequent giving of toys and reciprocal returning of toys (2% versus 1%, $p < .005$), and more frequent taking of toys (1% versus .5%, $p < .05$). It is perhaps not surprising that no significant group by inside–outside play interaction effects emerged, since the behaviors which were differentially affected by inside–outside play (except for vocalizing and taking toys) were different behaviors than those observed to differentiate children who had friends from children who did not have friends.

DISCUSSION

There are a number of parallels between the data from this study on the play behaviors of handicapped children who have friends versus handicapped children who do not have friends, and our previous study on normal preschool children who have and do not have friends (Roopnarine and Field, this volume). First, the distribution of children who have friends and children who do not have friends is approximately equivalent in both samples. Secondly, as in the study on normal preschool children, background factors such as age of child, height of child, and cognitive abilities of child based on developmental assessments did not differentiate children who had friends from those who did not. The only characteristic which differentiated those children in this study was the same characteristic that differentiated normal children who had friends, namely the extraversion rating. Although a difference in the distribution of children as a function of sex of child was not noted in the study of normal preschool children, the greater preponderance of boys among the sample of children with friends in this study may be a chance factor relating to the greater number of boys in the classroom. Finally, the parallel differences in play behaviors for the two samples of children with friends and children without friends are striking. Roopnarine and Field (this volume) reported more verbal behavior, more affective displays, both positive and negative (happy and angry), more assertive behaviors (labeled dominant behavior in that study) among children who had friends, and more watching the children's activities among children who did not have friends. These are virtually the same differences noted in this study on handicapped children with and without friends.

In both of these studies, four dimensions appeared to have emerged: assertiveness (characterized by approaching others, leading activity and leaving activity), vocal activity, affective expressivity (expressions of happy and angry affect, and laughter, which were reciprocated in kind), and extraversion. Because these dimensions have emerged in studies of both normal children and handicapped children, the question arises of whether those children with friends are simply more extraverted, or whether they have a more developed repertoire of social skills. This is a problem intrinsic to the "rate of interaction approach to assessment" in which the criterion is rate of interaction regardless of the quality or skillfulness of the interaction, as has been elaborated by Asher and his colleagues (Asher, Markell, & Hymel, 1981).

It is not clear in this study whether those children with friends are showing a greater number of social interaction behaviors because they have more social skills or because they are simply more extraverted, a construct which would include the greater frequency of behaviors such as assertiveness, vocal activity, and affective displays. Asher and Renshaw (1981) have suggested that, in order to determine whether children without friends are capable of affective social behavior, their social skillfulness needs to be assessed in a context that is independent of their current peer group. Although the grouping of handicapped with normal children was in part intended to produce a context that was different from the handicapped children's current peer group, it is clear that, for many of the children (at least five of the seven children whose friends were of their own peer group), this situation certainly was an extension of their peer group. Although use of hypothetical situations to independently determine the social skills of children with and without friends, by a number of investigators (Asher & Renshaw, in preparation; Gottman et al., 1975), indicated that children without friends indeed had fewer social skills, there is no a priori reason to suspect that the handicapped children in this sample who had friends were any more skillful socially than those without. As was noted earlier, on all background variables, the children with and the children without friends did not differ. This was also the case for our study on normal children with and without friends (Roopnarine & Field, this volume). Thus, the rate of interaction assessment may merely be differentiating those children who are extraverted from those who are not.

The generally lower frequency of these social behaviors amongst the entire group of handicapped children, relative to similar developmentally normal children, in the study reported by Field et al. (1981), suggests a lower level of social skillfulness among the handicapped children in general. This is not surprising, for all of the reasons that have been elegantly elaborated by Gottlieb and Leyser (1981). Gottlieb and Leyser suggest that developmental lags in speech and language are noted in these children, and that fewer displays of affective behaviors and assertiveness might be expected, due to fear of failure. A high expectancy of failure has been noted to lower the overall performance of children of this kind below the level that can be expected based on intellectual capacity alone. These factors may have contributed to the very small number (2 of 7) of handicapped–nonhandicapped friendship pairs. As has been noted by Field et al. (1981), children may select equal status or equivalent developmental level children as their friends. Although the developmental age of the handicapped and normal children in this study was approximately equivalent, as has been noted by Gottlieb and Leyser (1981), handicapped children are typically considered "lower status" among integrated groups of handicapped and normal children. Nonetheless, for at least two of the seven children, normal children were the playmate of choice. It is interesting that, in both of these cases, the most socially active handicapped children paired themselves with the most socially active normal children, as if the higher status children of both hierarchies were attracted to each other.

We had reason to believe at the outset of the study that the most optimal situation for facilitating friendship formation of these young handicapped children may be a mainstreamed situation in which they were grouped with normal children. This rationale was based on our previous study (Field et al, 1981), in which handicapped children, when grouped with normal children, were observed to emit a greater frequency of social behaviors toward their peers. In addition, we considered that much of the increase in social behaviors was facilitated by the imitation of social behaviors of normal children by the handicapped children. Although Gottlieb and Leyser (1981) have suggested that in only one study has it been reported that the handicapped child will imitate desired social behaviors as a result of interaction with more socially active children (Gample, Gottlieb, & Harrison, 1974), this infrequent finding may relate to high status children relating to each other and low status children relating to each other. Gottlieb and Leyser have suggested that, from a theoretical standpoint, the high status child will serve as a model for behaviors to be imitated by a low status child, and high status children will alter their attitudes toward the low status children after interacting with them. However, if the low status children are pairing themselves with low status children, and the high status with high status, the effects of modeling and imitation may be attenuated. This poses the perennial question of the most optimal intervention strategy.

Given that we can identify behaviors which occur at greater frequency among children who develop friends versus those who do not, what then do we do with this information? This question has been discussed at some length by a number of investigators (Asher & Renshaw, 1981; Gottlieb & Leyser, 1981), but the question still remains whether modeling and imitation, social reinforcement by teachers, peer or teacher interaction coaching techniques are the most optimal. Short of answering that question, and in the interim, it would appear that nothing can be lost by mainstreaming children in this fashion, and that "friends will be friends," despite our illusory attempts to understand that phenomenon.

ACKNOWLEDGMENTS

I would like to thank all the children and teachers who participated in this study. Further thanks go to Debra Cohen, Kerry Collins, and Reena Greenberg for assistance with data collection. This research was in part funded by a NIMH research scientist development award, No. 1k02MM00331-01.

REFERENCES

Asher, S. R., Markell, R. A., & Hymel, S. (1981). Identifying children at risk in peer relations: A critique of the rate-of-interaction approach to assessment. *Child development, 52,* 1239–1245.

Asher, S. R., & Renshaw, P. D. (1981). Children without friends: Social knowledge and social skill training. In S. R. Asher & J. M. Gottman (Eds.), *The development of children's friendships.* Cambridge: Cambridge University Press.

Asher, S. R., & Renshaw, P. D. (in preparation). *Social skills and social knowledge of high- and low-status kindergarten children.*

Buck, R. (1975). Nonverbal communication of affect in children. *Journal of Personality and Social Psychology, 31,* 644–653.

Cowen, E., Pederson, A., Babijian, H., Izzo, L., & Trost, M. (1973). Long-term follow-up of early detected vulnerable children. *Journal of Consulting and Clinical Psychology, 41,* 438–446.

Field, T., Roseman, S., DeStefano, L., & Koewler, J. (1981). Play behaviors of handicapped preschool children in the presence and absence of non-handicapped peers. *Journal of Applied Developmental Psychology, 2,* 49–58.

Gampel, D. H., Gottlieb, J., & Harrison, R. H. (1974). Comparison of classroom behavior of special-class EMR, integrated EMR, low IQ and nonretarded children. *American Journal of Mental Deficiency, 79,* 16–21.

Gottlieb, J., & Leyser, Y. (1981). Friendship between mentally retarded and non-retarded children. In S. R. Asher & J. M. Gottman (Eds.), *The development of children's friendships.* Cambridge: Cambridge University Press.

Gottman, J., Gonso, J., & Rasmussen, B. (1975). Social interaction, social competence and friendship in children. *Child Development, 46,* 709–718. Ladd, G. W., & Oden, S. L. (1979). The relationship between peer acceptance and children's ideas about helpfulness. *Child Development, 50,* 402–408.

Roff, J. (1963). Childhood social interaction and adult psychosis. *Journal of Clinical Psychology, 19,* 152–157.

Social Interactions and Patterns of Friendships in Normal and Emotionally Disturbed Children*

Carollee Howes

Ted climbs through the railing onto the ramp; Jacob follows. Ted says "Ooh, ooh, ooh" and runs to the door, then turns and runs down ramp. Jacob runs up ramp and says, "Play ball?" Ted: "Yeah." Jacob runs up ramp, pretends to slip, and falls down. Ted runs up and lays on ground next to Jacob. Jacob stands up, vocalizing: "Dawdee, dawdee, dawdee!" as he looks through the mailslot in the door. Ted imitates this sequence. Jacob looks through mailbox, vocalizes, rings door bell, then lies down. Ted goes over to the mail slot, looks in, vocalizes, and lies down next to Jacob. Both children giggle.

Vicki walks over to Rita, picks up a cup and says, "Cake," looking at Rita. Rita puts sand in Vicki's cup. Vicki picks up sand in a cup, looks up at Rita and says, "Cake?"

Ted and Jacob and Vicki and Rita are all toddlers who have been classified as friends. Ted and Jacob are normally developing toddlers who attend a community based day care center. Vicki and Rita are toddlers who have been severely physically abused, and have been ordered by the courts to attend an intervention program which includes day care.

The study of friendships in preverbal children is a fairly recent

* This research was supported by NIMH grant Nos. 5T32MH1424604 and IR03MH3555, and by grants from the Milton Fund of Harvard University and Children's Village USA. Special thanks to the staff and children who graciously permitted us to observe. Thanks also to Dr. Tad Mayeda, Robert Eldridge, Laura Beizer Seidner, Cheryl Morris, Michael Espinosa, and Chan Wen Chuan, who made comments on an earlier draft of this chapter.

phenomenon. Research on early peer interaction recognized that acquainted peers interacted differently from unacquainted (Doyle, Connolly, & Rivest, 1980; Mueller & Vandell, 1979). Acquaintance was sometimes interpreted as friendship. In fact, in a 1976 paper, Judith Rubenstein and I called dyads friends if their mothers reported that the toddlers often played together. Friendship, however, is more than being acquainted. It involves mutual affection, preference for the other, and reciprocity. In young children, these characteristics can be observed in behaviors present before the children have the cognitive and linguistic competencies to discuss friendship or to identify friends by sociometric techniques. For the past several years, I have been investigating the phenomena of friendships in very young children. In this chapter, I will report on two research programs on friendship formation in both normal and emotionally distrubed or abused young children.

In this work, friendship was defined as an affective tie between two children which has three necessary behavioral components: mutual preference, mutual enjoyment, and the ability to engage in skillful interaction (Howes & Mueller, 1980).

Friendships, or lack of friendships, in school-age children are important predictors of later mental health (Cowen, Pederson, Babigian, Izzo, & Trost, 1973). It is less likely that poor relationships with peers in the elementary school years cause adult maladjustment than that early peer rejection is indicative of limited social competence and the ability to develop relationships that would be present as early as the toddler period (Campbell & Cluss, 1982). Therefore, toddlers who have difficulty forming friendships with peers may be those who do not adapt to developmental demands.

However, if friendships can be facilitated between emotionally disturbed or abused children, such relationships may have therapeutic value for the later development of the children. The experience of a close emotional relationship with another person may alter the child's basic trust in others, and provide a positive expectation about human relationships. Programs which foster and teach peer relationships, as part of a larger program which give the child alternative attachment figures, may provide primary prevention for later emotional maladjustment.

The study of friendship formation in emotionally disturbed and abused children can also shed light on the mutual dependence or independence of parent–child and child–peer relationships. From a social network perspective (Lewis & Feiring, 1979) that assumes an independence of the two systems, we would expect that friends might become substitute attachment figures for children whose parents do not provide the warm and sensitive parenting that, according to attachment theorists (Ainsworth, Blehar, Waters, & Wall, 1978) facilitates secure attachment. Evidence for this perspective comes from the famous Freud and Dann (1951) study which describes intense positive emotional bonds between World War II orphans, and from Ipsa's (1981) study of Soviet day care children who demonstrated secure attachment relationships in Ainsworth's strange situation.

Alternatively, yet still from a social networks perspective, the social isolation of abusing parents, and of many parents of emotionally disturbed children, may serve to isolate the child from peer contacts. Thus, the emotionally disturbed or abused child may lack the skills and experience with peers to form friendships. Evidence for this point comes from George and Main's (1979) study of abused toddlers, in which abused toddlers were more likely to ignore other children than were controls.

From attachment theory perspective, the child who is emotionally disturbed or abused is unlikely to have a secure attachment relationship with the primary parent. Children who are securely attached are more likely to be able to explore the world of peer relationships and form friendships (Waters, Wippman, & Sroufe, 1979; Paster, 1981). Children with less secure attachments to their primary parent, according to this perspective, would have a difficult time forming friendships.

Beyond the issue of whether the qualitative nature of the parent—child relationship will facilitate or inhibit the formation of relationships with peers, we can ask whether there are particular interactive patterns or styles between parents and children which could then be transferred by the child into a peer interaction. Vandell and Wilson (1982) find no relationship between specific maternal behaviors with infants, and infant behavior with peers either at the same point in time or three months later. Yet infants who were more sociable with their mothers were more sociable with peers. Little comparable work has been done with children in the toddler period.

PATTERNS OF FRIENDSHIP PROJECT

The patterns of friendship study was designed to provide descriptions of friendship formation in very young children. The sample included children as young as 5 months old. At 6 months, research suggests that infants have the ability to engage in peer social encounters (Vandell & Wilson, 1982) and that there is some evidence of reciprocity in their contacts (Hay, Pedersen, & Nashe, 1982). But can children this young form friendships? The oldest normal children in the sample were 4 years old. Certainly these children were expected to form friendships. However, the extant research literature, when the project began, did not provide the descriptions of young preschoolers' friendships. Since then, work by Corsaro (1981), Rotheram and Phinney (1981), and Rubin (1980) have provided excellent accounts of preschool friendships. The sample of normally developing children was composed of three age groups of children enrolled in a community daycare facility. The youngest group consisted of seven infants ranging in age from 5 to 14 months (median = 10 months) when they entered the group program. The toddler group of eight children ranged in age from 16 to 23 months (median = 20 months) when they entered the group. The preschool group consisted of nine children ranging in age from 39 to 49 months (median = 42 months) when they entered the group. The day care center had just opened as the study began, so all children were new to the particular peer group. No children in the project had prior daily group experience with peers.

A second major purpose of the project was to compare friendship formation in normally developing children with that in emotionally disturbed children. The clinical population selected for study consisted of children who were enrolled in outpatient programs for study consisted of children who were enrolled in outpatient programs for emotionally disturbed children directed by the child psychiatry unit of a mental health hospital. These children were diagnosed as severely emotionally disturbed, with a predominance of nonorganic disorders. Two age groups were available for study: toddlers who ranged in age from 21 to 31 months at entry (median = 28 months), and preschoolers who ranged in age from 40 to 82 months at entry (median = 52 months). There were two subgroups of four toddlers and two subgroups of six preschoolers. All children in these groups were also new to the group and without prior daily peer contact.

The children were similar in their heterogeneous socioeconomic backgrounds. About half in each group came from intact families. The programs in which the children participated were similar in program content. Teacher–child ratios varied from 1 : 2 in the clinical groups to 1 : 4.5 in the preschool group. All programs were full day and full week.

Procedures

Each child was observed on 2 separate days for 15 minutes at 8-week intervals over a year. The two observations during each time period were combined. This procedure generated six 30-minute observations of each child.

The target of the observation was selected from a randomized list of children in the group. Observations took place during free play periods, stopped during caregiving and teacher directed activity, and were only collected when all of the children in the group were in attendance.

Each combined observation was composed of 360 intervals. A continuous coding observational procedure was followed. The observer recorded the presence and order of preselected behaviors on code sheets divided into intervals. Every 5 seconds, a beeper told the observer to move to the next interval. A social behavior was considered to be an initiation if there were no social behaviors in the preceding interval. An initiating social behavior was coded with a (1); the next social behavior in the same or subsequent interval was coded with a (2), and so on. A social behavior was considered to terminate an interaction if there was no response in the same or subsequent 5-second interval. The behavior of both the target child and any other child with whom the target interacted (the partner) were coded and ordered. For example, both the sequence (1) target child vocalized, (2) partner smiled, and the sequence (1) partner vocalized, (2) target child smiled, were recorded. If behaviors occurred simultaneously, for example, the target child vocalized and smiled, or the target child and partner both smiled, both behaviors were given the same order number. Coding was facilitated by limiting the number of social behaviors coded to offer objects, receive objects, vocalize smile or laugh, positive touch, imitate the ongoing activity of the other, take a toy, and physical aggression.

Pilot testing of the procedure established that 5-second intervals were the minimum length feasible for "in situ" recording of naturally occurring interaction while preserving the sequence of the interaction.

In addition to the presence and order of social behaviors, the level of peer social play was rated in every 5-second interval. The five scale points range from parallel play to complementary and reciprocal play (Howes, 1980). In level 1 play, children were engaged in similar activities but did not interact. In level 2 play, children were engaged in the same or similar activity and were in eye contact. In level 3 play, simple social play, each child directed a social behavior to the other while engaging in parallel activity. Level 4 involved complementary and reciprocal activity plus mutual awareness. Complementary and reciprocal activities are ones in which each child's action reverses the other's, demonstrating awareness of the role of the other. Examples include rolling a ball back and forth; chasing the other and then being chased; going down the slide and watching the other go up the steps of the slide, then going up the steps as the other goes down; one child offering a toy, the other receiving it and then offering it back; and engaging in mutually agreed upon fantasy play, for example, one child pushes a truck from the block structure to the shelves, where the second child loads the truck with blocks. Level 5 includes both contingent social behaviors and complementary activities.

Interobserver reliability on the observational codes was established by two coders on three infants, five toddlers, and five preschoolers who were not subjects in the study. Interobserver reliability was calculated (agreement on which behavior or scale-point-recorded–agreements-plus-disagreements plus omissions) for each interval. Only intervals in which at least one observer recorded behavior were included in the interobserver reliability calculations. Percent agreement on recording of the individual behaviors and scale points ranged from .85 to .99, (median = .94).

Interobserver reliability on the sequence of behaviors was calculated (agreement-on-sequence–agreement-plus-disagreements) for each interaction sequence. Interobserver reliability was 87%. Reliability was established prior to data collection, and monitored throughout the study.

Dyadic Transcripts

Following the observations, transcripts of the behaviors between every possible dyad in the group were prepared by collapsing across individuals. That is, the transcript for dyad A–B was prepared by combining all intervals from the code sheets in which A was the target child and B the partner with the intervals in which B was the target child and A was the partner. Care was taken to preserve the sequential nature of the data. Simultaneous behaviors (behaviors with the same order number) were placed on the same line, while subsequent behaviors were placed on subsequent lines. Lines of behavior belonging to the same 5-second interval were bracketed.

Transcripts were coded for complexity and content of dyadic interaction—that is, number of interactions, number of initiations that received a response within 10 seconds, number of elaborated exchanges, number of positive affective exchanges, and number of agonistic exchanges. Intercoder reliability ranged from .94 to .98% agreement; median .96.

PATTERNING OF FRIENDSHIPS

The first task of the project was to examine the patterning of friendships in each group. The behavioral criteria for friendship consisted of three necessary and mutually exclusive criteria: mutual preference, mutual enjoyment, and the ability to engage in skillful interaction.

Mutual preference was defined as a high probability that a dyadic interaction would follow a social initiation by either partner. On the average, 27% of social initiations resulted in interaction. Fifty percent dyadic success rate at initiating interaction was used as the criterion for the mutual preference component of friendship. Mutual enjoyment was defined as the ability to engage in positive affective exchanges. This social exchange involved ongoing prosocial activity while both partners expressed positive emotions. Only 38% of the dyads ever engaged in positive affective exchanges over the year. The third component, the ability to engage in skillful interaction, was operationally defined as the ability to engage in complementary and reciprocal play (level 4 or 5 in the Peer Play Scale). Only 57% of the dyads demonstrated this ability.

Each dyad was rated as a friend or nonfriend during each of the six time periods. To be judged a friend, a dyad had to be successful at initiating interaction at least 50% of the time, and have at least one positive affective exchange and at least one interval of complementary and reciprocal peer play. An analysis of observational periods in which dyads failed to meet the three component friendship criteria showed that the component of mutual preference was the hardest criteria to meet (Howes, 1983). This suggests that these friendships between young children are the result of an emotional bonding as opposed to a relationship based merely on advanced social skills.

Thirty-two (26%) dyads in the sample were rated as friends. Although friends were found in all groups studied, the patterning of friendship differed by age and whether the children were normal or disturbed (Howes, 1983).

The patterning of friendship style and the content of social behaviors used in friendly social interaction within the normal sample suggests a developmental progression. Infants had a limited number of very stable partners with whom they interacted primarily on the basis of object exchange rather than verbally. Toddlers initially had only stable partners, but by the second half of the year had formed short-term, time-limited relationships. Toddlers commonly formed more than one friendship. Toddler friendly interactions were less likely than infant interactions to be based on object exchanges, but they were not as likely to be verbal exchanges as were preschool friendly interactions. Preschoolers had two patterns of friendship. Preschool children were most likely to have several short-term or sporadic friendships, a pattern which existed in this group from the beginning of the year. However, some preschool friendships were stable. Preschool friendly interactions were based on verbal exchanges.

The major difference between the normal sample and the emo-

Table 1
Individual Differences in Styles of Interaction with Peers

	I	II	III	IV
		NORMAL SAMPLE		
	.92 number of elaborated exchanges	.84 proportion of group initiated to	.82 frequency agonistic	.84 frequency receive object
	.90 time positive affective exchanges	.74 proportion of group complementary and reciprocal play	.82 time agnoistic exchanges	.83 frequency offer object
	.87 frequency vocalization	.68 proportion of group interacted	.75 proportion of group in agonistic exchanges	
	.80 number successful initiations	.67 proportion of group simple social play		
	.76 frequency smile or laugh	.60 proportion of all interactions initiated		
	.74 number of initiation	.60 portion of group positive affective exchanges		

DISTURBED SAMPLE

.97 time positive affective
.94 frequency vocalization

.94 frequency smile or laugh
.88 number elaborated ex-
      changes
.75 proportion of group posi-
      tive affective exchanges
.70 number of successful initia-
      tions
.62 proportion of group in-
      teracted
.62 proportion of group com-
      plementary and recipro-
      cal play
.61 proportion of group simple
      social play
.61 proportion of group initi-
      ated to

.96 frequency offer object
.97 frequency receive object

.72 number of initiations

.97 frequency imitates
.65 number simple exchanges

.90 time agonistic exchanges
.77 proportion of group in ago-
      nistic exchanges

.71 agonistic frequency

tionally disturbed sample was in the patterning of friendships. Disturbed children only formed short-term friendships. However, while normal children formed new short-term friendships with different new partners, the disturbed children returned to the same partner following disruptions in their friendships.

The children in the disturbed sample were not more aggressive or antagonistic than the children in the child care sample. Although friendships were less frequent in the disturbed sample, behaviors in the dyads which formed friendships were quite similar. The children in the disturbed sample experienced smaller groups and a higher adult–child ratio than the children in the child care sample. These factors, as well as a more limited choice of compatible partners and more focused adult attention, may have reduced the number of friendships in the sample.

INDIVIDUAL DIFFERENCES

In order to analyze individual styles of interaction with peers, two types of measures, individual frequencies of social behaviors and sociability scores, were calculated for each child by summing across dyads and over time periods. Frequency measures of social behaviors were the number of initiations, the number of successful initiations (received a response within 10 seconds), the number of simple exchanges (2 units in length), the number of elaborated exchanges (more than 2 units in length), the number of vocalizations, smiles, or laughs, object offers, object receives, imitates other, physical aggression and toy takes directed to peers, and time in positive affective and agonistic exchanges. Sociability measures were the proportion of the group initiated to, engaged in any interaction, engaged in positive affective exchanges, engaged in agonistic exchanges, engaged in complementary and reciprocal play (levels 4 or 5), engaged in simple social play (level 3), engaged in simple exchanges and engaged in elaborated exchanges, and the proportion of all interactions initiated.

Two principal component analyses with varimax rotation were then used to derive independent factors for the normal and the disturbed groups. This analysis is presented in Table 1.

Individual styles of interaction with peers were more differentiated in the normal sample than in the disturbed. The first principal component, before rotation, accounted for 60.4% of the variance in the disturbed sample, as opposed to 39.7% of the variance in the normal sample. After the matrix was rotated, measures of sociability and measures of skillful prosocial interaction loaded on two independent factors in the normal sample, while in the disturbed sample measures of sociability and measures of skill loaded on the same factor. In both samples, object exchanges appeared as independent of skill and sociability. In the disturbed sample, frequency of initiations also loaded on the object exchange factor, while in the normal sample frequency of initiations and frequency of successful initiations loaded together. Agonistic behaviors appeared as a separate factor in both samples.

Given the small samples upon which these principal component analyses were based, the results can only be taken as tentative. The lack of differentiation of styles in approach to peers in the disturbed sample suggests that, for these children, peer interaction is an all or nothing phenomenon. If a child is going to interact with peers she or he is both sociable and skillful.

In the normal sample, sociability and skill appear as independent dimensions of a child's approach to peers. The independence of these factors is counter to previous research, which finds that sociability as measured by sociogram techniques is predicted by social skill (Asher, 1977). However, the independence of skill and sociability provides a partial explanation for the finding that increases in social skills via an intervention program do not necessarily change the sociometric ratings of social isolates (Renshaw & Asher, 1982). Perhaps, while skills may be perfected in dyadic interaction with a particular peer, the ability to engage with many different peers is a skill learned in other contexts or dependent on a particular orientation to peer relationships. A common evaluative response of older children to a more shy or reserved peer is, "She is really interesting, once you get to know her."

RELATIONSHIPS BETWEEN FRIENDSHIPS AND MOTHER–CHILD INTERACTION

The normal infant and toddler samples were observed at home 6 weeks prior to beginning daycare. Following a 15-minute warm up period, the mother was asked to complete a 10-minute questionaire and then resume her normal activities. The observer collected a 30-minute observation of the child's behavior with mother and toys. Twenty-three discrete social behaviors directed from the child to an adult, or an adult to a child, were coded as present or absent every 5 seconds, using a continuous coding format. Child behaviors were vocalize, smile, share a toy, touch, comply with a command, violate adult standards of behavior, cry, obstruct adult's task, demand, resist adult's command, and hit adult. Adult behaviors were talk, touch, cuddle, smile, direct attention to a toy, play with, comply with child's demand, reprimand, command, prohibit, restrain, and hit child. Interobserver reliability was established by two observers on ten independent subjects. Percent agreement (agreements/agreements + disagreements) was calculated for each time interval when adult–child interaction occurred, and then averaged across the whole observation for each subject. The range of mean percent agreement for the ten subjects was 86% to 93%, median 91%.

Using longhand transcripts of the coding sheets similar to the peer dyadic transcripts, each adult–child interaction was coded for content and duration. An interaction was defined as at least one behavior and a response by the partner in the same or subsequent 5-second interval. An interaction terminated when the partner did not respond with a social behavior in the same or subsequent 5-second unit. Prosocial interactions were coded as belonging to one of five mutually exclusive categories. These categories were

1. Simple affective exchanges—the child smiles and the adult smiles, cuddles, or talks.
2. Positive affective exchanges—the child smiles *and* either shares an object, vocalizes, touches, or engages in reciprocal play, and the adult smiles, cuddles, or talks.
3. Reciprocal play exchanges—the child and adult engage in play or a game.
4. Teaching exchanges—the child shares a toy or vocalizes, and the adult directs attention to a toy.
5. Simple verbal exchanges—the child and adult both vocalize without other social behavior.

Time spent in each category of interaction was calculated by summing the number of time intervals in all the interactions of that category.

The transcripts of one visit each of ten randomly selected subjects were independently coded by two coders. Percent agreement on the five categories ranged from 86% to 93%, median 89%.

Partial correlations, controlling for age of child, were computed between home visit scores and behaviors in day care. Children who engaged in frequent reciprocal play exchanges ($r(12) = .62$, $p < .05$), and had high frequencies of sharing toys with their mothers ($r(12) = .68$, $p < .01$) during the home visit, formed friendships with a high proportion of children in their group.

Although infants and toddlers who spent more time with adults in daycare spent less time in play with peers (Howes, 1982), pre-day-care mother–child harmonious interaction predicted both harmonious teacher–child interaction and a positive orientation to peers in day care. However, different elements of mother–child interaction predicted relationships with teachers versus peers. Time spent in positive affective exchanges with mother was related to time spent in positive affective exchanges with teachers ($r(12) = .85$, $p < .01$). Time spent in reciprocal play exchanges with mother was related to total frequency of prosocial bids to peers in daycare ($r(12) = .62$, $p < .05$). It is particularly interesting that the measure of positive affective exchanges with mother appears as an important predictor of relations with teachers, as it is conceptually linked to the measure "affective sharing" used to describe behavior in the preseparation episode of the Ainsworth strange situation (Waters et al., 1979). In both affective sharing and positive affective exchanges, infants are expressing positive emotions while engaging in complex interaction with mother. Waters et al. (1979) found affective sharing to differentiate securely and anxiously attached infants in the strange situation. Thus, it appears that infants who had established positive relationships with their mothers prior to day care were able to establish positive relationships with teachers in day care. The relationship between reciprocal play with mother, and both friendship formation and prosocial overtures to peers, suggests that the particular skills developed in mother–infant play are more important than the security implied in positive affective exchanges for facilitating peer interaction. The turn taking structure of reciprocal play with adults may be sufficiently similar to the turn taking structure of peer interaction to permit generalization of skills. Moreover, the experience of reciprocal play with mother is likely to develop an expectation that a playful overture will result in a positive interaction (Stern, 1979).

FRIENDSHIP AND PEER INTERACTION IN ABUSED TODDLERS

The study of peer interaction and friendship formation in abused children is particularly interesting because of its implications for the study of the relationship between parent–child and child–child relational and interactive systems. Abused children are known to have problematic relationships with at least one adult by virture of their diagnosis. The children I am now studying are all court referred to an intervention program because they have been severely physically abused or neglected. Additionally, research studies of parent–child attachment and interaction within abusing families report poor attachments and distorted interaction (Gaensbauer & Sands, 1979; Lewis & Schaeffer, 1981). Pastor (1981) reports that children rated as poorly attached as toddlers were initially less competent in peer interaction as preschoolers. Therefore, the first purpose of the abused toddlers project is to examine the question: Will abused children be able to establish relationships with peers or will they, due to their problematic parent–child relationships, be unable to do so? Previous research provides contradictory evidence. Lewis and Schaeffer (1981) found no differences in peer interaction between abused and control children, while George and Main (1979) report that abused children avoided their peers and behaved twice as aggressively toward them as did their controls. The abused children in the George and main study were in daycare centers for only abused children, while the abused children in the Lewis and Schaeffer study were integrated into a daycare center serving both abused and nonabused children. Perhaps the nonabused children served as peer therapists or models for the abused children.

The second purpose of the abused toddlers project is to investigate this hypothesis of nonabused toddler serving as intervention agents for their nonabused peers (Furman & Masters, 1980). The setting of the research is an intervention program that provides day care for both abused children and low income nonabused children. The children are divided into three homerooms. One homeroom consists of only abused children. The nonabused children are assigned to the other homerooms on the basis of available space. The children receive meals, baths, naps, and do quiet group play activities in their homerooms. During about half of the children's awake periods, all homerooms are brought together for "free mix." "Free mix" resembles free play periods at nursery schools and daycare. Children are free to choose a variety of play materials. While teachers supervise play, they do not structure activities. During "free mix" periods, abused and nonabused children have opportunities to interact.

Procedure

Observations of peer interaction and friendship formation are collected in several ways. Over a 10-week period, naturalistic observations are collected daily during the free mix period. These observations are made in two ways: Eight 5-minute observations on each target child are made using the identical codes and procedures for collecting, transcribing, and coding used in the patterns of friendship study.

Eight additional 5-minute observations are collected on each target child using a narrative method. Narratives are collected by an observer who records in short-hand verbatim fashion the content and context of all peer contacts. Peer contacts are defined according to Corsano's (1981) definition of an interactive unit. They are sequences of behavior that begin with the acknowledged presence of two children in an ecological area, and end with the physical movement of interactants from

Table 2
Measures of Peer Contacts

Easy entry into activity	Either child A is engaged in an activity, child B approaches, and both engage in joint activity, Child A and B turn parallel activity into a mutual games; or Child A tries to recruit Child B into the activity and Child B agrees.
Difficult entry into activity	Either Child A is engaged in an activity, Child B approaches, and is rebuffed; or Child A tries to recruit Child B and Child B ignores Child A.
Sustained play	The dyad persists in maintaining joint activity for an extended time, or stays together during several activities.
Shared meanings	The activity of the dyad reflects shared themes of meaning. Agonistic themes are object possession struggles and aggression. Cooperative themes include motor copy, run-chase, peek-a-boo, adult fantasy imitation.
Prosocial behavior	Comfort child who is hurt or distressed, help a child finish a task, teach another child.

the area, which terminates the originally initiated activity. If a peer contact continues beyond the end of the 5-minute observation, observers continue to record until the contact terminates. Immediately following the observation, the narratives are transcribed and elaborated. Each peer contact in the narrative is coded for the measures presented in Table 2. Reliability was established on 60 peer contacts of toddlers not included in the sample which were independently recorded and coded by two observers. Percent agreement ranged from .78 to 1.00 (median = .875). Reliability is being monitored throughout the data collection to maintain acceptable levels.

A third set of observations are made in a structured setting. All possible dyads of target children are observed for 20 minutes each in a laboratory playroom. Social interactive behaviors and emotional expressiveness are recorded using the same procedures for data collection, transcribing, and coding as the free mix code sheet observations. These observations are the basis of Robert Eldredge's dissertation, and will not be reported here. All observations were made by trained observers who were unaware of the abused or nonabused classification of the children.

In this chapter, I will report a preliminary analysis of free mix observations collected on the first cohort of toddlers in the study. The design of the project is to observe, using the three procedures, four cohorts, each consisting of five abused and five nonabused children selected to match the abused group on the basis of age, developmental status, and family background. The five abused toddlers in Cohort One are all physical abuse cases. They range in age from 16 to 28 months (median age 19 months). Four of the abused toddlers are female; one is male.

As all observations come from the free mix setting, 7 additional abused and 18 additional nonabused toddlers appeared as peer partners in the data. The 12 abused toddlers who appeared in the total sample range in age from 8 to 26 months (median age = 16.5 months); and the 23 nonabused toddlers range in age from 9 to 28 months (median age = 17 months). All the toddlers in the sample come from low income homes, and the majority from single parent homes. The children are Hispanic, black, anglo, and Asian in ethnic background.

Eighty-nine different dyads contributed to the code sheet observations, and 72 different dyads to the narrative observations. Sixty-five dyads appeared in both code sheet and narrative records.

Friendship Formation

Friendships were defined and identified from free mix code sheet data using the same criteria of friendship as in the patterns of friendship project: mutual preference, mutual enjoyment, and skillful interaction. A comparison of friendship formation both within the different groups of the abused toddler study and between the abused toddler study and the patterns of friendship study is presented in Table 3.

Table 3
Comparison of Friendship Formation in Abused and Patterns of Friendship in Study

		Friendships	
	Number of dyads	Number	Proportion
Abused study total	89	3	.03
Abused–Abused	19	1	.05
Nonabused–Nonabused	40	2	.05
Same homeroom	27	2	.07
Different homeroom	13	0	0
Abused–Nonabused	30	0	0
Patterns of Friendship			
Time Period One			
Total	122	8	.07
Toddlers	35	4	.11
Normal	22	2	.09
Disturbed	13	2	.15

Friendships appeared in similar proportion in both the abused group and in the nonabused dyads who shared a homeroom. No friendships were found between abused and nonabused children, or between non-abused children who did not share a homeroom.

The children in the abused study formed only one quarter as many friendships as did the toddlers in the patterns of friendship study during the first time period of that study. There are several possible explana-tions for this difference. Program, teaching styles, and philosophy dif-fered somewhat between settings. Although little research has been conducted on the influence of adult direction on peer interaction, we can speculate that, more or less, teacher intervention or direct teaching about peer interaction may change the nature of the relationships formed. Analysis of the narrative observations in the abused study showed that teachers were five times as likely to intervene into a peer contact if the contact was between abused–nonabused toddlers than if the contact was between abused toddlers or between nonabused tod-dlers (χ^2 (1) = 5.17, p < .05). Interventions were just as likely to involve prosocial as conflict strategies. Therefore, teachers were monitoring peer contacts between abused and nonabused toddlers and changing the frequency of their intervention on the basis of their knowledge of the child's abused–nonabused classification.

The toddlers in the abused study were from lower SES back-grounds than the toddlers in the patterns of friendship study. Social class has been reported to change the character of school age friend-ships (Berg & Medrich, in press), but little is known about the influence of social class on young children's peer interaction.

Alternatively, the difference may be an artifact of the observation procedure. If friendships had been identified from behaviors within the homeroom instead of within the free mix area, more friendships might have been identified. Support for this explanation comes from the find-ing that all friendships were formed between members of the same homeroom.

Complexity and Content of Peer Interaction

Comparisons of complexity and content in peer interaction were drawn from both the narrative and code sheet observations. These com-parisons are presented in Table 4. The 95 peer contacts described in the narratives were proportionally divided between abused–abused, non-abused–nonabused, and abused–nonabused contacts. This distribu-tion suggests that abused toddlers were no more likely than nonabused toddlers to either ignore or to engage with peers. Contacts between abused and nonabused toddlers were five times more frequent than

Table 4
Comparisons of Peer Interaction by Dyad Composition

	Homeroom			
	Same		Different	
Peer Interaction	Abused	Nonabused	Abused–Nonabused	Nonabused–Nonabused
Proportion of contacts	.29	.26	.36	.07
Proportion of dyads	.22	.29	.31	.15
Number of interactions	17	26	4	5
Success rate of initiation	.24	.46	.36	.38
Proportion of contacts with				
Easy entry	.39	.32	.15	.14
Difficult entry	.07	.16	.24	.29
Number of simple exchanges	2.3	4.9	1.6	.9
Number of elaborated exchanges	10.8	11.1	2.2	4.1
Proportion of contacts with sustained play	.32	.04	.03	00
Time in complementary and reciprocal peer play	5.5	4.3	1.3	1.5
Proportion of contacts with complementary and reciprocal peer play	.40	.19	.14	.00
Proportion of contracts with				
shared meaning	.46	.32	.67	.29
cooperative themes	.32	.20	.29	00
agonistic themes	.14	.12	.38	.29
Number of agonistic exchanges	2.7	1.1	3.1	2.4
Proportion of contacts with				
agonistic behavior	.30	.24	.50	.43
physical agression	.11	.08	.21	.14
toy take	.19	.16	.29	.29
Frequency of aggression	5.5	4.3	6.5	3.9
Frequency of toy take	3.2	3.6	5.9	1.9
Number of positive affective exchanges	4.9	5.9	3.4	3.2
Proportion of contacts with prosocial behavior	.04	.04	.00	.00

contacts between nonabused toddlers from different homerooms (χ^2 (1) = 17.05, p < .001). Only seven (7%) of the peer contacts were between nonabused toddlers from different dyads. This pattern was also found in the code sheet observations. Thirteen different dyads (15%) were involved in abused–nonabused interactions, as opposed to an average of 25 (27%) different dyads in the other categories. As will be described below, peer contacts between abused–nonabused dyads were not particularly smooth or harmonious, but the toddlers chose to engage rather than to ignore each other as did the nonabused dyads from different homerooms.

When rates and complexities of interaction, that is, actually engaged in social bids and responses as opposed to merely being in contact, are considered, the toddlers from the same homerooms demonstrated greater social competencies than toddlers from different homerooms. Toddlers in the abused and nonabused same homeroom groups engaged in more interactions than toddlers in the abused–nonabused and nonabused different homeroom groups (F(3, 88) - 3.80, p < .01, Scheffe = .05). The increased rates of interaction are partially explained by the finding that same homeroom dyads had a higher proportion of peer contacts with easy entry into joint activity ($\chi^2(1)$ = 3.87, p < .05). Abused–abused dyads had a smaller proportion of peer contacts with difficult entry into joint activity than any other group (Fisher Exact = .05). The results suggest that same homeroom dyads were able to form relationships that facilitated joint activity and peer interaction.

Toddlers from the same homeroom had a greater number of elaborated exchanges than toddlers from different homerooms. Abused and non-abused toddlers from the same homeroom did not differ in number of elaborated exchanges (F(3, 88) = 4.11, p < .01, Scheffe = .05). Elaborated exchanges are interactions that are sustained beyond a simple social bid and response. Another measure of sustained interaction is sustained activity, which is the extent to which a peer dyad persists in maintaining joint activity or a sequence of joint activities. Abused dyads had a greater proportion of contacts with sustained play than any other group ($\chi^2(3)$ = 12.15, p < .01).

Difference in time in complementary and reciprocal peer play between toddlers from same and different homerooms did not reach significance (p = .07), but abused dyads had a higher proportion of contacts with complementary and reciprocal peer play than any other group ($\chi^2(2)$ = 10.84, p < .01).

These results suggest that one of the goals of the intervention program for the abused toddler was achieved. The abused toddlers were able to form peer relationships and engage in skillful and sustained interaction. Informal observations and conversations with the staff suggest that the abused toddlers were simultaneously forming attachments to their adult caregivers. It is beyond the scope of our data base to determine if the peer relationships were mediated by or independent of the children's attachments to adults. Since facilitating peer relationships was a goal of the intervention program, the abused toddlers may have received more structuring of and reinforcement for peer interaction during homeroom periods than the nonabused toddlers received in their own homerooms. If this was so, it could partially explain the greater number of peer contacts with sustained play and complementary and reciprocal play in the abused dyads.

Toddlers in the same homeroom had more positive affective exchanges than toddlers in different rooms ($F(3, 88) = 7.78$, $p < .01$). Abused–abused toddlers were no different from non-abused toddlers from the same homeroom. Toddlers from the same homerooms were the only dyads to demonstrate prosocial behaviors—that is, comforting, helping, or teaching the other peer. Toddlers in both the abused–abused and nonabused same homeroom were no different in proportion of contacts with prosocial behaviors.

These results add more strength to the general trend that toddlers, regardless of their abused or nonabused classification, who shared a homeroom interacted in friendlier and more complex ways than toddlers who belonged in different homerooms. This suggests that the toddlers may have perceived a sense of "primary groupness" or "family" based on shared experiences of meals, baths, naps, and quiet group activities. Perhaps it was this type of mundane experiences that facilitated the bonding described by Freud and Dann (1951). It is interesting that such behavior occurs outside of the toddler's primary peer group, since their own experiences of being victims of physical aggression occured within the family. Perhaps aggression directed outside of the primary peer group is safer than aggression inside the peer group for children who are in the process of forming relationships. Lee (1973) in an early study of social networks within an infant group, reported that one particularly aggressive child was avoided by the other infants in the group. Perhaps the children learned that aggression would disrupt relationships.

Alternatively, aggression may be considered exploratory behavior. Certainly the nonabused toddlers encountered by the abused children in the free mix setting were less familiar than the other abused toddlers. Perhaps the increase in aggressive contacts were trial and error behavior preliminary to establishing routines for interaction or to establishing dominance heirarchies. However, this explanation does not explain why the abused–nonabused dyads were more aggressive than the equally unfamiliar nonabused dyads from different rooms. An alternative explanation would suggest that, because the free mix setting is a less controlled environment than the homeroom, the abused children become involved in aggressive contacts because they have fewer internal controls on aggressive behaviors than the nonabused children. Free mix involves more children than homeroom periods. It is also noisier. Adults caregivers talk to each other and are less focused on the children. All these factors contribute to fewer external behavioral constraints. In this situation, abused children were more likely than nonabused to become involved in aggressive peer contacts.

Abused–nonabused dyads had a higher proportion of contacts in which a meaning or theme was shared (a concept developed by Brenner & Mueller, 1982) than any other group ($\chi^2(3) = 6.70$, $p < .05$). When the content of the theme was analyzed, this difference could be accounted for by agonistic themes. Abused–nonabused dyads had a higher proportion of contacts with an agonistic shared theme than any other group ($\chi^2(3) = 8.12$, $p < .05$). Toddlers from different homerooms (abused–nonabused dyads and nonabused from different homerooms,) had a greater proportion of contacts with agonistic behavior, shared or not, than toddlers from the same homeroom ($\chi^2(2) = 11.31$, $p < .001$). Abused–nonabused dyads had higher proportions of contacts with agonistic behavior than nonabused dyads from different homerooms ($\chi^2(1) = 14.78$, $p < .001$). Abused–nonabused dyads and nonabused dyads from different homerooms had equal proportions of contacts with toy taking, but abused–nonabused dyads had higher proportions of contacts with physical aggression than nonabused dyads from different homerooms (Fisher Exact $p = .05$). There were no differences between groups in number of agonistic exchanges, frequency of aggression, or frequency of toy taking. These results suggest that the abused toddlers are either initiating physical aggression or are being victims of physical aggression in their peer contacts with nonabused children. Future analyses will separate the roles of the abused and nonabused toddler in the aggressive contacts.

These preliminary results suggest two conclusions. First, toddlers in the abused sample, as well as the nonabused, were establishing relationships and engaging in peer interaction. For both the abused and nonabused toddlers, relationships were friendlier and interaction more complex when dyads shared a homeroom. Nonabused toddlers from different homerooms tended to ignore each other and have few peer contacts, while abused–nonabused dyads tended to be disruptive and physically aggressive.

CONCLUSIONS

The results of these two research programs examining young children's friendships and their antecedents suggest two conclusions. First, both normally developing children and emotionally disturbed children are capable of forming preferential emotional bonds or friendships. There are differences between the emotionally disturbed children and the normally developing children in their approach to peers. Emotionally disturbed children may be less differentiated in skill and sociability styles, and they do form relationships less frequently, but once friendships are established they are remarkably similar groups.

Second, some aspects of the parent–child relationship appear to be transferred to the peer relationship. Normally developing children who had experienced reciprocal play interactions with their mothers were more peer oriented and more likely to form friendships. Abused children engaged in higher levels of physical aggression with peers outside their primary groups.

REFERENCES

Ainsworth, M., Blehar, M., Waters, E., & Wall, S. (1978). *Patterns of attachment.* Hillsdale, NJ: Erlbaum.

Asher, S. (1977). Children's friendships in school settings. In L. Katz (Ed.), *Current topics in early childhood education.* Norwood, NJ: Ablex.

Brenner, J., & Mueller, E. (1982). Shared meaning in boy toddler peer relations. *Child Development, 53,* 380–391.

Berg, M., & Medrich, E. (in press). Children in four neighborhoods. *Environment and behavior.*

Campbell, S., & Cluss, P. (1982). Peer relationships of young children with behavior problems. In Rubin, K. & Ross, H. (Eds.), *Peer relations and social skills in childhood.* New York: Springer-Verlag.

Corsaro, W. (1981). Friendship in the nursery school. In S. Asher & J. Gottman (Eds.), *The development of children's friendships.* New York: Cambridge.

Cowen, E., Pederson, A., Babigian, H., Izzo, L. & Trost, M. (1973). Long-term follow-up of early detected vulnerable children. *Journal of Consulting and Clinical Psychology, 41,* 438–446.

Doyle, A., Connolly, J., & Rivest, L. (1980). The effect of playmate familiarity on the social interaction of young children. *Child Development, 51,* 217–223.

Freud, A., & Dann, S. (1951). An experiment in group upbringing. *Psychoanalytic Study of the Child,* 197–268.

Furman, W., & Masters, J. (1980). Peer interactions, sociometric status, and resistance to deviation in young children. *Developmental Psychology, 16,* 229–336.

Gaensbauer, T., & Sands, K. (1979). Distorted affective communications in abused/neglected infants and their potential impact on caretakers. *Journal of the American Academy of Child Psychiatry, 18,* 236–250.

George, C., & Main, M. (1979). Social interactions of young abused children. *Child Development, 50,* 306–318.

Hay, D., Pedersen, J., & Nash, A. (1982). Dyadic interaction in the first year of life. In K. Rubin and H. Ross (Eds.), *Peer Relationships and Social Skills in Childhood.* New York: Springer-Verlag.

Howes, C. (1980). Peer play scale as an index of complexity of peer interaction. *Developmental Psychology, 16*, 371–372.

Howes, C. (1983). Patterns of friendship. *Child Development, 54*, 1041–1053.

Howes, C., & Mueller, D. (1980). Early peer friendships. Their significance for development. In W. Spiel (Ed.), *The psychology of the twentieth century*. Zurich: Kindler.

Howes, C. (1982). *Individual differences in young children's peer interaction and friendship formation*. Paper presented at the International Conference on Infant Studies, Austin, TX.

Ispa, J. (1981). Peer support among soviet daycare toddlers. *International Journal of Behavioral Development, 4*, 255–269.

Lee, L. C. (1973). *Social encounters of infants*. Paper presented at the International Society for the Study of Behavioral Development, Ann Arbor, MI.

Lewis, M., & Feiring, C. (1979). The child's social network. In M. Lewis and L. Rosenblum (Eds.), *The Child and its Family*. New York: Plenum.

Lewis, M., & Schaeffer, S. (1981). Peer behavior and mother-infant interaction in maltreated children. In M. Lewis & L. Rosenblum (Eds.), *The Uncommon Child*. New York: Plenum.

Mueller, E., & Vandell, D. (1978). Infant-infant interaction. In J. D. Osofsky (Ed.), *Handbook of infant development*. New York: Wiley.

Pastor, D. (1981). The quality of mother-infant attachment and its relationship to toddler's initial sociability with peers. *Developmental Psychology, 17*, 326–335.

Renshaw, P., & Asher, S. (1982). Social competence and peer status. In K. Rubin & H. Ross (Eds.), *Peer relationships and social skills in childhood*. New York: Springer-Verlag.

Rotheram, M., & Phinney, J. (1981). *Patterns of social overtures among preschool friends and non-friends*. Paper presented at the Society for Research in Child Development.

Rubenstein, J., & Howes, C. (1976). The effect of peers on toddler interaction with mother and toys. *Child Development, 47*, 597–605.

Rubin, Z. (1980). *Children's friendships*. Cambridge, MA: Harvard University Press.

Stern, D. (1977). *The first relationship*. Cambridge, MA: Harvard University Press.

Vandell, P., & Wilson, K. (1982). Social interaction in the first year. In K. Rubin & H. Ross (Eds.), *Peer relationships and social skills in childhood*. New York: Springer-Verlag.

Waters, E. (1978). The reliability and stability of individual differences in infant-mother attachment. *Child Development, 49*, 483–494.

Waters, E., Wippman, J., & Sroufe, A. (1979). Attachment, positive affect, and competence in the peer group. *Child Development, 50*, 821–829.

11

Social Interactions of Handicapped Preschoolers in Developmentally Integrated and Segregated Settings: A Study of Generalization Effects*

Phillip S. Strain

My colleagues in this book have described, with great sensitivity and rigor, the here-and-now regarding the development of friendships and how this important peer relation occurs (or does not occur) among normal and handicapped children. In this chapter, I would like to explore what may be if one takes an active, interventionist's approach to the *purposeful* development of social relations between normal and handicapped children. While this chapter, like several others in the volume, has a single study as its focus, it is important also to frame the present outcome study in a conceptual and historical context. Therefore, I would like to preface my data presentation with a brief discussion of a behavioral approach to peer relations, handicapped children's peer relations, and specific intervention efforts that led to the current "friendship-building" intervention.

BEHAVIORAL APPROACH TO PEER RELATIONS

Two characteristics of the behavioral approach to peer relations are most relevant to this discussion. These are (a) precise and intensive

* Support for this chapter was provided, in part, by Contract No. 300–82–0368 (Early Childhood Research Institute) from the Department of Education to the University of Pittsburgh. However, the opinions expressed herein do not necessarily reflect the position or policy of the U.S. Department of Education, and no official endorsement by the Department should be inferred.

measurement of observable, ongoing social exchanges, and (b) careful analysis of events and behaviors that co-occur with social exchanges.

Precise and Intensive Measurement of Behavior

Because social exchanges are so complex, it is necessary that their assessment and treatment be grounded in a measurement methodology that insures unambiguous analysis. Agreement between observers (i.e., two or more persons agree that they see the same interpersonal skills at the same point in time) is essential, particularly when we are concerned with competencies that are open to multiple, sometimes conflicting interpretations. Of course, the development of observational systems that can produce close agreement between observers is a longstanding tradition in the behavioral approach to peer relations.

Unambiguous measurement first becomes critical to the interventionist at the level of target behavior selection. If the goals and objectives related to social relations cannot be precisely defined and measured, the treatment cannot be faithfully implemented or evaluated. It is very doubtful that good instruction can follow on the heels of ill-defined objectives.

Table 1 below offers some examples of social skill definitions found in behavioral treatment studies.

In addition to their complexity, social relations present a significant measurement challenge, due to the extreme variability in the performance of skills across days and settings. Therefore, brief and few behavior samples are difficult to interpret because of the notorious instability of social behavior. We know, for example, that a host of subtle environmental events can have a profound impact on the daily rate, duration, and complexity of social behavior. An abbreviated list of these "controlling" events include: (a) number and kinds of toys available, (b) sex and developmental level of children available for interaction, (c) teacher proximity, (d) density of children in the environment, (e) teacher's instructions to play together, and (f) availability of designated play areas (e.g., doll corner, dress-up area, kitchen area). In treatment settings, the control of these events is not logistically feasible, and probably not desirable if one wants to know the level and type of social skills produced in a *noncontrived* setting. Given the unpredictable influence of the above-mentioned events, multiple behavior samples, distributed across several consecutive days, must be used to insure the representativeness of the data. For assessment and treatment purposes, the intensive (daily) measurement of target skills associated with the behavioral approach provides a reliable basis for the interpretation of children's social relations.

Careful Analysis of Co-occuring Events and Behaviors

A fair assumption is that children's social skills are influenced by the social context of assessment. That is, the amount and quality of manifested skills can vary in accordance with the social responsiveness or "support" available in any particular setting. For example, any assessment of a handicapped child's social skills in settings populated exclusively by handicapped children will invariably result in underestimations of competence (Strain & Fox, 1981). Where available social partners are not generally responsive to peers, the assessment of social skills is a bit like measuring telephone-answering behavior in a setting without telephones.

In order to take into account the influence of social partners on target children's interpersonal skills, it is necessary to collect data on specific behaviors as they occur as "initiated" or "responded" events in an interaction sequence. Previously, ourselves and other behavioral researchers (Strain & Timm, 1974; Greenwood, Walker, Todd, & Hops, 1979) have demonstrated the validity of the following definitions for initiated and responded events:

Initiated—the target child or an interacting peer emits any of the predesignated behaviors (for example, as in Table 1), either 3 seconds *before* or *after* another child's social behavior.

Responded—the target child or an interacting peer emits any of the predesignated behaviors (for example, as in Table 1) *within* 3 seconds following another child's social behavior.

By assessing target skills according to their distribution as initiated or responded events, interventionists can answer the following vital questions regarding social skill assessment and intervention effects:

(a) To what extent do peers respond in a positive fashion to the social initiations of target children?

(b) To what extent do peers initiate positive contact with target children?

(c) To what extent do target children respond in a positive fashion to the social initiations of peers?

(d) To what extent do target children initiate positive contact with peers?

(e) Are patterns of social contact more reciprocal (i.e., initiations typically are followed by positive responses) following intervention?

Table 1
Sample Definitions of Socially Isolate and Cooperative Behaviors

Author(s)	Behavior Category	Definition
Dy, Strain, Fullerton & Stowitschek (1981)	Motor–gestural	• This included all positive physical contacts, such as brushing another person's arm while reaching for something; cooperative use of an object, such as looking at a book with another person, exchanging pens, taking turns placing puzzle pieces; touching and/or manipulating the same object or parts of the same object; all other gestural movement directed to another person, such as handing an object, pointing, motioning to "Come" or "Go away," shaking head to indicate "Yes" or "No," and waving.
	Vocal–verbal	• This included all positive vocal expressions or verbalizations which, by virtue of content, e.g., "Hey you," "Uh-huh" (while nodding), clearly indicated that the person was directing the utterance to another individual.
Gable, Hendrickson, & Strain (1978)	Approach Gestures	• Consisted of any deliberate behavior of the child which involved the hand(s), arm(s), or other body parts in a motion directed to another child, e.g., an inward circular hand and arm motion, repeated bending and straightening of forefinger while arm extended towards a peer.
	Positive Physical Contact	• Consisted of any deliberate behavior which brought the hand(s), arm(s), feet or other parts of the body into direct physical contact with another child in a positive manner, e.g., a soft touch, a pat, a hug, stroking or grasping-shaking hands, in a positive manner.

	Cooperative Play	• Consisted of any discrete interactive pattern engaged in by two or more children, e.g., mutual playing and/or physically interacting with the same object or materials, or set of objects materials with a common purpose.
Ragland, Kerr, & Strain (1981)	Ball play	• This included the following motor behaviors: passing a ball to a peer and catching a ball thrown by a peer.
	Physical assistance	• This included helping a peer onto and off some climbing apparatus.
Strain & Ezzell (1978)	Social Isolation	• Sitting idly in a secluded part of a room, ignoring social initiations by peers and adults, remaining on the periphery of a group, and physical withdrawal from strangers.
Strain, Shores, & Kerr (1976)	Motor–Gestural	• All movements emitted that cause a child's head, arms, or feet to come into direct contact with the body of another child; that involve waving or extending arms directly toward another child; or that involve placing of hands directly upon a material, toy or other movable apparatus that is being touched or manipulated by another child.
	Positive	• Touch with hand or hands; hug; holding hands; kiss; wave; all cooperative responses involved with sharing a toy or material.

Limitations of Behavioral Approach

With few exceptions, behavioral interventions for improving children's peer relations have yet to produce other than transient, setting-specific behavior change. Moreover, it has become clear that promoting substantial increases in the frequency of children's globally defined social behaviors cannot be equated with making the social interactions of target youngsters "look like" or "function like" those of nonhandicapped peers. Finally, we have found (via sequential analysis of observational data) that adult behaviors such as prompts and reinforcing events in treatment studies, and in the more natural course of events, can both increase *and* limit the amount, duration, and complexity of interaction between children (Strain, Shores, & Timm, 1977).

While this summary is not overly encouraging, it is possible to pinpoint a number of conceptual and assessment limitations that very likely contributed to the disappointing outcome of current treatment approaches.

First, early efforts to improve handicapped children's peer relations promoted a "cart-before-the-horse" approach that led to the application of behavioral technologies prior to a full understanding of what competent behavior was in the first place. Even in its best understood and dissected form, behavioral procedures will never be more than a cluster of teaching tactics to be applied to a sequence of target behaviors. It is ironic that the sequence of behavior, logically the foundation of sciences dealing with the analysis of behavior, would be so little understood. Previously, it was suggested that failures to effectively teach social skills were a function of faulty procedures (cf. Tremblay, 1981). While that may be the case, it is also likely that the a priori selection of treatment targets has resulted in: (a) the inadvertant choice of nonfunctional behavior targets, and/or (b) the choice of treatment targets that have essential behavioral prerequisites, behavioral prerequisites that are *not* included in the intervention program.

Second, earlier research promoted a rather narrow conceptualization of peer relations as a bundle of operant responses with obvious antecedents and consequences. And although they (antecedents and consequences) may be there, no one using interaction data as the units of measurement has yet to find them. Notwithstanding the apparent absence of clearly identifiable antecedents and consequences, an array of antecedents (verbal prompts, physical prompts, instructions) and consequences (praise statements, token reinforcement, edibles) have been applied to discrete behaviors with the predictable outcome— short, discrete interaction episodes that bear little resemblance to nontrained interaction patterns (Strain & Kerr, 1981).

Third, and finally, the behavioral literature in general has emphasized singular solutions to what is an exceedingly complex phenomenon. The poorly developed peer relations of handicapped children can emerge and be maintained by a variety of biological, interpersonal, and environmental events. Some children may have suffered such a profound insult to their central nervous systems that they cannot readily engage in those basic social exchange behaviors (e.g., passing a toy, praising another's efforts, greeting a friend) that comprise social interactions. At the other end of the etiological continuum, children may be neurologically intact but, because of their classification as handicapped, they become the objects of verbal abuse, scapegoating, and social rejection by their peers (see Gottlieb, 1975). Of course, overt rejection and abusiveness often set into motion a vicious cycle in which the victims of negative stereotypes engage in retaliatory behavior, which in turn makes them even less accepted. Against this complex background of skill deficits interacting with peer rejection, it should not be too surprising that interventions focused *exclusively* on skill building with handicapped children are less than a complete success.

HANDICAPPED CHILDREN'S PEER RELATIONS

Poorly developed social skills, peer rejection, and few friendships are major defining characteristics of handicapped children. Furthermore, they are *persistent* characteristics, not subject to spontaneous recovery or easy treatment. While the case has been made by others in this symposium (cf. Berndt and Furman) of the developmental significance of friendships for normally developing children, it may be argued that friendships are even more important for handicapped children's language, cognitive, sexual, and academic development.

A number of behavior patterns commonly found among handicapped children make them particularly vulnerable to not having positive social relations and to experiencing the long-term negative consequences of the absence of friends. For example, as Strain and Kerr (1981) suggest, handicapped children:

1. Do not engage generally in behaviors that are reinforcing to peers (e.g., verbal compliments, offering to share prized items). As a consequence, handicapped children seldom are sought out for interaction by developmentally more advanced youngsters.
2. Do not respond generally to the infrequent approach behaviors of normally developing children. As a result, handicapped chil-

dren may quickly extinguish attempts to interact and establish a friendship.
3. Often misread subtle social cues and, as a result, behave in ways that are viewed as bizarre and unpredictable.

The social isolation and active rejection that often results from the above listed behavior patterns set into motion a far too predictable chain of events, with handicapped children having limited access to more appropriate and advanced behavior models, spontaneous peer tutoring, and encouragement for good performance. For children with multiple, often severe skill deficits, these missed social and educational opportunities portend an ever increasing discrepancy between their social repertoire and that of nonhandicapped children.

INTERVENTIONS TO IMPROVE HANDICAPPED CHILDREN'S SOCIAL RELATIONS

There is a substantial literature which shows rather impressive changes in normally developing children's social skills following systematic training (e.g., Hops & Greenwood, 1981). Coaching children in certain skills (Asher & Taylor, 1977), and establishing cooperative learning experiences (Slavin, 1980) have all been used successfully to increase nonhandicapped children's social participation and relations. There is also some evidence that long-term behavior change may result from such interventions (e.g., O'Connor, 1972). The treatment outcome data on handicapped children (i.e., children with cognitive impairments or severe behavior disorders) is far less impressive.

There have been three primary forms of behavioral intervention designed to improve social relations in young handicapped children. These include the use of adult (usually teacher) prompting and social reinforcement, the provision of particular toys or activities that set the occasion for social interaction, and the use of peers as agents of change. As noted by Strain and Fox (1981), the three modes of treatment represent, in the above order, both a historical trend as well as a movement toward more naturalistic methods of treating social withdrawal.

An impressive number of studies has shown that contingent teacher attention, along with occasional prompts, can successfully modify children's isolate behavior (e.g., Allen, Hart, Buell, Harris, & Wolf, 1964; Hart, Reynolds, Baer, Brawley, & Harris, 1968; Strain, Shores, & Kerr, 1976; Strain & Timm, 1974; Strain & Wiegerink, 1975; Timm, Strain, & Eller, 1979; Whitman, Mercurio, & Caponigri, 1970). Children treated successfully include those diagnosed as mentally retarded, behaviorally disordered, learning disabled, and disadvantaged. Several commonalities are evident among these adult-mediated studies. First, all the change agents were highly skilled behavioral practitioners. Second, all children engaged in some positive interactions with peers prior to treatment. Thus, in most studies it was not necessary to use intensive prompting or some elaborate shaping procedure to set the occasion for positive responding that could then be reinforced. Third, several types of collateral behavior change have been reported. Without direct programming, negative behaviors of target children have been reduced during intervention conditions (e.g., Strain & Timm, 1974). Also, a "spillover" of treatment effect has been noted with selected target children and peers. Specifically, Strain and Timm (1974) and Strain et al. (1976) found that children in the same setting who were not directly reinforced also increased their level of positive social behavior. Target children and peers for whom "spillover" effects obtained were all characterized by (a) some level of positive behavior during baseline conditions, (b) a generalized imitative repertoire, (c) a history of response acquisition using contingent social attention, and (d) physical proximity to reinforced children. Finally, none of these studies show that long-term behavior change followed treatment.

Efforts to improve the social relations of handicapped children by providing toys or activities that set the occasion for social interaction have been limited in number. Quilitch and Risley (1972) demonstrated that various commercially available toys clearly were divisible into those which did and did not promote social interaction. Several studies have been done in which training isolate children to play competently with certain toys or equipment resulted in a collateral increase in social interaction. For example, Buell, Stoddard, Harris, and Baer (1968) modified the socially isolate behavior of a 3-year-old girl by prompting and reinforcing her use of outdoor play equipment. Similar results were obtained by Johnston, Kelly, Harris, and Wolf (1966), who increased a withdrawn boy's level of positive social interaction by reinforcing his use of a jungle gym.

Use of play activities as an antecedent to social interaction has involved the provision of interdependent role behaviors to target children and peers. During a story-time period that immediately preceeded a free-play session, Strain and Wiegerink (1976) assigned a character role taken from children's stories to each preschool child present. If the story being read on a particular day was Goldilocks and the Three Bears, character roles would include Goldilocks, Grandmother, Papa Bear, Mama Bear, etc. During the course of the story-telling, each child was prompted and reinforced for engaging in two role-related behaviors. No programmed intervention took place during free-play. Results indicated a threefold increase in the amount of time the children engaged in social play during the free-play period. These results were replicated by Strain (1975) and Shores, Hester, and Strain (1976).

Although the provision of certain play materials and activities has produced substantial changes in the social behaviors of withdrawn preschool children, these strategies have not been wholly effective or efficient. For example, quite transient behavior change has accompanied the use of play materials and interdependent activities. Strain (1975) and Strain and Wiegerink (1976) report that the vast majority of positive social behaviors accompanying the provision of interdependent activities occurred within the first 5-minute segment of daily, 25-minute free-play sessions.

A final, and most critical limitation of activity-based interventions concerns the logistical feasibility of applying these tactics in classroom situations with several withdrawn children. The provision of interdependent activities has been characterized by teachers' close monitoring of target children only.

In part as a response to the shortcomings of earlier intervention strategies, recent research efforts have focused on the utilization of peers as social behavior intervention agents. The available literature on the use of peers as intervention agents for handicapped children has focused primarily on peer social initiations, a tactic employed in the study that follows.

SOCIAL INTERACTIONS OF HANDICAPPED PRESCHOOLERS IN DEVELOPMENTALLY INTEGRATED AND SEGREGATED SETTINGS: A STUDY OF GENERALIZATION EFFECTS

A consistent and troublesome finding in the literature on children's social behavior modification is the absence of generalized behavior change. Rather transient, setting-specific treatment effects are the norm, even where functional skills are taught (Hendrickson, Strain, Shores, & Tremblay, 1981), where naturalistic treatments have been used (Strain, Kerr, & Ragland, 1979), and where procedures to promote generalization are included in the treatment package (Strain, 1981).

In the more notable examples of the absence of post-treatment effects, researchers have used developmentally segregated settings (only developmentally disabled children present) to study target behavior generalization. Strain and Kerr (1981) suggest that developmentally segregated settings may inhibit post-treatment responding, due to handicapped peers' lack of social responsiveness. Since sustained social contact, by definition, demands skillful behavior by at least two persons, it seems reasonable to predict that trained children's social behavior may be actively ignored and quickly extinguished by non-trained, skill-deficient classmates (Strain, 1981).

Of course, the potential deleterious effect of developmentally seg-regated programming is particularly relevant to the national movement toward and debate about educating disabled children with nonhan-dicapped peers. To date, only one study has been conducted which systematically compares the effects of segregated and integrated pro-gramming on generalized behavior change. This study was designed to test the notion that a developmentally integrated setting would yield superior generalized behavior change than would a developmentally segregated setting (Strain, 1983). Four autistic boys served as target subjects. Each day, three 20-minute play sessions were conducted. One setting was devoted to peer-mediated training, one to integrated gener-alization assessment, and one to segregated generalization assessment. The order of the three sessions was counterbalanced across the days of the study. The study employed a multiple baseline design across sub-jects to demonstrate experimental control over the subjects' positive social interaction, and a combined multiple baseline and simultaneous treatment (generalization in this case) design to evaluate the impact of developmentally segregated and developmentally integrated settings on generalized behavior change. During the Baseline condition, each boy engaged in low levels of positive interaction during all sessions. During the Peer Social Initiations I condition, each boy was exposed sequentially to a peer-mediated treatment package. Only when the boys were exposed to the intervention did their level of positive interaction increase during training sessions. For each boy, clearly superior gener-alization effects were obtained during integrated sessions. In the final condition of the study, the treatment continued without alteration. However, now *both* generalization sessions were integrated. The simul-taneous generalization component of the design showed that integrated session data was clearly superior to segregated session data.

The present study was designed to replicate and expand the find-ings of this prior study by: (a) exposing a larger number of subjects to the peer-mediated intervention, (b) examining the effects of interaction history on social behavior change by assessing children's behavior in developmentally-segregated settings with unfamiliar peers, and (3) ex-amining the effects of trained peers on the generalization of target chil-dren's social behavior in integrated settings.

Subjects

The primary subjects were 6 autistic-like boys who were enrolled in a specialized class that served 12 severely disabled children, age 3 to

6 years. Each boy was identified by his teacher as having significant deficits in peer social skills. Pre-baseline observations confirmed the teacher's judgments. Like the target subjects, the remaining six children in the specialized class (3 girls, 3 boys) engaged in some form of stereotypic behavior, and two of the peers were self-injurious. Assessments using the McCarthy Scales of Children's Abilities showed that none of the youngsters exhibited age-appropriate skills in verbal, cognitive, or social domains. On the average, the children functioned developmentally below a 24-month level. In one treatment generalization setting, this intact group was assessed during a brief play period.

In another of the generalization settings, the six target children were integrated with six similarly handicapped children who were enrolled in another classroom in the same school building. Prior to this study, children in these two classes were not a part of any common activity. In still another generalization setting, the six boys were integrated for a brief play period with six normally developing kindergarten boys. In a final generalization setting, the six boys were integrated for another brief play period with six different, normally developing kindergarten boys who were instructed to "try their best to get the new children to play with you."

Settings

This study took place in five distinct settings. First, all peer social initiation treatment sessions were conducted in a 3 × 4 m playroom that was equipped with toys and athletic materials available to the target subjects in their classroom. Four generalization assessment sessions took place daily. These settings were as follows:

1. *Indigenous Setting* (developmentally segregated)—the six target boys were observed during a 6-minute play period with their six classmates.
2. *New Developmentally Segregated Setting*—the six boys were observed during a 6-minute play period with six similarly handicapped children who were enrolled in a separate specialized class.
3. *New Developmentally Integrated Setting*—the six boys were observed during a 6-minute play period with six normally developing kindergarten boys.
4. *New Developmentally Integrated with Trained Peers Setting*—the six boys were observed during a 6-minute play period with six different normally developing kindergarten boys who had been instructed by their teacher to "try their best to get the new children to play with you."

Each of the four generalization sessions was conducted in the school gym, with identical play items available.

General Procedures

Each day the six boys were escorted, one at a time, to the treatment setting room for a 6-minute intervention. The order in which the children were taken for intervention was counterbalanced across experimental days.

After all intervention sessions had been completed, the six target subjects were escorted to the school gym, where the four generalization sessions were held daily. The daily order of exposure to the four generalization sessions was counterbalanced across experimental days.

Behavioral Measures

Social interactions involving the target subjects with other study participants were assessed using an observational system described in detail by Strain and Timm (1974) and Strain, Shores, and Kerr (1976). Four broad categories of positive interaction (initiated vocal–verbal, responded vocal–verbal, initiated motor–gestural, responded motor–gestural) are observed with this protocol. Initiated behaviors included those events that occurred either 3 seconds before or after another child's social behavior. Responded behaviors included all designated events that occurred within 3 seconds of another child's social behavior.

Two categories of adult behavior were also coded in this study: (a) verbal and physical prompts to engage in positive interaction, and (b) social praise delivered contingent upon target subjects' positive interaction. Specific definitions can be found in Strain et al. (1976).

Observational Procedures

During intervention setting observations, each target child was the focus of observation for 6 consecutive minutes, yielding 36 total minutes of observation in this daily setting. The order in which the subjects were observed was counterbalanced across all days. Each day, two observers were present. They recorded behaviors continuously within 10-second interval blocks, thus preserving absolute frequency data and the initiated–responded dimension of interaction episodes. Interobserver agreement was calculated daily by dividing the total number of target behaviors recorded in agreement by that number plus those recorded in disagreement, then multiplying by 100. Agreement was reached only when both observers marked the same behavior, the same general category of behavior (positive motor–gestural, positive vocal–verbal), and the same initiated or responded dimension, all within the same 10-second interval on the recording sheet. Five consecutive days of agreement above 80%, while coding the high frequency interactions of the second graders, preceded formal data collection.

Observational procedures described above were duplicated during each of the four daily generalization assessments, with the following exception. During each of the 6-minute generalization sessions, only one subject was the focus of observation for a given minute. Thus, a 1-minute sample was obtained for each subject (in a counterbalanced fashion) for each generalization session daily.

Intervention Procedures

A 7-year-old boy who was described by his teacher as socially skilled and patient in his interactions with peers served as the intervention–training agent for the six autistic children. This second-grade peer confederate had a measured IQ of 121, and his mid-year achievement testing showed that he was reading and doing arithmetic 1 year above expected grade-level. This child agreed to participate (of course, his parents gave their permission also) after he was thoroughly informed about the study and what his role would be.

Prior to the first intervention condition, the experimenter and the peer confederate participated in six 20-minute training sessions in which specific social approach behaviors were trained and rehearsed. Based upon prior naturalistic observation of children's social encounters (Tremblay, Strain, Hendrickson, & Shores, 1981), the following social initiations were targeted for training: (1) verbal play organizers (e.g., "Let's play trucks," "You sit there and I'll hand you a block"); (2) sharing of play items; and (3) physical assistance related to play (e.g., pulling a playmate who is seated in a wagon). A training format identical to that outlined in Table 1, Strain, Shores, and Timm (1977) was used with the peer confederate during the six training sessions. Basically, the experimenter encouraged the peer confederate to initiate designated social initiations while he (the experimenter) engaged in behaviors that were typical of the target youngsters. When the experimenter did not respond to an initiation, he reminded the confederate that many such attempts would not be responded to favorably by the target subjects either.

Experimental Design

In order to assess the functional effects of peer social initiations on the social behavior of the 4 autistic-like boys an AB, single subject design was used.

The procedures in each condition are presented below:

Nontrained (Baseline)

The confederate and six target subjects participated daily in a 6-minute play session (training environment) for 10 days. No attempt was made to influence the behavior of the confederate during interaction with the autistic-like boys. The accompanying teacher was instructed not to interact with the children except in situations that appeared dangerous.

Trained (Intervention)

The confederate was instructed prior to each session to try his best to get a certain child to play by using the social initiations taught previously. The accompanying teacher was reminded once again to limit her contact with the boys during this training session. Training was in effect for 10 days.

The influence of developmentally integrated and segregated environments, along with familiarity of play partners and the training of peers to promote the generalization of behavior change, was assessed by a modified simultaneous treatment (generalization in this case) design (Kazdin & Geesey, 1980). This design employed two phases. First, during Non-Trained or Baseline sessions, all generalization sessions were held daily. Next, during the training sessions, the four different generalization sessions were continued as in Baseline. The peer confederate was never present during a generalization session.

Observer Agreement

Mean percent of agreement across 20 days of the study ranged from 82 to 100% across all behavior codes, with a mean of 92%. Observer agreement did not vary as a function of the settings for observation.

Adult Behaviors

Across the 20 days of the study, four prompts were delivered to the autistic boys to encourage their interaction with the confederate. All events occurred during one nontraining and one training session. No instances of adult praise for positive interaction were recorded.

Confederate Behavior

Table 2 presents the range and mean number of target social initiations (play organizers, shares, assists) emitted by the confederate toward each of the six boys for each experimental phase. As indicated in Table 2, the behavioral rehearsal sessions with the peer confederate resulted in a substantial increase in the number of target initiations directed to each boy. Also, the actual number of initiations directed to each boy was quite similar within conditions.

Target Subjects' Behavior in Treatment Setting

Table 3 presents the percent of intervals in which the target subjects were engaged in positive interaction with the confederate across all experimental conditions. Each target subject percentage data point depicts the 10-day average of the total number of intervals containing initiated or responded, vocal–verbal or motor–gestural behaviors of a positive nature, divided by the number of 10-second intervals coded (36) during daily intervention sessions.

Baseline data on all subjects show that positive peer encounters occurred very infrequently. When the treatment was begun, each subject's level of positive interaction during training sessions substantially

Table 2
Range and Mean Number of Target Social Initiations by Confederate Toward Target Subjects for Each Experimental Condition

Experimental Conditions	Range	Mean
Nontrained		
Confederate toward		
Subject 1	0–2	.1
Subject 2	0–2	.2
Subject 3	0–5	.3
Subject 4	0–4	.2
Subject 5	0–3	.1
Subject 6	0–2	.2
Trained		
Confederate toward		
Subject 1	8–23	17.5
Subject 2	5–30	20.2
Subject 3	6–31	22.2
Subject 4	4–22	17.9
Subject 5	9–31	20.2
Subject 6	6–28	19.5

Table 3
Range and Mean of 10 Sec Intervals in which Target Subjects Engaged in Positive Social Interaction with the Confederate during Each Experimental Session

Experimental Conditions	Range	Mean
Nontrained		
Subject 1	0–5%	1.8%
Subject 2	0–9%	.8%
Subject 3	0–3%	1.5%
Subject 4	0–3%	1.2%
Subject 5	0–9%	2.2%
Subject 6	0–3%	1.1%
Trained		
Subject 1	10–80%	45%
Subject 2	28–90%	55%
Subject 3	50–80%	60%
Subject 4	33–75%	49%
Subject 5	22–85%	62%
Subject 6	37–92%	60%

increased, with the group as a whole engaged in positive interaction about one-half of the time.

Target Subjects' Behavior in Generalization Settings

Figure 1 shows the mean percent of intervals that target children were engaged in positive interaction during daily generalization sessions. The data for each setting represents a 10-day average for the treatment group. The left-hand portion of Figure 1 depicts the level of positive behavior of subjects prior to their participation in the peer-mediated treatment. As can be seen, extremely low levels of social participation were evident in both developmentally-segregated settings, averaging less than 3% of the time engaged in positive interaction. In the new developmentally-integrated setting (peers not trained), social participation averaged 9%. Only in the integrated setting with trained peers did the subjects' level of social participation begin to approach (23%) that of nonhandicapped children. The 24% to 100% range depicted in Figure 1 represents the average level of social participation by the 6 normally developing boys in the "trained" group when they were playing with *their* class peers only in the same gym setting. The dashed line at 44% indicates the mean for this group.

In the right hand portion of Figure 1, generalization data are from the 10-day period in which the peer-mediated training of the 6 boys

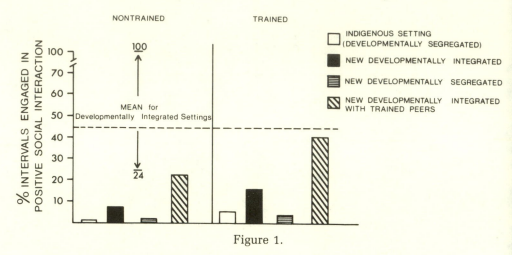

Figure 1.

took place. Several important comparisons are relevant here. First, after training, the boys' generalized behavior change in both segregated settings was *below* the level of social participation in both pretraining developmentally integrated settings. Second, in the integrated setting in which peers were not used to engage the handicapped children in social interaction, the level of generalized behavior change was *below* that exhibited prior to peer-mediated treatment in the trained-peer integrated setting. Finally, only after peer-mediated treatment, and in the company of trained peers, did the subjects' behavior change (40% participation) reach what could be considered a socially acceptable level.

Discussion

The results of this study show the following:

1. Developmentally integrated settings are clearly associated with greater social participation (both prior to and following skill training for severely handicapped young children) than developmentally segregated settings.
2. The lack of social participation in segregated settings is not attributable to interaction history, as evidenced in the similar levels of social interaction by target subjects with familiar and unfamiliar handicapped peers.
3. The social-initiation intervention produced large and consistent differences in all subjects' level of social participation in the treatment settings.
4. The minimal training offered to peers in order to support gener-

alized behavior change increased subjects' level of social participation to a level approximating that of normally developing children.

The findings mentioned above have a number of implications for the assessment and treatment of young handicapped children's social isolation. First, the substantial differences in subjects' level of social participation across generalization settings highlight the fragile nature of young children's social exchanges, and the caution one must take when interpreting outcomes from single-setting assessments. While the variability in children's social behavior should take no one by surprise, it is still the case that clinical judgments and experimental assignments to treatment protocols follow, almost exclusively, from the assessment of social encounters in single environments (e.g., Hart et al., 1968; O'Connor, 1972; Whitman et al., 1970).

Second, the differential responding found across generalization settings provides further evidence in support of Strain and Fox's (1981) contention that the absence of generalized treatment effects on young children's social behaviors can be attributed, in part, to the developmentally-segregated settings of assessment. While the precise behavioral mechanisms responsible for improved generalization in integrated settings are unknown, it seems reasonable to postulate that modeling opportunities, social initiations, and social responsiveness of peers are all enhanced in integrated environments.

While the present data clearly show that greater generalization is achieved in integrated as opposed to segregated settings, the social significance of this effect is questionable. Only when integrated setting peers were requested to engage handicapped children in interaction did the level of generalized behavior change approach the level of social participation characteristic of nonhandicapped youngsters. In effect, the data on integrated setting generalization versus integrated setting with trained peers suggests that *both* handicapped and nonhandicapped children be involved in treatment if substantial behavior change is to occur. While it may be questionable to assume that nonhandicapped children will willingly participate in intervention efforts for prolonged periods of time, there is mounting evidence that nonhandicapped children often go to great lengths in their attempts to communicate with disabled peers (Guralnick, 1981). The peer-mediated intervention described in this study provides one option for increasing the success of those communicative attempts.

REFERENCES

Allen, K. E., Hart, B. M., Buell, J. S., Harris, F. R., & Wolf, M. M. (1964). Effects of social reinforcement on isolate behavior of a nursery school child. *Child Development, 35,* 511–518.

Asher, S., & Taylor, A. (1981). The social outcomes of mainstreaming: Sociometric assessment and beyond. *Exceptional Education Quarterly, 1,* 43–59.

Gottlieb, J. (1975). Public, peer, and professional attitudes toward mentally retarded persons. In M. J. Begab & S. A. Richardson (Eds.), *The mentally retarded and society.* Baltimore: University Park Press.

Greenwood, C. R., Walker, H. M., Todd, N. H., & Hops, H. (1978). *Description of withdrawn children's behavior in preschool classes.* (Report No. 40). Eugene: Center at Oregon for Research in the Behavioral Education of the Handicapped, University of Oregon.

Guralnick, M. J. (1981). The social behavior of preschool children at different developmental levels: Effects of group composition. *Journal of Experimental Child Psychology, 31,* 115–130.

Hart, B. M., Reynolds, N. J., Baer, D. M., Brawley, E. R., & Harris, F. R. (1968). Effect of contingent and non-contingent social reinforcement on the cooperative play of a preschool child. *Journal of Applied Behavior Analysis, 1,* 73–76.

Hendrickson, J. M., Strain, P. S., Shores, R. E., & Tremblay, A. (1981). Functional effects of peer social initiations on the interactions of behaviorally handicapped children. *Behavior Modification, 5,* 340–367.

Hops, H., & Greenwood, C. R. (1981). Social skill deficits. In E. J. Mash & L. G. Terdal (Eds.), *Behavioral assessment of childhood disorders.* New York: Guilford Press.

Kazdin, A. E., & Geesey, G. (1980). Enhancing classroom attentiveness by preselection of back-up reinforcers in a token economy. *Behavior Modification, 4,* 98–114.

O'Connor, R. D. (1972). The relative efficacy of modeling, shaping, and the combined procedures for the modification of social withdrawal. *Journal of Abnormal Psychology, 79,* 327–334.

Quilitch, H. R., & Risley, T. R. (1972). The organization of day-care environments: Required vs. optional activities. *Journal of Applied Behavior Analysis, 5,* 405–420.

Shores, R. E., Hester, P., & Strain, P. S. (1976). The effects of amount and type of teacher-child interaction on child-child interaction. *Psychology in the Schools, 13,* 171–175.

Slavin, R. E. (1980). Cooperative learning. *Review of Educational Research, 50,* 315–342.

Strain, P. S. (1975). Increasing social play among severely mentally retarded preschool children with socio-dramatic play activities. *Mental Retardation, 13,* 18–19.

Strain, P. S. (1981). Modification of sociometric status and social interaction with mainstreamed developmentally disabled children. *Analysis and Intervention in Developmental Disabilities, 1,* 157–169.

Strain, P. S. (1983). Generalization of autistic children's social behavior change: Effects of developmentally-integrated and segregated settings. *Analysis and Intervention in Developmental Disabilities, 3,* 23–34.

Strain, P. S., & Fox, J. E. (1981). Peers as behavior change agents for withdrawn classmates. In A. E. Kazdin & B. Lahey (Eds.), *Advances in child clinical psychology.* New York: Plenum Publishing Company.

Strain, P. S., & Kerr, M. M. (1981). Modifying children's social withdrawal: Issues in assessment and clinical intervention. In M. Hersen, R. M. Eisler, & P. M. Miller (Eds.), *Progress in behavior modification* (Vol. 2). New York: Academic Press.

Strain, P. S., Kerr, M. M., & Ragland, E. U. (1979). Effects of peer-mediated social initiations and prompting/reinforcement procedures on the social behavior of autistic children. *Journal of Autism and Developmental Disorders, 9,* 41–54.

Strain, P. S., Shores, R. E., & Kerr, M. M. (1976). An experimental analysis of "spill-over" effects on social interaction among behaviorally handicapped preschool children. *Journal of Applied Behavior Analysis, 9,* 31–40.

Strain, P. S., Shores, R. E., & Timm, M. A. (1977). Effects of peer initiations on the social behavior of withdrawn preschoolers. *Journal of Applied Behavior Analysis, 10,* 289–298.

Strain, P. S., & Timm, M. A. (1974). An experimental analysis of social interaction between a behaviorally disordered preschool child and her classroom peers. *Journal of Applied Behavior Analysis, 7,* 583–590.

Strain, P. S., & Wiegerink, R. (1975). The social play of two behaviorally disordered preschool children during four activities: A multiple baseline study. *Journal of Abnormal Child Psychology, 3,* 61–69.

Timm, M. A., Strain, P. S., & Eller, P. H. (1979). Effects of systematic, response-dependent fading and thinning procedures on the maintenance of child-child interaction. *Journal of Applied Behavior Analysis, 12,* 308.

Tremblay, A., Strain, P. S., Hendrickson, J. M., & Shores, R. E. (1981). Social interactions of normally developing preschool children: Using normative data for subject and target behavior selection. *Behavior Modification, 5,* 237–253.

Whitman, T. L., Mercurio, J. R., & Caponigri, V. (1970). Development of social responses in two severely retarded children. *Journal of Applied Behavior Analysis, 3,* 133–138.

Handicapped Preschool Children: Peer Contacts, Relationships, or Friendships?

Nicholas J. Anastasiow

THIMBLES AND FRIENDSHIPS

Somewhere in my earlier training, I recall a professor who presented a model of research excellence by analogy to the following anecdote. As I remember it, Whitehead (hopefully not Nero Wolfe) selected his research assistants by placing them in a well-furnished room and asking them to find a lost thimble. The students who were rejected were those who stood and gazed around the room, making eye sweeps and occasionally examining a section of the room. The students who were accepted as graduate assistants were those who went to a specific area, such as a table, and began a systematic search.

Although the story is probably apocryphal, it was offered as an example of the most prestigious method of research: specific deductive hypothesis testing, which leads to findings of validity if not merit. The strength of the systematic, discrete, small-step search lies in the increased probability of positive results (here, finding the thimble); however, it should be noted the model assumes that the problem is clearly defined and that the thimble, once found, is easily recognizable, whether it be of gold, brass, or glass. Furthermore, the ecological settings of thimbles have been well documented as being in sewing baskets, drawers, or on floors.

The anecdote came to mind as I began to think about the various levels of research presented at the conference reported in this book, and the degree of specificity that some of the research workers were able to talk about regarding the variables under study and the continued search for the relevant variables. Those who talked about friendships of normally developing children, and peer interactions in general, have behind them a long line of developmental research, which has identified relevant target variables. On the other hand, those who were interested in ameliorating handicapped children's social deficits were more concerned with intervention strategies; their discussions did not focus on friendships among handicapped and normal peers, but rather focused on contacts among normal and handicapped preschoolers.

What these two groups had in common was the belief that friendships and peer relationships are good things to establish and have positive correlates in mental health. As Field notes in her chapter, those children who do not establish friendships are more likely to be isolated in life and have associated problems of juvenile delinquency and adult psychoses. The fact that handicapped children have gross social deficits concerns the interventionist, for fear that these children will suffer additional social deficits later in life.

The researcher working with normally developing children appears to be concerned with identifying the processes by which friendships are established and the antecedent conditions related to the outcome. There are some definitional problems regarding what a friendship is, but in general, like thimbles, one seems to recognize one when one sees one.

For the special educator, it is not only the thimble that is being sought but also pins, needles, rulers, zippers, and scissors that occupy the same space as thimbles. That is, the research worker who is studying the impact of placing handicapped children in integrated settings with normally developing children looks broadly at the communication skills, cognitive development, and expressive speech development of the handicapped child in such settings, and in addition attempts to determine how the normally developing children are relating to and accepting the handicapped children as peers. The special educator draws upon developmental psychology for a wide set of positive effects that might be derived from the environments in which normal children are placed, in contrast to the restrictive environments into which handicapped children have traditionally been placed.

In the section that follows, I examine some of the issues involved in establishing friendships, and the benefits children derive from peer relationships, which may or may not occur in integrated settings. First, however, I would like to make clear what I believe are the concerns of special educators in their research of the impact of mainstreaming.

THE VARIABLES OF THE SPECIAL EDUCATOR

Guralnick argues in his paper that the handicapped child can potentially derive major benefits from being placed in a setting with normally developing children. These benefits include the gains that can occur from observational learning, when children interact with other children more capable than themselves; the greater gains that are made in a responsive rather than a restrictive environment; and the cognitive and affective benefits derived from supportive environments. As Guralnick has argued, if there are multiple benefits to be gained, then it is critical that research workers document these anticipated outcomes by well-designed research studies, utilizing a developmental framework in the design of these studies.

Guralnick has been largely concerned in his own research with the effects of mainstreaming on developmentally delayed or mentally retarded children. His findings suggest that these children not only are delayed in cognitive functioning but also have major deficits in social skills, expressive language, and social interactions. Guralnick elegantly points out that placing a delayed child in an integrated setting does not per se do much to remediate the social deficits; placement in a stimulating and supportive environment is valuable, but limited for handicapped children's cognitive and social growth, and is not in itself sufficient to secure the development of desired peer relationships and social skills. Guralnick suggests that placement in integrated settings is intervention but not necessarily treatment. The reason that placement does not per se have the impact hoped for by proponents of mainstreaming can be explained, Guralnick feels, by examination of the child development and peer friendship formation literature. In that research, it has been well documented that children tend to choose as friends peers who are like themselves cognitively and who are high in social status. Even when handicapped children are matched on MA with normally developing peers, they rarely have high social status within the group and are less likely to be sought out. Guralnick has analyzed the research on peer relationships more extensively elsewhere (Guralnick, 1981). What appears to be happening in integrated settings, Guralnick points out, is that the high status normal child begins to relate to the delayed child as if the normal child were the adult and the handicapped child the child. These interactions are more control-and-demand oriented, and although they may hold some positive value for the handicapped child (and perhaps leadership qualities in the normal child), they are not the type of interactions that lead to friendship formations.

Guralnick sees the researcher who is concerned with the delayed child as seeking practical clinical solutions and highlighting the need for the remediation of social deficits that the handicapped child possesses. The work of Strain is an example of a line of research that is focusing on the nature of the intervention necessary to do so.

STRAIN'S INTERVENTIONS

In his chapter, Strain summarizes earlier behavioral research that focused on training the handicapped child to produce social interactions that resemble the peer interactions of normally developing children; he indicates that the findings have not been encouraging. Although the programs have resulted positively in reducing and making less noxious the undersirable behaviors emitted by delayed and/or disturbed children, the resulting behaviors are not the mature behaviors that are achieved in the normal course of development by normal preschoolers. Strain suggests that the major problem with the earlier research was that it promoted too narrow a view of what the construct of friendship contained. Rather, friendship formation involves a complex set of interacting processess that implies an array of antecedents and consequences.

In Strain's opinion, the earlier studies were excellent examples of how to control undesirable behaviors, but did not necessarily modify the basic disorder of the child. To make Strain's point clear, I am reminded of an example of an autistic child who was treated in a behavioral program, who had a tendency to climb up on the roof of her parent's home whenever she was able to do so. Utilizing behavioral techniques, the research workers reduced the child's roof climbing and increased her in-class sitting. In actuality, they managed to change the child's location in space, but effected little impact on her autistic state. Strain would interpret this finding as a singular solution applied to a complex phenomena.

As Strain indicates, in the case of friendship formations, single-variable studies minimize the fact that friendships are based on biological, interpersonal, and environmental events not all of which have been well specified for the normal child, let alone for the handicapped child. Strain suggests that the earlier behavioral research preceded rather than followed what should have occured; that is, a study or task analysis of the behaviors under question would have resulted in a definition of the construct of friendship and some notion of the processes and settings enhancing its occurence. Poor peer relationships are a common characteristic of most handicapped children, according to Strain. But how different handicapped children arrive at poor peer relationships may be due to neurological issues, cognitive deficits, and/or environmental constraints. Some of these issues are discussed in more detail below.

RESEARCH ON NORMAL DEVELOPMENT OF FRIENDSHIPS

Several chapters in this book discuss the manner in which friendships are formed, along with the attendant measurement issues. What is clear from the research available in the child development literature is that a cuddly, warm, agreeable infant will develop firm and loving attachments with a mentally healthy basic caregiver, and go on to establish interactions with peers that lead to the establishment of friendships which last from elementary school to the fifth generation of life (Elardo, Bradley, & Caldwell, 1975; Valliant, 1978; Werner & Smith, 1981). When a normal child does not develop such friendships, questions are raised about the child's temperament (a genetically based individual difference characteristic, Eibl-Eibesfeldt, 1975); the appearance of the fixed behavioral pattern of emotional signals and cues, such as the smile and cry; the characteristics of child-rearing practices of the caregiver (Werner & Smith, 1981); the nature of attachment (Ainsworth, 1973); the nature of separation (Bowlby, 1977); and the opportunity for peer interaction, and so on. If all of these events and practices fall within a reasonable normal range, then the child who fails to form friendships is suspected of being handicapped. The question remains: How do handicapped children begin and maintain friendships? Some insight is offered by the Field study. Field notes that some handicapped children can make friends and that the characteristics of the handicapped child who does so are very much like those of the normal child who makes friends. These attributes are mainly on an extroversion dimension of being more verbal, more affective, and more assertive.

Howe, working within a tight definition of friendship (an affective tie between two children that has three necessary behavioral components: mutual preference, mutual enjoyment, and the ability to engage in skillful interactions), reports that emotionally disturbed preschoolers were able to form preferential emotional bonds or friendships. She found some support for the nature of the interaction of the parent–child relationship as predictive of the peer relationship. Abused children engaged in higher levels of physical aggression with peers. Further findings indicated that the emotionally disturbed child was less likely to form friendships.

These studies offer us some direction into the nature of the problem and the difficulty of the research worker who approaches this area. There are other pertinent questions as well.

Cognitive and linguistic competence is an attribute of the normal child's friendships, but to what level of cognitive competence does the handicapped child have to achieve to be sufficient for friendship formation?

Attachment has been identified as a construct related to adequate peer relationships in the normal. Attachment in handicapped children is an under-investigated field (Ulrey, 1981). We do not know how attachments are formed in the handicapped child, nor how to detect poor attachment and poor separation techniques disentangled from the issues associated with the child's sensory impairments.

An additional issue involves the abused child. How does one treat the abused child, and is this treatment different from the treatment of the neurologically impaired child—whose social deficits may resemble each other? The neurologically impaired and the learning disabled child often have difficulty reading other's emotional cues of acceptance or rejection, and often emit cues that are atypical (Rourke, 1982). The common assumption is that emotional cues are fixed action patterns which are genetically based and common in man unless society requires suppression of their natural expression, such as the restriction of the smile among the Japanese (Ekman, 1971).

Two of the conference participants (Jeff Seibert and Ann Hogan of the University of Miami) stress the importance of not lumping all handicapped children into the same pot when talking about forming friendships. If the social skills are below what one would expect considering the child's MA, Seibert and Hogan suggest that it is likely a problem of the child's total set of spontaneous behaviors, suggesting a motivational deficit which would require a different treatment than with the cognitively delayed child, who may never be able to achieve mature adultlike affective relationships. In either case, Seibert and Hogan, as Guralnick, question throwing the handicapped child in with normal peers for free play without providing a supportive structure that encourages specific types of interaction that would benefit the handicapped child. To Seibert and Hogan, the implications of the Guralnick finding that the normal peer may be too didactic with the handicapped child might serve as a warning to the teacher of the handicapped child: In the days of stress on specific behavioral objectives, the teacher might approach the social skill development of these children in a didactic manner with clearly defined situations and promts, which would lead to the single variable acquisition Strain describes, and hinder the interaction and communication skills that might be developed through interactive games at the water table or sand box. Seibert and Hogan's own work in developing the "Early Social-Communication Scales" (Seibert & Hogan, 1982) addresses both the initiating and maintaining of skills that they believe teachers need to balance in eliciting controlled teacher-directed responses and spontaneous child-initiated responses. Attention needs to be given to how teachers are trained to be sensitive to both.

SUMMARY

To return to the thimble introduced at the onset, one is reminded that Mark Twain invented a thimble-throwing test to detect whether it was a boy or girl wearing a skirt. Common sense led him to believe experience would lead a girl to spread her skirt to catch the thimble whereas a boy, used to wearing trousers, would put his legs together for the same reason. Ethnologists might offer a very different hypothesis about sex differences in leg positions than the commonsense position would generate.

Special educators have been in a similar position of operating out of the commonsense position that it would be a good thing, for a host of "morally" good reasons, to place handicapped children in settings with normally developing children. As we have seen earlier, this is too simplistic a view. There are major differences between the terms "least restrictive" and "most facilitative" in defining environments, yet the intent of those who advocate each is the same—that is, provide as near as possible a normal placement for children with sensory impairments. The reduction of active rejection does not necessarily lead to active acceptance. As one of the normal children in Strain's sample said: "I won't throw rocks at them, but do I have to play with them?" It is a less difficult value question to answer the child when the handicapped child is autistic, emotionally disturbed, or excessively disordered than it is when the child is cognitively normal and wheelchair-bound, cerebral palsied, or spina bifida or any other of a host of low-incidence disorders that leave the children with disordered bodies and faces but intact cognitive functioning. It appears to be no accident that handicapped adults and parents of handicapped children have chosen the civil rights movement on which to base their case for free access to buildings and public transportation, and thereby to occupational and cultural opportunities. Active acceptance of the handicapped, as with minority groups, has not resulted when legal means have been secured only to prevent harassment. Gaining equality of education, and freedom of choice in life styles and occupations, is still an issue to be resolved. Developing the social skills demanded by society for such access is an important issue, since, as we have seen, the handicapped child typically has social deficits that need to be remediated. Thus, we return to the essential issue of this book: how to facilitate the handicapped person's social skills early in life so as to enable a larger percentage of these persons to have access to the full range of events in our society when they are adults.

The work presented in this volume suggests that we should modify our expectations of what might be achieved with delayed children by placing them in integrated classrooms. This still leaves open the question of what can be achieved with impaired children who are cognitively able. As we have seen above, matching MAs does not solve the problem of the cognitive deficit. A 12-year-old who has a 6-year-old's IQ is likely to have behaviors that teachers and 6-year-olds consider abnormal (finger movements, lack of eye contact, general nervousness). These behaviors can be reduced, but the individual is still viewed as being retarded. A 3-year-old in a wheelchair who is cognitively normal may have deficits in experience outside the home, experience oversolicitation and lack autonomy, have parents who have undergone grief and mourning in having a handicapped child; but this 3-year-old will be able to emit normal behavior in curiosity, language, and cognition which will elicit different responses from teachers and peers. As the contributors to this book suggest, it is time to become more specific about what can be accomplished, and with whom.

REFERENCES

Ainsworth, M. (1973). The development of infant-mother attachment. In B. Caldwell & H. Ricciuti (Eds.), *Review of Child Development Research* (Vol. 3). Chicago: University of Chicago Press.

Bowlby, J. (1977). The making and breaking of affectional bonds. *British Journal of Psychiatry, 130,* 201–210.

Eibl-Eibesfeldt, I. (1975). *Ethology: The biology of behavior.* New York: Holt, Rinehart & Winston.

Ekman, P. (1971). Universals and cultural differences in facial expressions of emotion. Pp. 207–283 in J. K. Cole (Ed.), *Nebraska symposium on Motivation.* Lincoln NE: University of Nebraska Press.

Elardo, R., Bradley, R., & Caldwell, B. N. (1975). The relation of infants' home environment to mental tests performance from six to thirty-six months: A Longitudinal analysis. *Child Development 46,* 71–76.

Guralnick, M. J. (1981). The development and role of child-child social interactions. In Anastasiow, N. J. (Ed.), *Socioemotional Development,* San Francisco: Jossey-Bass.

Rourke, B. P. (1982). Central processing deficiencies in children: toward a developmental neuropsychological model. *Journal of Clinical Neuropsychology, 4,* 1–18.

Seibert, J. M., & Hogan, A. E. (1982). A model for assessing social and object skills and planning interventions. In D. P. McClowry, A. M. Guilford, & S. O. Richardson (Eds.), *Infant Communication.* New York: Grune and Stratton.

Ulrey, G. (1981). Emotional development in the young handicapped child. In N. J. Anastasiow (Ed.), *Socioemotional Development.* San Francisco: Jossey-Bass.

Valliant, G. E. (1978). *Adaptations to life.* Boston: Little, Brown.

Werner, E. E., & Smith, R. S. (1981). *Vulnerable but invincible. A longitudinal study of resilient children and youth.* New York: McGraw-Hill.

Author Index

Numbers in italic indicate pages upon which the complete references can be found.

Subject Index